1001

MOST POPULAR

Wedding
Questions

From

WedSpace.com

By Alex and Elizabeth Lluch

WS Publishing Group
San Diego, California

1001 Most Popular Wedding Questions from WedSpace.com

By Alex and Elizabeth Lluch

Published by WS Publishing Group
San Diego, California 92119
Copyright © 2010 by WS Publishing Group

Designed by WS Publishing Group:
David Defenbaugh, Sarah Jang

For Inquiries:
Log on to www.WSPublishingGroup.com
E-mail info@WSPublishingGroup.com

ISBN 13: 978-1-934386-88-0

Printed in China

About

WedSpace.com

1001 Most Popular Wedding Questions
was created by compiling the top questions from
thousands of brides on WedSpace.com.

WedSpace.com is the fastest-growing bridal
community online, designed for both engaged
and married couples to connect with other brides,
friends, family, wedding vendors and much more.

WedSpace.com is an invaluable resource for
engaged couples, offering wedding planning
articles, news, polls, events, and groups.

WedSpace.com members can:
- Video chat live with guests and vendors
- Upload wedding music, photos, and videos
- Create blogs
- Post their wedding planning questions for
  experts and other brides to answer

Introduction

FINDING THE PERSON YOU LOVE, making plans to the spend the rest of your lives together, creating your perfect wedding day ... about 5 million people each year tie the knot, and many of them are asking the same questions when it comes to wedding planning.

In this book, renowned wedding experts Alex and Elizabeth Lluch answer the 1001 most commonly asked questions, compiled from thousands of couples registered on WedSpace.com, the first and only social networking site for engaged couples, their guests, and wedding vendors. Alex and Elizabeth are the authors of 30 of the top-selling wedding planning books in North America, so they are thrilled to help engaged couples everywhere with their most pressing wedding questions.

1001 Most Popular Wedding Questions from WedSpace.com explores every important topic in wedding and honeymoon planning, from budgeting, to understanding the responsibilities of the wedding party members, to choosing a ceremony and reception site, to wedding traditions and etiquette.

If you have a wedding or honeymoon planning question you don't see here, log on to WedSpace.com. Then search our Questions & Answers section or ask your questions on our forum to get answers from wedding professionals and other couples just like you! Enjoy the wedding planning process on the way to the most incredible day of your life: your wedding day!

CHAPTER 1

Getting Started

1. What is the first thing a couple should do to start planning the wedding?

   The first thing a couple should do is sit down and have an open and honest conversation about what type of wedding they would like to have, how much money they would like to spend, who is going to pay for what, and any other priorities they have for the wedding.

2. How do I determine the total cost of my wedding?

   Start with the amount of money you would like to spend on your wedding. Now, estimate how much money you will spend on certain parts of or items in the wedding, such as your dress, the food and beverages, the music, etc. Add these amounts together. That subtotal is your projected wedding budget. As you go, you should record how much you actually end up spending on these items. This will help you stay within your budget.

3. What is the average cost of a wedding in the U.S.?

   The average U.S. wedding costs slightly more than $21,000.

4. How should my wedding budget break down?

   Here is how an average wedding budget typically breaks down for each aspect. Naturally, you may choose to splurge or save in certain areas, so this breakdown can be adjusted as need be.

   Ceremony = 5% of Budget
   Wedding Attire = 10% of Budget
   Photography = 9% of Budget
   Videography = 5% of Budget
   Stationery 4% of Budget
   Reception = 35% of Budget
   Music = 5% of Budget
   Flowers = 6% of Budget
   Decorations = 3% of Budget
   Transportation = 2% of Budget
   Rental Items = 3% of Budget
   Gifts = 3% of Budget
   Miscellaneous (Marriage license, taxes, etc.) = 4% of Budget

5. How can we tell people about our engagement?

   Traditionally, couples would place an engagement announcement in their local newspaper; however, this is not as common anymore. Modernly, many couples will alert friends, family, and coworkers with an email or by sending a link to a wedding website they create.

6. What are the benefits of creating a wedding website?
Building a wedding website gives your guests a place to go to see all the details of your wedding, from your proposal story to the members of the wedding party to your registry to the details of the "what, where, when" of the wedding day.

7. How can we tell our guests about our wedding website?
You can include the URL in your Save the Date cards or on your invitations and tell your guests to visit your site for complete details of the wedding. Just remember that some older people, like grandparents, may not be Internet-savvy, so you may still want to include maps and such with your invitations.

8. What are the benefits of a wedding planning book?
A good wedding planning book can help you stay organized, store information from various vendors, and make notes of what needs to be completed. WS Publishing Group publishes 30 of the top-selling wedding planners on the market — many come complete with slots for business cards, 3-hole punches, zippered pouches for storing paperwork, and helpful worksheets.

9. How do I figure in taxes on all the taxable items I purchase for my wedding?
Many people make a big mistake by not figuring out the taxes they will have to pay for their wedding expenses. For example, if you are planning a reception for 250 guests with an estimated cost of $60 per person for food and beverages, your pretax expenses would be $15,000. A sales tax of 7.5% would mean an additional expense of $1,125! Find out what the sales tax is in your area and which items are taxable, and figure this expense into your overall budget.

10. What is a wedding consultant?
Wedding consultants are professionals whose training, expertise, and contacts will help make your wedding as close to perfect as it can possibly be. They can save you considerable time, money and stress when planning your wedding. Wedding consultants have information

on many ceremony and reception sites as well as reliable service providers such as photographers, videographers and florists, which will save you hours of investigation and legwork. Wedding consultants can provide facilities and service providers to match your budget. They can also save you stress by ensuring that what you are planning is correct and that the service providers you hire are reliable and professional. Most service providers recommended by wedding consultants will go out of their way to do an excellent job for you so that the wedding consultant will continue to recommend their services. You can have a wedding consultant help you do as much or as little as you think necessary. A consultant can help you plan the whole event from the beginning to the end, helping you formulate a budget, and select your ceremony and reception sites, flowers, wedding gown, invitations, and service providers, or he or she can help you at the end by coordinating the rehearsal and the wedding day. Remember, you want to feel like a guest at your own wedding. You and your family should not have to worry about any details on that special day. This is the wedding consultant's job!

11. Should I hire a wedding consultant?

Strongly consider engaging the services of a wedding consultant. Contrary to what many people believe, a wedding consultant is part of your wedding budget, not an extra expense! A good wedding consultant should be able to save you at least the amount of his or her fee by suggesting less expensive alternatives that still enhance your wedding. In addition, many consultants obtain discounts from the service providers they work with. If this is not enough, they are more than worth their fee by serving as an intermediary between you and your parents and/or service providers. When hiring a wedding consultant, make sure you check his or her references. Ask the consultant if he or she is a member of the Association of Bridal Consultants (ABC) and ask to see a current membership certificate. All ABC members agree to uphold a Code of Ethics and Standards of Membership.

12. What is a wedding designer? Is this different from my wedding consultant?

They actually serve much of the same purpose — both are types of event planners who will help you create the wedding of your dreams. The difference is a wedding designer is usually a person with specific formal training and experience in floral arrangements, interior design, or even fashion who can help you create an overarching theme or "brand" for your wedding that flows through every aspect, from the invitations to the centerpieces. This person gives you creative ideas that you can use to lend a cohesive theme to your wedding.

13. How much does a wedding consultant cost?

Wedding consultants can cost from $500 to $10,000. It depends who you hire and for how long, and also if they charge hourly or set a flat rate. Some people hire a consultant for the entire wedding planning process and some hire one only for the Big Day.

14. What kind of questions do I ask a wedding consultant when I'm considering hiring him or her?

- What is the name of the wedding consultant?
- What is the website and e-mail of the wedding consultant?
- What is the address of the wedding consultant?
- What is the phone number of the wedding consultant?
- How many years of professional experience do you have?
- How many consultants are in your company?
- Are you a member of the Association of Bridal Consultants?
- What services do you provide?
- What are your hourly fees?
- What is your fee for complete wedding planning?
- What is your fee to oversee the rehearsal and wedding day?
- What is your payment policy?
- What is your cancellation policy?
- Do you have liability insurance?

15. When should I hire a professional wedding planner or consultant?

Nine months before the wedding.

16. Do I need to invite my wedding planner to parties like the bridal shower, etc?

You are not obligated to invite your wedding planner, unless you choose to.

17. Do I need to tip my wedding coordinator?

You do not need to tip your wedding coordinator unless he or she has gone above and beyond what is expected and you wish to thank that person with a monetary gift. It is also acceptable to send a nice arrangement of flowers or a gift certificate as a thank you.

18. Should I plan to incorporate do-it-yourself projects in my wedding planning?

DIY wedding projects can save money at times and may give your wedding a personal touch, but they can also become stressful for the couple. A good tip is to look online at different design sites and wedding blogs and find DIY projects that brides have posted. Brides will post materials to buy, cost, and the timeline for the projects. That way you can get a feel for how long a project will take and how labor-intensive it will be.

19. How much time should I allot for DIY projects?

The DIY projects a couple tackles should be determined by their proximity to the wedding date, size of guest list, and scope of the project. Any DIY project that you take on in close proximity (within a week or two) to your wedding date should be small, only a few hours worth of work, to avoid unnecessary stress. However, consider that you will have so many other details to think about at that time. These are the kind of situations where you might want to enlist friends and family to help out. If you have a large guest list, consider that it may not be worth the time spent to create a handmade favor or place card for a large number of people.

20. What are some Do's for my wedding that I should know?

Here is a list of some important Do's for your wedding:

· Hire a professional wedding consultant.
· Maintain a sense of humor.
· Maintain open communication with your fiancé and with both sets of parents, especially if they are financing the wedding.
· Be receptive to your parents' ideas, especially if they are financing the wedding.
· Be flexible and keep your overall budget in mind.
· Maintain a regular routine of exercise and eat a well-balanced diet.
· Register for gifts; consider a price range that your guests

can afford.
- Break-in your shoes well before your wedding day.
- Practice with makeup and various hairstyles for your wedding day.
- Check recent references for all of your service providers.
- Get everything in writing with your service providers.
- Assign your guests to tables and group them together by age, interests, acquaintances, etc.
- Consider drawing up a prenuptial agreement and a will.
- Send thank-you notes as soon as you receive gifts.
- Give a rose to each of your mothers as you walk down the aisle during the recessional.
- Try to spend some time with each of your guests and personally thank them for coming to your wedding.
- Encourage the bride's parents to introduce their family and friends to the family and friends of the groom's family, and vice-versa.
- Toast both sets of parents at the rehearsal dinner and/or at the reception. Thank them for everything they have done for you and for giving you a beautiful wedding.
- Eat well at the reception, especially if you will be drinking alcohol.
- Keep a smile on your face; there will be many photographs taken of both of you.
- Expect things to go wrong on your wedding day. Most likely something will go wrong, and no one will notice it but you. Relax and don't let it bother you.
- Preserve the top tier of your wedding cake for your first anniversary.
- Send a special gift to both sets of parents, such as a small album containing the best photographs of the wedding. Personalize this gift by having it engraved with your names and the date of your wedding.

21. What are some important Don'ts for my wedding?

Here is a list of some important Don'ts when you are planning your wedding:
- Don't get involved in other activities; you will be very busy planning your wedding.
- Don't make any major decisions without discussing it openly with your fiancé.
- Don't be controlling. Be open to other people's ideas.
- Don't overspend your budget; this can be extremely stressful.

- Don't wait until the last minute to hire your service providers. The good ones get booked months in advance.
- Don't try to make everyone happy; it is impossible and will only make your wedding planning more difficult.
- Don't try to impress your friends.
- Don't invite old boyfriends or girlfriends to your wedding, unless both you and your fiancé are friendly with them; you don't want to make anybody uncomfortable.
- Don't arrive late to the ceremony!
- Don't try to do "everything." Delegate responsibilities to your fiancé, your parents, and to members of your wedding party.
- Don't rely on friends or family to photograph or videotape your wedding. Hire professionals!
- Don't assume that members of your wedding party know what to do. Give them direction with your Wedding Party Timeline and *Wedding Party Responsibility Cards*, available at most major bookstores.
- Don't assume your service providers know what to do. Give each of them a copy of your detailed Service Provider Timeline.
- Don't schedule your bachelor party the night before the wedding. You don't want to have a hangover on your special day!
- Don't drink too much during the reception; you don't want to make a fool of yourself on your most special day!
- Don't allow your guests to drive drunk after the reception; you may be held responsible.
- Don't rub cake in the face of your spouse during the cake-cutting ceremony; your spouse might not appreciate it!
- Don't overeat; this may upset your stomach or make you sleepy.
- Don't leave your reception without saying good-bye to your family and friends.

CHAPTER 2

Who Pays for What?

22. What do the bride and her family traditionally pay for in a wedding?
    · Engagement party
    · Wedding consultant's fee
    · Bridal gown, veil and accessories
    · Wedding stationery, calligraphy and postage
    · Wedding gift for bridal couple
    · Groom's wedding ring
    · Gifts for bridesmaids
    · Bridesmaids' bouquets
    · Pre-wedding parties and bridesmaids' luncheon
    · Photography and videography
    · Bride's medical exam and blood test
    · Wedding guest book and other accessories
    · Total cost of the ceremony, including location, flowers, music,
    · Rental items, and accessories
    · Total cost of the reception, including location, flowers, music,
    · Rental items, accessories, food, beverages, cake, decorations, favors, etc.
    · Transportation for bridal party to ceremony and reception
    · Own attire and travel expenses

23. What do the groom and his family traditionally pay for in a wedding?
    · Own travel expenses and attire
    · Rehearsal dinner
    · Wedding gift for bridal couple
    · Bride's wedding ring
    · Gifts for groom's attendants
    · Medical exam for groom including blood test
    · Bride's bouquet and going away corsage
    · Mothers' and grandmothers' corsages
    · All boutonnieres
    · Officiant's fee
    · Marriage license
    · Honeymoon expenses

24. What do the bridal party and attendants traditionally pay for in a wedding?
    · Own attire except flowers
    · Travel expenses

- Bridal shower paid for by Maid of Honor and bridesmaids

25. What expenses are the groom's attendants responsible for?
- Own attire except flowers
- Travel expenses
- Bachelor party paid for by Best Man and ushers

26. Who pays for the honeymoon?
Traditionally the groom is responsible for the honeymoon. Nowadays, many couples find it necessary for both the bride and groom to contribute to the cost in order to experience the honeymoon of their dreams. (Today, the average newlywed couple spends $2,500-$3,500 on their honeymoon.)

Some couples create a honeymoon registry, which allows guests to contribute to the activities and cost of the honeymoon.

Another tradition is the Dollar Dance at the reception. The bride and groom dance with their guests while accepting the dollar "dance fee" as a contribution to their honeymoon.

27. How many couples pay for their own weddings?
With couples getting married later in life than decades past, more and more people are paying for their own weddings. A recent survey showed that 30 percent of couples are paying for all or part of their weddings.

✳ Notes

....
....
....
....
....
....
....
....
....
....
....
....
....
....
....
....
....
....
....
....
....
....
....

CHAPTER 3

Ceremony

28. What are some options for a ceremony site?
Here are some different options for your ceremony site: churches, cathedrals, chapels, temples, synagogues, private homes, gardens, hotels, clubs, halls, parks, museums, yachts, wineries, and beaches. Just check with church or city officials to make sure you are allowed to book the location for a ceremony and to obtain any permits.

29. What is the ceremony site fee?
The ceremony site fee is the fee to rent a facility for your wedding. In churches, cathedrals, chapels, temples, or synagogues, this fee may include the organist, wedding coordinator, custodian, changing rooms for the bridal party, and miscellaneous items such as kneeling cushions, aisle runners, and candelabras.

30. How much is the ceremony site fee?
The ceremony site fee usually costs $100 to $1,000.

31. How do I know what the ceremony site fee includes?
Prior to booking a facility, ask the church official or the person in charge of planning events at the facility what is included in the ceremony site fee, whether it is an organist, chairs, candelabra, etc.

32. When should I reserve the ceremony and reception sites?
Nine months before the wedding, or earlier.

33. What should I consider when looking at or booking a ceremony site?
Your selection of a ceremony site will be influenced by the formality of your wedding, the season, the number of guests expected and your religious affiliation. Consider issues such as proximity of the ceremony site to the reception site, parking availability, handicapped accessibility, and time constraints.

34. If we want a beach wedding, do we need a permit?
Yes, you should contact the city hall of the area and find out what permits you need to attain and how much they cost.

35. If we have our ceremony in a park, what do we need to consider?

You should consider that you will need to obtain the correct permits from the city, as well as rent everything your guests need to be comfortable. This includes chairs and extras like portable bathrooms.

36. What are some restrictions or guidelines I should think about when choosing a ceremony site?

Make sure you ask about restrictions or guidelines regarding photography, videography, music, decorations, candles, and rice or rose petal tossing.

37. How can I save money when booking my ceremony site?

Have your ceremony at the same facility as your reception to save a second rental fee. Set a realistic guest list and stick to it. Hire an experienced wedding consultant. At a church or temple, ask if there is another wedding that day and share the cost of floral decorations with that bride. Membership in a church, temple or club can reduce rental fees. At a garden wedding, have guests stand and omit the cost of renting chairs.

38. What are some questions I should ask when looking at or booking a ceremony site?

- What is the name of the ceremony site?
- What is the website and e-mail of the ceremony site?
- What is the address of the ceremony site?
- What is the name and phone number of my contact person?
- What dates and times are available?
- What is the ceremony site fee?
- What is the payment policy?
- What is the cancellation policy?
- Does the facility have liability insurance?
- What are the minimum and maximum numbers of guests allowed?
- What is the denomination, if any, of the facility?
- What restrictions are there with regards to religion?
- Is an officiant available? At what cost?
- Are outside officiants allowed?
- Do vows need to be approved?
- Are any musical instruments available for our use?
- If so, what is the fee?

- What music restrictions are there, if any?
- What photography restrictions are there, if any?
- What videography restrictions are there, if any?
- Are there are any restrictions for rice/petal tossing?
- Are candlelight ceremonies allowed?
- What floral decorations are available/allowed?
- When is my rehearsal to be scheduled?
- Is there handicap accessibility and parking?
- How many parking spaces are available for my wedding party?
- Where are they located?
- How many parking spaces are available for my guests?
- What rental items are necessary?
- What is the fee?

39. What are ceremony accessories?

Ceremony rental accessories are additional items needed for the ceremony but not included in the ceremony site fee.

You may need to consider renting audio equipment, aisle stanchions, candelabra, candles, candle-lighters, chairs, heaters, a gift table, a guest bookstand, and a canopy. If you plan to rent any accessories for your ceremony, make sure the rental supplier has been in business for a reasonable period of time and has a good reputation. Reserve the items you need well in advance. Find out the company's payment, reservation and cancellation policies. Some companies allow you to reserve emergency items such as heaters or canopies without having to pay for them unless needed, in which case you would need to call the rental company a day or two in advance to request the items. If someone else requests the items you have reserved, the company should give you the right of first refusal.

40. What is an aisle runner?

The aisle runner is a thin rug made of plastic, paper or cloth extending the length of the aisle. It is rolled out after the mothers are seated, just prior to the processional. Plastic or paper doesn't work well on grass; but if you must use one of these types of runners, make sure the grass is clipped short. You may need to rent this for your ceremony.

41. What is a kneeling cushion?

A kneeling cushion is a small cushion or pillow placed in front of the altar where the bride and groom kneel for their wedding blessing. You may need to rent or purchase a kneeling cushion for your ceremony.

42. What is the arch in a Christian wedding?

The bride and groom exchange their vows beneath a white lattice or brass arch, often decorated with flowers and greenery. If your ceremony site does not have an arch, you may be able to rent or build one.

43. What is a chuppah in a Jewish ceremony?

A chuppah is a canopy under which a Jewish ceremony is performed, symbolizing cohabitation and consummation. If your ceremony site does not have a chuppah, you may be able to rent or build one.

44. How much do ceremony accessories cost?

They can cost from $100 to $500 or more, depending upon what you are renting.

45. How can I save money on ceremony accessories?

When considering a ceremony outside of a church, figure the cost of rental items. Negotiate a package deal, if possible, by renting items for both the ceremony and the reception from the same supplier. Consider renting these items from your florist so you only have to pay one delivery fee.

46. What is the guest book at the ceremony for?

The guest book is a formal register that your guests sign as they arrive at the ceremony or reception. It serves as a memento of who attended your wedding. This book is often placed outside the ceremony or reception site, along with an elegant pen and penholder.

47. What is important to consider in having a guest book at my ceremony?

Make sure you have more than one pen in case one runs out of ink. If you are planning a large ceremony (over 200 guests), consider having more than one book and pen so that your guests don't have to wait in line to sign in.

48. What are a guest book attendant's duties?
A guest book attendant is responsible for inviting all guests to sign in. A younger sibling or close friend who is not part of the wedding party may be well suited for this position.

49. What is a unique alternative to a traditional guest book?
You can have a wishing tree; provide a small potted tree and a basket of small cards with a loop of ribbon or string. Guests write loving wishes on the cards and hang them on the tree. The bride and groom plant the tree as a special reminder of their wedding day.

50. How much does a guest book and pen usually cost?
Guest books and pens usually range from $30 to $100, depending upon their quality.

51. How much do ring bearer pillows usually cost?
Ring bearer pillows can cost anywhere from $15 to $75, depending on the style and fabric used.

52. How much does a flower girl's basket cost?
A flower girl's basket usually costs $20 to $75.

53. What are pew cards?
Pew cards may be used to let special guests and family members know they are to be seated in the reserved section on either the bride's side or the groom's side. These are most typically seen in large, formal ceremonies. Guests should take this card to the ceremony and show it to the ushers, who should then escort them to their seats. Pew cards may indicate a specific pew number if specific seats are assigned, or may read "Within the Ribbon" if certain pews are reserved but no specific seat is assigned.

54. What do I need to consider when purchasing pew cards?
Pew cards may be inserted along with the invitation, or may be sent separately after the RSVPs have been returned. It is often easier to send them after you have received all RSVPs so you know how many reserved pews will be needed.

55. How can I personalize my ceremony?
Regardless of your religious affiliation, there are numerous ways in which you can personalize your wedding ceremony to add a more creative touch. If you're planning a religious

ceremony at a church or temple, be sure to discuss all ideas with your officiant. Here are some other ideas to help personalize your ceremony:

- Invite the bride's mother to be part of the processional. Have her walk down the aisle with you and your father, as in a traditional Jewish processional.
- Invite the groom's parents to be part of the processional also.
- Ask friends and family members to perform special readings.
- Ask a friend or family member with musical talent to perform at the ceremony.
- Incorporate poetry and/or literature into your readings.
- Change places with the officiant and face your guests during the ceremony.
- Light a unity candle to symbolize your two lives joining together as one.
- Drink wine from a shared "loving" cup to symbolize bonding with each other.
- Hand a rose to each of your mothers as you pass by them during the recessional.
- If the ceremony is held outside on a grassy area, have your guests toss grass or flower seeds over you instead of rice.
- Publicly express gratitude for all that your parents have done for you.
- Use a canopy to designate an altar for a non-church setting. Decorate it in ways that are symbolic or meaningful to you.
- Burn incense to give the ceremony an exotic feeling.
- Fill a glass vase or urn with two different colors of sand, one to represent the bride and one to represent the groom, to symbolize the blending of marriage.
- Say your vows in more than one language to incorporate your heritage and foreign speaking family members.

56. What should we consider if we are going to do a dove release after being pronounced husband and wife?

You should find a reputable company in your area that will handle the dove release in an ethical way. This means not releasing doves at night, in bad weather, inside a building, or beyond where they can easily fly back.

57. What should we know if we are considering a butterfly release?

You should find a company that specializes in butterfly releases for weddings. The butterflies will arrive in a package with instructions about how to keep them dormant until the wedding. You should only release butterflies when it is a clear day, not at night or in inclement weather. Many times, butterflies will land on your dress or bouquet!

58. What are the formations for the processional in a Christian wedding ceremony?

During the processional, the order of people who enter the church is as follows (the groom and Best Man begin at the front of the church):

- Ushers — the ushers escort all the guests to their seats and then return to the back of the church to enter one by one
- Bridesmaids — the bridesmaids wait at the back of the church and enter after the ushers
- Maid of Honor — the Maid of Honor enters after all the bridesmaids have gone down the aisle
- Ring Bearer — if you have a ring bearer in your wedding, he enters after the Maid of Honor
- Flower Girl — the flower girl enters after the ring bearer, strewing petals down the aisle
- Bride's Father and Bride — the bride's father stands on the left side of the bride and they walk down the aisle together

59. What are the formations for the recessional in a Christian wedding ceremony?

The formations for the recessional of a Christian wedding ceremony are as follows, from first to last (all the women stand to the right side of the men):

- Bride and Groom — the bride and groom walk down the aisle and out of the church first
- Flower Girl and Ring Bearer — they are next to take their exit after the bride and groom
- Maid of Honor and Best Man — they follow the ring bearer and flower girl down the aisle
- Bridesmaids and Ushers — they are next to recede down the aisle
- Bride's Mother and Bride's Father — they follow after the bridesmaids and ushers

· Groom's Mother and Groom's Father — they are the last to exit down the aisle of the church

60. **What are the formations for the processional of a Jewish wedding ceremony?**

During the processional of a Jewish wedding ceremony, the order of the people who enter is as follows:

· Ushers — they escort people to their seats and then return to the back of the synagogue to enter one by one
· Best Man — he enters after the ushers
· Groom's Father, Groom and Groom's Mother — they walk together down the aisle, the groom's father to the left of the groom, and the groom's mother to the right of the groom
· Bridesmaids — they enter after the groom and his parents
· Maid of Honor — she follows the bridesmaids down the aisle
· Ring Bearer and Flower Girl — they enter together after the Maid of Honor, the ring bearer standing on the left side of the flower girl
· Bride's Father, Bride, Bride's Mother — they walk together down the aisle, the bride's father standing to the left of the bride, and the bride's mother standing to the right of the bride

61. **What are the recessional formations for a Jewish wedding ceremony?**

During the recessional of a Jewish ceremony, the order of the people leave as follows (all the men stand to the right of the women):

· Groom and Bride — the groom and bride leave first, the groom standing to the right of the bride
· Bride's Father and Bride's Mother — they follow the groom and bride out of the synagogue
· Groom's Father and Groom's Mothers — the groom's father stands to the right of the groom's mother as they exit
· Ring Bearer and Flower Girl — they follow the groom's parents next down the aisle
· Best Man and Maid of Honor — the Best Man stands on the right of the Maid of Honor
· Ushers and Bridesmaids — they are the last to leave the synagogue

62. **How can I personalize my marriage vows?**

As with all your ceremony plans, be sure to discuss your ideas for marriage vows with your officiant. The following are some ideas that you might want to consider when planning your marriage vows:

· You and your fiancé could write your own personal marriage vows and keep them secret from one another until the actual ceremony.
· Incorporate your guests and family members into your vows by acknowledging their presence at the ceremony.
· Describe what you cherish most about your partner and what you hope for your future together.
· Describe your commitment to and love for one another.
· Discuss your feelings and beliefs about marriage.
· If either of you has children from a previous marriage, mention these children in your vows and discuss your mutual love for and commitment to them.

63. **How can we honor a loved one who has passed away during our ceremony?**

Ultimately, how you choose to honor a lost loved one is up to you and your fiancé; however you might consider keeping a seat at the ceremony empty and placing a flower or photo on the chair. You might also ask the officiant to say a prayer for that person or mention him or her during the ceremony.

64. **Who gives the bride away if the father isn't present?**

Anyone meaningful to the bride can walk her down the aisle, such as her mother, both parents, her step-father, or any other special person in her life. The bride can also walk alone if she prefers.

65. **What does the bride need to bring to the ceremony?**

· Aspirin/Alka Seltzer
· Bobby pins
· Breath spray/mints
· Bridal gown
· Bridal gown box
· Cake knife
· Going away clothes
· Clear nail polish
· Deodorant
· Garter
· Gloves

- Groom's ring
- Guest book
- Hair brush
- Hair spray
- Head piece
- Iron
- Jewelry
- Kleenex
- Lint brush
- Luggage
- Makeup
- Mirror
- Nail polish
- Panty hose
- Passport
- Perfume
- Personal camera
- Plume pen for guest book
- Powder
- Purse
- Safety pins
- Scotch tape/masking tape
- Sewing kit
- Shoes
- Something old
- Something new
- Something borrowed
- Something blue
- Sixpence for shoe
- Spot remover
- Straight pins
- Tampons or sanitary napkins
- Toasting goblets
- Toothbrush & toothpaste

66. What does the groom need to bring to the ceremony?
    - Airline tickets
    - Announcements
    - Aspirin/Alka Seltzer
    - Breath spray/mints
    - Bride's ring
    - Going away clothes
    - Cologne
    - Cuff links

❋ Ceremony

- Cummerbund
- Deodorant
- Hair comb
- Hair spray
- Kleenex
- Lint brush
- Luggage
- Neck tie
- Passport
- Shirt
- Shoes
- Socks
- Toothbrush & paste
- Tuxedo
- Underwear

CHAPTER 4

Ceremony Music

✿ Ceremony Music

67. When should I play music at my ceremony?

Ceremony music is the music played during the ceremony; i.e., prelude, processional, ceremony, recessional and postlude. Prelude music is played 15 to 30 minutes before the ceremony begins and while guests are being seated. Processional music is played as the wedding party enters the ceremony site. Ceremony music is played during the ceremony. Recessional music is played as the wedding party leaves the ceremony site. Postlude music is played while the guests leave the ceremony site.

68. When should I book the musicians for the ceremony?

Nine months before the wedding.

69. Should I hire a vocalist or soloist to perform the music at my ceremony?

Couples who want special hymns or songs to be performed during their ceremony often hire a vocalist. A vocalist is a singer who can perform songs either with or without musical accompaniment. You will need to be sure that the vocalist you choose can perform the songs that you want — often songs are written in specific pitches for a certain type of singer (i.e., soprano or tenor). Be sure to listen to your vocalist sing the exact song you want before signing any contracts. Be sure that any songs you might choose are appropriate for your ceremony site. Also, check with your ceremony site's wedding coordinator to see if he or she has any recommendations. Many churches have choir members who might be perfectly suited to perform at your wedding. Vocalists typically charge by the hour and can range from $50 per hour to $400 per hour.

70. What should I consider when hiring a vocalist or soloist to perform at my ceremony?

When choosing a soloist or vocalist to perform at your wedding, there are a few things to consider: When and for how long do you want them to perform? Do you need them for the entire ceremony? Do you want them to perform during the cocktail and dinner hours of your reception? The longer you need a vocalist or soloist to perform, the more music they need to have in their repertoire. Someone who only performs during the interlude and postlude will not have to have as varied a song list as one who needs to perform during the processional and recessional as well.

Also, consider the songs you have chosen for the different parts of your ceremony and ask yourself how they will sound when performed by a single person or instrument.

71. Should I ask to come to hear a vocalist perform or ask for an audition?

Ask the vocalist or soloist to provide you with a demo tape containing performances of typical wedding music they have recently performed. You can also ask if it is possible to have an in-person audition. This is especially important if your musical choices are unusual. In that case, you will want to hear the vocalist perform your specific songs. Be prepared to pay a small fee if your vocalist or soloist does not usually provide auditions.

72. Should I hire a trio or quartet to perform the music at my wedding?

A popular choice for ceremony music is to hire a trio or quartet. This is a small group of musicians, three in a trio and four in a quartet, performing with instruments from the same family, or ones that complement each other. Choices may include guitar trios, string quartets (featuring a violin, viola, and cello), or a combination of stringed instruments and flutes. Because trios and quartets have more instruments, there is a fuller sound to their performances and their repertoire is more extensive then a soloist's might be. Be sure to listen to the musicians as a group before hiring them, and be sure that the musicians you audition are the same ones who will perform at your wedding. Also, check that the group can perform your musical selection. Many classical pieces, as well as popular songs, have been arranged for performance by trios and quartets, so check on the availability of sheet music before deciding on a group. Trios and quartets often set prices based on the number of people in the group and range from $50 to $500 per hour, per person.

73. What should I consider when hiring a trio, quartet, or ensemble to perform at my ceremony?

Before choosing a trio, quartet or ensemble, you must again ask yourself some questions. How long do you want them to play? What types of music are you interested in having at your ceremony? Do you want the musicians to perform during your reception? If you have a song list for your ceremony that includes both classical pieces and instrumental versions of popular songs, you will want to check to make sure that the musicians are familiar with your popular song selections.

74. **Should I ask for an audition from the live musicians I am considering hiring?**

If you have unusual or unique song selections, ask your musicians to audition performing one of your selections. If an in-person audition is not something that the musicians typically offer, you may have to pay a small fee, or they may provide a demo tape. If your musicians provide a demo recording, be sure to ask if the same musicians featured on the recording are the ones who will be performing at your wedding.

75. **Should I hire a chamber ensemble to perform the music at my wedding?**

Chamber ensembles are groups of classical musicians who perform a specific type of classical music. Chamber music is classical music written to be played in a small room or venue as opposed to a large symphony concert hall. This makes for a perfect choice for many wedding ceremonies, as well as the cocktail and dinner hours of your reception. The music available for chamber ensembles is varied, including pieces written just for chamber musicians, as well as pieces originally written for larger orchestras that have been arranged for the smaller ensemble. The cost for chamber ensembles is usually set based on the number of people in the group, and range from $50 to $500 per hour, per person.

76. **Can I ask my chamber ensemble to play a few instrumental versions of popular songs at my ceremony?**

Chamber ensembles often only play classical pieces and may not have experience with instrumental versions of popular songs. For instance, if you have chosen "Wind Beneath My Wings" as the song that will be playing while your mother takes her seat, a chamber ensemble may not be a good choice. Also, if there will be dancing at your reception, a chamber ensemble will not be appropriate, so you may have to hire different musicians for your reception.

77. **Can I use recorded music at my ceremony?**

Some couples choose to use recorded music during their

ceremonies. Your ceremony site's wedding coordinator or a close friend can queue up specific songs. This can be a great way to save money on a live band or ensemble.

78. How much does ceremony music cost?
Hiring musicians to play your ceremony music can cost anywhere from $100 to $900 or more.

79. What is the prelude?
The prelude is the period of time before the ceremony begins. During the prelude your guests will be arriving and taking their seats. You want to make sure that there is music playing as soon as your first guests arrive so you should begin playing your prelude music as early as possible. Prelude music sets the tone for your wedding and gives your guests their first impression of what type of ceremony to expect. You may choose chamber music pieces for a formal ceremony, or smooth jazz for a less formal ceremony. In general, the music should be non-intrusive.

80. When should I start playing prelude music at my ceremony?
Deciding when to start playing the music for your prelude will depend on such things as how long you are allowed to use your ceremony site (one or two hours before the ceremony) and how the prelude music will be provided. If you have hired musicians who get paid by the hour, you may want your prelude to start later than if you are playing a CD.

81. What music should I play during the prelude of my ceremony?
We have compiled a list of songs that are popular selections for prelude music:
- Adagio For Strings, Op.11 - Barber
- Air On A G String - Bach
- All I Ask Of You - Andrew Lloyd Webber
- Ave Verum Corpus - Mozart
- Cavarelli Rusticana Intermezzo - Mascagni
- Clair De Lune - Debussy
- Four Seasons - Vivaldi
- Fur Elise - Beethoven
- The Gift - Jim Brickman
- Larghetto From Xerxes - Handel
- Scene By The Brook - Beethoven

· Romance No. 2 - Beethoven
· Symphony No. 28 Andante - Mozart

82. What is the pre-processional?
The pre-processional is the time just before the procession of the wedding party begins. This is the time when important family members, such as the mother-of-the-bride, are ushered to their seats. Changing the music from prelude to pre-processional lets your guests know that the ceremony is about to begin and is a way to honor family members who are especially important to you.

83. How do I select the music I should play during the pre-processional?
The choices for pre-processional music are endless. You may choose a piece of chamber music, an instrumental version of a contemporary ballad, or something that has special meaning to you and your family, such as a version of a lullaby your mother used to sing, or a favorite hymn of your grandmother's. While the choice is yours, keep in mind the tempo of the piece and how it will fit in with your other ceremony musical choices. A song that is vastly different in style from your prelude and processional may make your ceremony music seem disconnected.

84. What music should I play during the pre-processional?
We have compiled a list of songs that are popular selections for pre-processional music:
· Air - Water Music Suite - Handel
· Canzon V - Giovanni Gabrieli
· Emperor's Hymn - Haydn
· Son. No 3 Detta Del Niccolini - Girolamo Fantini
· Ø Sunrise, Sunset - Sheldon Harnick & Jerry Bock
· Trumpet Voluntary - Jeremiah Clarke
· Winter Largo, Four Seasons - Vivaldi

85. When is processional music played?
Processional music is played as the bridal party walks down the aisle. When the wedding party appears at the top of the aisle, the music should switch from pre-processional to processional. As soon as the bride appears at the top of the aisle, the music should switch to the piece you have chosen for the bride's entrance. This is the moment that you, and all of your guests, have been waiting for. Your music should be

dramatic and sweeping. Feel free to consider music besides the traditional wedding march, such as instrumental versions of favorite ballads and contemporary love songs. Keep in mind the tempo and how the piece will be performed.

86. How do I select the music I should play during the processional?

The processional piece should have a tempo that allows the bridesmaids and groomsmen to walk down the aisle at a measured pace and heightens the suspense for the wedding guests as they wait to see the bride. Many people use classical pieces for this part of the ceremony. When choosing a piece, keep in mind how the music will be played. A piece that is perfect in full orchestral form may not have the same presence if performed by a string quartet.

87. What music should I play during the processional?

We have compiled a list of songs that are popular selections for processional music:
  · Air from Water Music Suite - Handel
  · Bridal Chorus - Wagner
  · Canon In D - Pachelbel
  · Canzon V - Giovanni Gabrieli
  · Guitar Concerto In D Major - Vivaldi
  · Gymnopedie No.1 - Satie
  · Larghetto (From Xerxes) - Handel
  · Oboe Concerto (Slow Movement) - Handel
  · Overture (From Royal Fireworks Music) - Handel
  · Pathetique Sonata - Beethoven
  · Promenade (From Pictures At An Exhibition) - Mussorgsky
  · See The Conqu'ing Hero - Handel
  · Sonatas For Organ, Op. 65, No. 3 - Mendelssohn
  · Te Deum - Charpentier
  · To A Wild Rose - Macdowell
  · Toccata (From L'orfeo) - Monteverdi
  · Trumpet Concerto In D (Iv-Allegro) - Telemann
  · Trumpet Tune - Purcell
  · Trumpet Voluntary - Clarke
  · Winter, Largo - Vivaldi

88. What is the lighting of the unity candle?

During the ceremony, the bride and groom each use a lit candle to light the unity candle, which symbolizes two becoming one. The candle has no religious significance so it can be used in ceremonies of every denomination.

89. Should I play music during the lighting of the unity candle?

Many couples choose to set the lighting of their unity candle to music. You may want to consider having a favorite song or a special hymn to play as background music or having a vocalist perform a song that has significance to you as a couple. Again, be sure to check with the wedding coordinator at your ceremony site to determine if there are any restrictions on what music is allowed.

90. What music should I play during the lighting of the unity candle?

We have compiled a list of songs that are popular selections to play during the lighting of the unity candle:
- All People On Earth Do Dwell - Various
- Amazing Grace - Mahalia Jackson
- Ave Maria - Shubert
- Beautiful In My Eyes - Joshua Kadison
- Because We Are In Love - The Carpenters
- Morning Has Broken - Eleanor Farjeon
- The Wedding Song (There Is Love) - Petula Clark
- The Wedding Song - The Lennon Sisters
- You Are The One - Debbie Friedman

91. When is recessional music played?

Recessional music is played as the wedding party leaves the ceremony site.

92. How do I select the music to play during the recessional?

As soon as you are pronounced husband and wife your recessional music will begin. This is the moment you and your new spouse will walk back up the aisle as a married couple. You should choose music that is joyous and conveys your feelings of excitement and happiness. There is an unlimited variety of classical and contemporary music to choose from — everything from a traditional wedding march to a contemporary pop song. Use this time to create a feeling of celebration, but consider how your musical choice will be performed, what is appropriate for your ceremony site, and how formal your wedding is.

93. What music should I play during the recessional?
We have compiled a list of songs that are popular selections to play during the recessional:
- Arrival Of The Queen Of Sheba - Handel
- Brandenburg Concerto No.4, Allegro - Bach
- Concerto For Two Trumpets In B- Allegro - Vivaldi
- Crown Imperial - Walton
- Fugue In E-Flat Major - Mendelssohn
- Hallelujah Chorus - Handel
- Hornpipe (From Water Music) - Handel
- Hornpipe (From Concerto Grosso Op. 6, No. 7) - Handel
- Ode To Joy - Beethoven
- Spring, Allegro (The Four Seasons) - Vivaldi
- Toccata - Widor
- Trumpet Concerto In B, Allegro - Telemann
- Trumpet Concerto In D, Ii Allegro - Telemann
- Wedding March - Mendelssohn

94. What is the interlude/postlude?
The interlude, or postlude, is the time between the end of the ceremony and the beginning of the reception. Many couples use this time to take wedding party pictures or to greet their guests in a receiving line.

95. How do I select the music for the interlude/postlude?
The music you choose for the interlude should be non-intrusive to allow for conversation while your guests mingle and enjoy refreshments and hors d'oeuvres. You may choose to have smooth jazz, a string quartet, or a CD of instrumental or New Age music playing. If you have hired a band, be sure that they perform at an appropriate volume for the interlude and avoid songs with vocals unless they are performing far from the receiving line. The interlude may be a good time to showcase you and your fiancé's musical tastes.

96. What music should I play during the interlude/postlude?
We have compiled a list of songs that are popular selections to play during the interlude/postlude:
- Alleluia (From Exsultate Jubilate) - Mozart
- Arabesque - Debussy
- Ave Maria - Schubert
- Carillon De Westminster - Vierne
- Claire De Lune Classical - Debussy
- Greensleeves - Traditional

- Jesus, Joy Of Man's Desiring - Bach
- Minuet In G - Beethoven
- Musetta's Waltz, La Boheme - Puccini
- Pastoral Symphony - Handel

97. What are popular ceremony music selections for a Christian wedding?

We have compiled a list of songs that are popular selections to play for a Christian wedding:

- Trumpet Voluntary - Purcell
- The Bridal Chorus - Wagner
- Wedding March - Mendelssohn
- Postlude In G Major - Handel
- Canon In D Major - Pachelbel
- Adagio In A Minor - Bach

98. What are popular ceremony music selections for a Jewish wedding?

We have compiled a list of songs that are popular selections to play for a Jewish wedding:

- Erev Shel Shoshanim
- Erev Ba
- Hana' Ava Babanot

99. Is music included in the ceremony site fee?

Music may or may not be included as part of the ceremony site fee. Be sure to check with your ceremony site about restrictions pertaining to music and the availability of musical instruments for your use. Discuss the selection of ceremony music with your officiant and musicians.

100. What factors should go into selecting my ceremony music?

When selecting ceremony music, keep in mind the formality of your wedding, your religious affiliation, and the length of the ceremony. Also consider the location and time of day. If the ceremony is outside where there may be other noises such as traffic, wind, or people's voices, or if a large number of guests will be attending your ceremony, consider having the music, your officiant, and your vows amplified. Make sure there are electrical outlets close to where the instruments will be set up.

101. How can I save money on ceremony music?

Hire student musicians from your local university or high school. Ask a friend to sing or play at your ceremony; they will be honored. If you're planning to hire a band for your reception, consider hiring a scaled-down version of the same band to play at your ceremony, such as a trio of flute, guitar, and vocals. This could enable you to negotiate a "package" price. If you're planning to hire a DJ for your reception, consider hiring him or her to play pre-recorded music at your ceremony.

❋ Notes

....
....
....
....
....
....
....
....
....
....
....
....
....
....
....
....
....
....
....
....
....
....
....
....

CHAPTER 5

Officiant

❁ Officiant

102. When should I select and book my officiant for the wedding?
Nine months before the wedding, or earlier.

103. Who can officiate my wedding?
Here are some of the options you have when considering who to officiate your wedding: a priest, clergyman, minister, pastor, chaplain, Rabbi, judge, or Justice of the Peace.

104. Can we have a friend or family member preside over our ceremony?
It is becoming increasingly popular to have a friend or loved one become ordained and act as your officiant. Make sure this person goes through an accredited program or online program, and double-check that it will be legal.

105. What is the officiant's fee?
The officiant's fee is the fee paid to the person who performs your wedding ceremony.

106. How much is the officiant's fee?
The officiant's fee can range anywhere from $100 to $500.

107. What is the officiant's gratuity?
The officiant's gratuity is a discretionary amount of money given.

108. How much is the officiant's gratuity?
The officiant's gratuity is usually $50 to $250.

109. When should we give the Best Man the officiant's fee to pass along?
At the rehearsal dinner.

110. What should I do if the officiant refuses to accept the fee?
Some officiants may not accept a fee, depending on your relationship with him or her. If a fee is refused, send a donation to the officiant's church or synagogue.

111. Should I include my officiant on my guest list?
Your officiant and his or her partner should be invited to your reception, so don't forget to include them on your guest list and seating chart.

CHAPTER 6

Wedding Gowns

112. **What are some important things I should consider when selecting a wedding dress?**
In selecting your wedding dress, keep in mind the time of year and formality of your wedding. It is a good idea to look at bridal magazines to compare the various styles and colors. If you see a dress you like, call boutiques in your area to see if they carry that line. Always try on the dress before ordering it.

113. **What is the price range of wedding dresses?**
Wedding dresses can range anywhere from $300 to $10,000, depending on the designer.

114. **What is the most flattering dress style for a short, heavy figure?**
To look taller and slimmer, avoid knit fabrics. Use the princess or A-line style. Chiffon is the best fabric choice because it produces a floating effect and camouflages weight.

115. **What is the most flattering dress style for a short, thin figure?**
A shirtwaist or natural waist style with bouffant skirt will produce a taller, more rounded figure. Chiffon, velvet, lace and Schiffli net are good fabric choices.

116. **What is the most flattering dress style for a tall, heavy figure?**
Princess or A-line are the best styles for slimming the figure; satin, chiffon and lace fabrics are recommended.

117. **What is the most flattering dress style for a tall, thin figure?**
Tiers or flounces will help reduce the impression of height. A shirtwaist or natural waist style with a full skirt are ideal choices. Satin and lace are the best fabrics.

118. **What questions need to be asked at the bridal boutique where I am buying my bridal gown?**
   · What is the name of the bridal boutique?
   · What is the website and e-mail of the bridal boutique?
   · What is the address of the bridal boutique?
   · What is the name and phone number of my contact person?
   · What are your hours of operation? Are appointments

needed?
- Do you offer any discounts or giveaways?
- What major bridal gown lines do you carry?
- Do you carry outfits for the mother of the bride?
- Do you carry bridesmaids' gowns and/or tuxedos?
- Do you carry outfits for the flower girl and ring bearer?
- What is the cost of the desired bridal gown?
- What is the cost of the desired headpiece?
- Do you offer in-house alterations? If so, what are your fees?
- Do you carry bridal shoes? What is their price range?
- Do you dye shoes to match outfits?
- Do you rent bridal slips? If so, what is the rental fee?
- What is the estimated date of delivery for my gown?
- What is your payment policy/cancellation policy?

119. When should I order my wedding dress?

You should order your wedding dress at least four to six months before your wedding, especially if it has to be specially ordered and fitted.

120. What should I do if I can't afford my dream dress?

Consider shopping online for a secondhand gown that is similar or from the same designer. Find sample sales where you can buy designer gowns for much less money. Purchase the floor model gown, which will be cheaper than ordering a brand-new gown. Find an excellent tailor who you trust and have him or her make a dress similar to the dream dress.

121. What should I bring to the bridal boutique?

Always call and make an appointment before stopping in. Bring your mother, sister, Maid of Honor, or Mother-in-Law along with you. Also bring something to tie your hair back with, a strapless bra, and a shoe with a heel about the height of what you will wear on your Big Day. It is also helpful to bring in tear sheets from magazines so you can show the boutique staff what you have in mind for your gown. Bring a digital camera and have someone take pictures of you in each dress, from different angles.

122. How many dresses should I look at before choosing?

There is no set rule about how many dresses you should try on. It is great to get a nice selection to get a sense of how different styles and shapes look on you, but many brides buy the first gown they try on!

123. **What should I keep in mind when ordering my bridal gown?**

When ordering a gown, make sure you order the correct size. If you are between sizes or prone to weight gain, order the larger one. You can always have your gown tailored down to fit, but it is not always possible to have it enlarged or to lose enough weight to fit into it! Don't forget to ask when your gown will arrive, and be sure to get this in writing.

124. **What should I be wary of when buying a gown?**

Some gown manufacturers suggest ordering a size larger than needed. This requires more alterations, which may mean extra charges. It is a good idea to locate a few tailors in your area and ask for alteration pricing in advance. Many boutiques offer tailoring services but you will often find a better price by finding an independent tailor specializing in bridal gown alterations. Also, gowns often fail to arrive on time, creating unnecessary stress for you. Be sure to order your gown with enough time to allow for delivery delays. And be sure to check the reputation of the boutique before buying.

125. **What shade of white should I wear?**

In the old days, wearing white symbolized purity and virginity, but modernly white is just the most traditional gown color. You can wear any shade you prefer that complements your skin tone. Some options include stark white, diamond white, ivory, champagne, and blush.

126. **How can I incorporate color in my wedding attire?**

Try a colorful sash, piece of jewelry, or shoe. Some brides are going so far as to wear colored wedding gowns. Pink, blue, gold, red, and even gray hues are showing up on many brides who like to their personality to show through their dress.

127. **What should I consider when getting alterations on my wedding dress?**

Alterations usually require several fittings. Allow four to six weeks for alterations to be completed. However, do not alter your dress months before the wedding. Your weight may fluctuate during the final weeks of planning and the dress might not fit properly. Alterations are usually not included in the cost of the dress. You may also want to consider making some modifications to your dress such as shortening or lengthening the train, customizing the sleeves, beading and so forth. Ask your bridal boutique what they charge for the modifications you are considering.

128. Should I have my gown bustled?

Brides bustle their gowns after the ceremony to keep the dress off the floor. This prevents anyone from stepping on the train and keeps it from getting dirty. Creating a bustle for a gown is a simple alteration. Decide if you want or need a bustle and, if so, have the bridal boutique salesperson show your mother or Maid of Honor how to bustle your gown.

129. How can I make sure the alterations are correct?

Be sure you can move, walk, sit, and dance freely in the dress you choose. If you feel comfortable and there is no wrinkling, puckering, gapping, bulging, pulling at the seams, or any other issues that indicate problems with the fit, you will look and feel beautiful in that gown.

130. How much do alterations usually cost?

Alterations can cost anywhere from $75 to $500, depending upon the amount of work you need done to your dress.

131. How can I save money on alterations?

Consider hiring an independent tailor. Their fees are usually lower than bridal boutiques.

132. How many dress fittings do I need to have?

You should have at least 3 fittings. The first fitting should be 6 months before, the second fitting should be 1 month before, and the final fitting is 1 to 3 weeks before.

133. When should I arrange for a final fitting of my and my attendants' dresses?

One to three weeks before the wedding or more.

134. What should I do if I notice something I don't like at one of my fittings?

Speak up! Your wedding gown is a very large financial investment and should be perfect. Speak up if you spot a problem or there is something that isn't up to par. Have as many fittings as it takes to get the dress right.

❀ Notes

....

....

....

....

....

....

....

....

....

....

....

....

....

....

....

....

....

....

....

....

....

....

CHAPTER 7

Veils, Headpieces & Hairstyles

135. What should I consider when buying a veil or headpiece?

The headpiece should complement but not overshadow your gown. In addition to the headpiece, you might want a veil. Veils come in different styles and lengths. Select a length that complements the length of your train. Consider the total look you're trying to achieve with your gown, headpiece, veil, and hairstyle. If possible, schedule your hair "test appointment" the day you go veil shopping so you'll be able to see how your veil looks on your hairstyle.

136. What are the types of veils to consider?

The types of veils include a Blusher, Fingertip, Birdcage, Ballet or Waltz, Mantilla, Pouf, Chapel, and Cathedral. Veils vary in length, material, and formality.

137. What is a Blusher veil?

A Blusher is a single layer veil that is worn over the face during the ceremony, and then flipped back over the head.

138. What is a Fingertip veil?

This is the most common veil length, reaching to the fingertips. It can be worn with a variety of dress styles.

139. What is a Birdcage veil?

A vintage look, a Birdcage veil is made of lace or French netting that covers the face.

140. What is a Ballet or Waltz veil?

A Ballet or Waltz veil is long and flows from the headpiece down to the ankles. It is a good option for a dress without a train.

141. What is a Mantilla veil?

A Mantilla veil is a Spanish-inspired veil that drapes over the head and is usually made of lace.

142. What is a Pouf veil?

A Pouf veil has gathered material at the point where it connects to the headpiece, creating added volume.

143. What is a Chapel veil?

A Chapel veil is a formal look, extending 2½ yards from the headpiece, flowing down over the train of the dress.

144. What is a Cathedral veil?

The most formal veil, a Cathedral extends 3½ yards from the headpiece.

145. What is an appropriate veil for getting married outdoors?

A long veil is too formal for an outdoor wedding; thus, choose a shorter veil like a Fingertip or Blusher.

146. Can I remove my veil after the ceremony?

Yes, many brides remove their veils for the reception. Have your wedding consultant or Maid of Honor find a safe place for it.

147. What veil should I wear if I still want to show off the back of my dress?

You can wear a veil that falls as far as mid-thigh; then remove it after the ceremony to reveal the back of your dress.

148. What is a headpiece?

The headpiece attaches the veil, or the bride can wear a decorative headpiece, such as a headband, without a veil.

149. What are some different types of headpieces I can buy?

Some options for a headpiece include a profile, garden hat, headband, Juliet Cap, tiara, hairpins, or wreath.

150. What type of headpiece is a profile?

A profile is an ornamental comb that can accent a sophisticated updo, such as a French twist or chignon. Profiles are generally worn without a veil.

151. What type of headpiece is a garden hat?

A garden hat is a wide-brimmed hat that makes a dramatic statement, especially well suited for an outdoor summer wedding.

152. What type of headpiece is a headband?

A headband is a popular headpiece made from satin, lace, or the same material as your dress. It can be a simple strip of fabric or can incorporate a silk flower. A headband is generally worn without a veil.

153. What type of headpiece is a Juliet Cap?

This Old World-style headpiece sits on the crown of your

head and is generally adorned with pearls or beading.

154. What type of headpiece is a tiara?

A great headpiece if you want to feel like a princess on your Big Day, a tiara can be worn with a veil and kept on after the veil is removed. If you have short hair, have a hairdresser help you wire the hairpiece so it will stay.

155. What type of headpiece are hairpins?

Hairpins can be a simple and beautiful way to adorn wedding hair with pearls, crystals, flowers, butterflies and more. Hairpins are perfect for any length hair.

156. What type of headpiece is a wreath?

Ask your florist to create a wreath for you using greenery or the same flowers from your bouquet for an ethereal look. Choose long-lasting flowers that won't wilt. High-quality silk flowers are also an option.

157. How much do headpieces usually cost?

Headpieces can cost anywhere from $60 to $500.

158. How can I save money on a headpiece?

Some boutiques offer a free headpiece or veil with the purchase of a gown. Make sure you ask for this before purchasing your gown.

159. Can I make my own headpiece?

A headpiece like a headband or flower hairpin can be easy to make from materials found at a local crafts store. Look for pretty ribbon, high-quality silk flowers, lace, French netting, and other materials.

160. What should I consider if I want to wear fresh flowers in my hair?

Choose a hardy bloom like daisies or roses. Delicate flowers like sweet peas and tulips will wilt quickly. Another popular flower to wear in the hair is the gardenia, which has a soft, pretty scent.

161. What should I keep in mind when getting my hair professionally done for the wedding day?

Consider having your professional hairdresser experiment with your hair and headpiece before your wedding day so there are no surprises. Most hairdressers will include the cost of a sample session in your package. They will try several styles on you and write down the specifics of each one so that things go quickly and smoothly on your wedding day. On the big day, you can go to the salon or have the stylist meet you at your home or dressing site. Consider having him or her arrange your bridal party's hair for a consistent look.

162. Do I want to get a haircut or highlights before my wedding?

Get a trim a couple of weeks before your wedding to get rid of any split ends. If you color or highlight your hair, do this well enough in advance so your hair has time to look natural after the treatment. Don't get a brand-new haircut or color you've never tried before right before the wedding. You want to look like yourself!

163. Should I have my hair or makeup done first on my wedding day?

You should always have your hair done first.

164. If I want my bridesmaids and Maid of Honor to have their hair and makeup done on my wedding day, do I need to pay for them?

The wedding party usually pays for their own hair and makeup; however, you can pay as a gift to them if you like.

165. How can I save money when I get my hair done for my wedding day?

Negotiate having your hair arranged free of charge or at a discount in exchange for bringing your mother, your fiancé's mother and your bridal party to the salon.

✽ Notes

....
....
....
....
....
....
....
....
....
....
....
....
....
....
....
....
....
....
....
....
....
....
....
....

CHAPTER 8

Shoes & Accessories

166. How much do shoes for my wedding cost?

This all depends upon the designer and what type of shoe you are looking for, but they can run anywhere from $50 to $500.

167. What do I need to consider when buying shoes for my bridal gown?

Make sure you select comfortable shoes that complement your gown, and don't forget to break them in well before your wedding day. Tight shoes can make you miserable and ruin your otherwise perfect day!

168. What shoe is best for an outdoor wedding?

A high heel will probably sink into the grass, sand, or soft ground at an outdoor wedding, so it is best to wear a pretty flat shoe or a wedge.

169. With what type of dress is it appropriate to wear gloves?

Gloves add a nice touch with either short-sleeved, three-quarter length, or sleeveless gowns.

170. What are some of my options for gloves?

Gloves come in various styles and lengths. Depending on the length of your sleeves, select gloves that reach above your elbow, just below your elbow, halfway between your wrist and elbow, or only to your wrist.

171. What should I consider when buying gloves?

You may want to consider fingerless mitts that allow the groom to place the wedding ring on your ring finger without having to remove your glove. You should not wear gloves if your gown has long sleeves, or if you're planning a small, at-home wedding.

172. How much do gloves typically cost?

Gloves can cost anywhere from $15 to $100.

173. Should I wear nylons or panty hose underneath my bridal gown?

You can, but it is not necessary. If you do choose to wear nylons, they should be selected with care, especially if the groom will be removing a garter from your leg at the reception. Consider having your Maid of Honor carry an extra pair, just in case you get a run.

174. What types of undergarments should I wear on my wedding day?

You will want to consider wearing a thong, body slimmer, or bustier. Always wear flesh-colored or nude-colored undergarments and have someone check that they don't show through your dress in sunlight and with the photo flash. Wear your undergarments to your dress fittings to be sure you know what looks and fits best with your gown.

175. What is the bridal slip?

The bridal slip is an undergarment that gives the bridal gown its proper shape. Be sure to wear the same slip you'll be wearing on your wedding day during your fittings. Many bridal salons rent slips. Schedule an appointment to pick up your slip one week before the wedding; otherwise, you run the risk of not having one available on your wedding day. If rented, the slip will have to be returned shortly after the wedding. Arrange for someone to do this for you within the allotted time. Rent a slip rather than purchasing one; chances are you will never use it again.

176. What kind of jewelry should I wear with my bridal gown?

Think about selecting pieces of jewelry that can be classified as "something old, something new, something borrowed, or something blue." Brides look best with just a few pieces of jewelry — perhaps a string of pearls and earrings with a simple bracelet. Purchase complementary jewelry for your bridesmaids, to match the colors of their dresses. This will give your bridal party a coordinated look.

177. How much does bridal jewelry usually cost?

The cost of the jewelry all depends upon what you want, but it can range anywhere from $60 to $2,000.

✿ Notes

....

....

....

....

....

....

....

....

....

....

....

....

....

....

....

....

....

....

....

....

....

....

....

....

CHAPTER 9

Engagement Rings & Bands

178. What do diamonds symbolize?
Throughout the world, diamonds are used to symbolize love and the unbreakable bond of marriage.

179. Why does the engagement ring go on the left hand?
In the past it was believed that the ring finger on the left hand held a vein that ran directly to the heart. A ring on this finger meant that the marriage between the two people would be a long, loving and happy one.

180. What is the average size of the diamond engagement ring today?
Today, the average size of the diamond on an engagement ring is about .75 carats.

181. What are the different shapes of diamonds?
There are various shapes of diamonds. The most popular is the round cut, known as "brilliant." Close to 75 percent of diamonds sold are round. This is mainly because they tend to sparkle more than the other shapes. Other shapes, such as marquise, oval, emerald, princess (or square), and the pear shape, are known as "fancy."

182. What are the different kinds of metals to choose from?
Platinum is the most expensive metal for a ring. Palladium is an alternative to platinum that is less expensive. White gold also looks similar to platinum, but costs about half as much. You might also talk to a jeweler about yellow gold, rose gold, and other unique metal options.

183. What do I need to know before I buy a diamond?
Before purchasing a diamond, you will need to know your fiancée's taste. If you are planning to surprise her, try to purchase your diamond from a reputable source that offers a money back guarantee or at least allows exchange. In addition, make sure you get a detailed appraisal of the diamond in writing. Also get in writing any other policy such as money-back or trade-in as well as whether the purchase is subject to verification of GIA certification.

184. What does the term "boat" mean when I go to buy a diamond?
The boat is a piece of paper used to hold the diamond upright (in a V-shape) so one can look at the diamond.

This paper is extremely white so it allows you to see the diamond's true color.

185. What does the term "brilliance" mean when I go to buy a diamond?

Brilliance is the amount of sparkle a diamond possesses.

186. What does the term "chip" mean when buying a diamond?

Chips are external nicks in the girdle of the diamond.

187. What does the term "cloud" mean when I go to buy a diamond?

Clouds refer to a cloudy area inside the diamond.

188. What does the term "crown" mean when I go to buy a diamond?

The crown is the part of the diamond above the girdle.

189. What does the term "culet" mean when I go to buy a diamond?

The culet is the minute bottom facet of the stone.

190. What does the term "facet" mean when I go to buy a diamond?

Facets are the planes on a diamond which direct light through the stone.

191. What does the term "feather" mean when I go to buy a diamond?

Feathers are used to describe a central crack with little cracks along its side.

192. What does the term "fire" mean when I go to buy a diamond?

Fire is the intensity of colors created by a diamond.

193. What does the term "girdle" mean when I go to buy a diamond?

The girdle is the rim or edge of the stone having the largest diameter.

194. What does the term "inclusion" mean when I go to buy a diamond?

Inclusions are the carbon spots inside a diamond that reflect light, making the spot look black.

195. What does the term "scratch" mean when I go to buy a diamond?

A scratch is a mark on the face of the diamond. Scratches can usually be polished out.

196. What does the term "pavilion" mean when I go to buy a diamond?

The pavilion is the part of the diamond below the girdle.

197. What does the term "table" mean when I go to buy a diamond?

The table is the broad top facet of the diamond.

198. What does the term "color" mean in terms of a diamond?

A diamond's color scale ranges from D to Z. Keep in mind that the slight color of near colorless diamonds is usually visible only through a magnifying lens and from the underside of the diamond. Therefore, minor shades of color, are hard to see in mounted stones.

D to F: Colorless
G to J: Near colorless
K to M: Faint yellow
N to R: Very light yellow
S to Z: Light yellow
Z+: Fancy or colored

199. What does the term "cut" mean in terms of a diamond?

Cut is the most important element of a diamond. It is what gives the diamond fire and sparkle. Most women would agree that a smaller diamond with a lot of fire and sparkle is better than a bigger diamond without any flair. A diamond that is cut too shallow may appear larger than a properly cut diamond of the same size, but it may have less sparkle. On the other hand, a diamond that is cut too deep may appear smaller than a properly cut diamond of the same size, but it may look darker. Prices can vary as much as 50 percent between a well-cut stone and a poorly-cut stone.

200. What does the term "clarity" mean in terms of a diamond?

The clarity of the diamond is very important as it allows you to see the diamond's level of perfection. The more imperfections in a diamond, the less fire or sparkle it has. The less imperfections in a diamond, the more light that can pass through it. Clarity is graded on a scale of Flawless (FL), Internally Flawless (IF), Very Very Slight Inclusion (VVS1 and VVS2), Very Slight Inclusion (VSl and VS2), and Slight Inclusion (SI1-SI3). Clarity is always graded under a jeweler's loupe (10x magnification) and always with an experienced eye. All diamonds have one or more inclusions, whether visible or not, but no two diamonds have the same inclusion in the same are Therefore, flaws or inclusions are often referred to as the "fingerprint" of the diamond.

· Flawless (FL): An FL diamond contains no imperfections. These diamonds are extremely rare and therefore very expensive.

· Internally flawless (IF): An IF diamond has no internal inclusions and very few minor external inclusions.

· Very Very Slight Inclusions (VVS1): A VVS1 diamond has very small inclusions, mainly externally. These inclusions are so small that they are hard to find even with a jeweler's loupe.

· Very Very Slight Inclusions (VVS2): A VVS2 diamond has a little larger inclusion than the VVS1 but it is still hard to see under a jeweler's loupe.

· Very Slight Inclusions 1 (VS1): A VS1 diamond has small inclusions, usually around the edge of the stone. It is not easy to see these inclusions under a jeweler's loupe.

· Very Slight Inclusions 2 (VS2): A VS2 diamond has small inclusions, usually around the heart of the stone. These inclusions may be a little difficult to see under a jeweler's loupe.

· Slight Inclusions 1 (SI1): An SI1 diamond has few inclusions, usually around the edge of the diamond. These inclusions are easy to locate under a jeweler's loupe.

· Slight Inclusions 2 (SI2): An SI2 diamond has inclusions, usually around the table of the diamond. These inclusions are very easy to locate under a jeweler's loupe.

· Slight Inclusions 3 (SI3): An SI3 diamond has inclusions, usually under the table of the diamond. These inclusions are very easy to locate under a jeweler's loupe.

· Inclusions 1 (I1): An I1 diamond has several inclusions inside the diamond that are very easy to locate under a jeweler's loupe and may even be seen with the naked eye.

· Inclusions 2 (I2): An I2 diamond has several inclusions,

usually in the heart of the stone. These inclusions are easily seen by the naked eye.

· Inclusions 3 (I3): An I3 diamond has several inclusions that are very easily seen by the naked eye.

201. **What does the term "carat" mean in terms of a diamond?**
Carat is the unit used to measure the weight of a diamond. It is equal to 200 milligrams or 142 carats to the ounce. The cost of a diamond increases exponentially as its size or weight increases. For example, a two-carat diamond costs much more than two one-carat diamonds. This is because bigger diamonds are harder to find. The price point for a carat is about .85-carat. This means that an .80-carat diamond will cost much less than a .90-carat diamond, but a .90-carat diamond will cost almost the same as a 1-carat diamond. So if you have the choice, buy either a .80 carat diamond or, if you can afford it, a 1 carat diamond. To save money, set a small side diamond on each side of the center diamond; this will make the center stone look much bigger. Or buy an oval diamond, which is the least expensive shape. Buy your diamond after Christmas or Valentine's Day to take advantage of sales. Summer is also a good time to buy a diamond since jewelers are usually slow during this time. Keep in mind that color is not too crucial since it is difficult to discern color differences once the diamond is mounted. Always buy from a reputable jeweler who offers a money-back guarantee or at least gives you the option of trading-in your diamond for another one.

202. **Should I get the diamond GIA certified?**
Definitely make your purchase subject to verification by GIA certification. Do not rely on verification by a GIA-certified agent recommended by the jeweler who sold you the diamond. Try to find an independent agent or go directly to the GIA. The GIA is the only independent organization that will tell you the true, unbiased characteristics of your diamond without having an interest in selling you something.

203. **What should I get in writing before I buy a diamond?**
Before you purchase a diamond, make sure you get a detailed appraisal of the diamond in writing. Also get in writing any other policy such as money-back or trade-in as well as whether the purchase is subject to verification of GIA certification.

204. What kind of insurance do I need to protect my engagement ring?
Often, wedding jewelry is covered under basic homeowners' insurance, but should probably be itemized separately.

205. When should we begin shopping for wedding bands?
Two to four months before the wedding.

206. What should we consider when deciding what style of wedding bands to get?
The bride's wedding band should complement her engagement ring in style and metal. For the groom, consider his lifestyle when choosing a wedding band. Certain metals are stronger and will resist wear and tear better than others. For instance, if you work with your hands and will be wearing your wedding band every day, you will want to avoid any soft metals. A durable metal, like titanium, is a good choice.

207. When should we pick up our wedding bands?
Two to six weeks before the wedding.

CHAPTER 10

Makeup & Beauty

208. When should I book my hair and makeup appointment?

Six to eight weeks before the wedding.

209. How much does having my makeup done for my wedding day cost?

It depends upon the makeup artist you are using, but it can range from $30 to $150 per person.

210. What do I need to keep in mind when getting my makeup done?

It's smart to go for a trial run before the day of the wedding so there are no surprises. You can either go to the salon or have the makeup artist meet you at your home or dressing site. Consider having him or her apply makeup for your mother, your fiancé's mother and your bridesmaids for a consistent look. In selecting a makeup artist, make sure he or she has been trained in makeup for photography. It is very important to wear the proper amount of makeup for photographs. Consider having your makeup trial right before your hairdresser trial — that way you'll see how your hair looks with your makeup on. It can make a big difference.

211. What kind of makeup should I avoid on my wedding day?

Beware of using too much shimmer or glitter, as these types of makeup will cause you to appear shiny in your pictures. A light shimmer used to highlight certain areas such as your cheekbones and brow bones is OK, but you may want to take test photos before the wedding day to see how it is going to look. It is best to use a waterproof mascara and eyeliner, especially if you know you will be shedding a few tears on your Big Day. Finally, don't wear a ton of makeup if you don't normally. You want to look like yourself!

212. How do I make sure my makeup doesn't melt or run if I have oily skin?

You should consult a makeup professional who can suggest oil-free products and matte makeup products. Using blotting papers and a mattifying toner can help keep makeup fresh.

213. How can I save money when having my makeup done by a professional for my wedding day?

Try to negotiate having your makeup applied free of charge or at a discount in exchange for bringing your mother, your fiancé's mother and your wedding party to the salon.

214. My makeup artist suggested airbrush makeup. What is airbrush makeup?

Airbrush makeup is foundation that is applied with a spray tool that gives even, all-over coverage that won't streak, run, or fade during the day. Thus, it is a top choice for bridal makeup. It also provides beautiful coverage for photos.

215. Can I do my makeup myself?

If you are doing your makeup yourself you will want to practice many times, experimenting with colors, products, and techniques. Go to a makeup counter at your local department store to pick up some helpful hints and special products that will help you apply your makeup flawlessly. Have a makeup artist at the store show you to apply different products for the look you want.

216. Should I get a facial before my wedding to have clear skin?

If visiting an esthetician for facials, avoid extractions near your Big Day as this can often cause you to break out — the last thing you want right before your wedding. Rather, go in for extractions a month or two prior to your wedding and return for a follow-up facial without extractions a few days before the wedding.

217. How can I make sure my face looks flawless for my wedding day?

Drink a lot of water! Your skin will look clearer and more hydrated, and you will feel better all over. And get plenty of rest. This can be tough, especially in the few days leading up to the wedding. Try to leave the day before your wedding mostly open for rest to ensure you show your freshest face on your Big Day.

218. How long before the wedding should I get an eyebrow and lip wax?

Plan to get waxed a week or so before the wedding, then touch up the areas with tweezers the day or two before. Don't use tweezers on your Big Day as the area will be red.

219. When should I get a manicure or pedicure for my wedding?

A day or two before the wedding would be the best time to get a manicure or pedicure. That way, you don't risk ruining them before they dry the day of the wedding, and you have more time on the day of the wedding to get your hair and makeup done.

220. What should I keep in mind when getting a manicure or pedicure for my wedding?

Don't forget to bring the appropriate color nail polish with you for your appointment. You can either go to the salon or have the manicurist meet you at your home or dressing site. Consider having him or her give your mother, your fiancé's mother and your bridesmaids a manicure in the same color.

221. How can I save money on a manicure or pedicure?

Try to negotiate getting a manicure or pedicure free of charge or at a discount in exchange for bringing your mother, your fiancé's mother and your wedding party to the salon. Or, have a get-together with your bridesmaids and give each other manicures and pedicures.

CHAPTER 11

Groom's Attire

222. What should the groom wear at the wedding?

This is really up to you and is based on the formality of the wedding. For a semi-formal or formal wedding, the groom will need a tuxedo. A tuxedo is the formal jacket worn by men on special or formal occasions. When selecting a place to rent a tuxedo, keep in mind the reputation of the shop. Make sure they have a variety of styles and makes from which to choose.

223. What do I need to keep in mind when selecting the color and style of the groom's formal wear?

The most popular colors for suits are black, white, and gray. It also may depend upon where you are getting married. However, the groom should keep in mind formality, location, time of day, weather conditions and what the bride is wearing when selecting his attire. Consider darker colors for a fall or winter wedding and lighter colors for a spring or summer wedding.

224. How can the groom save money on a tuxedo?

Try to negotiate getting your tuxedo for free or at a discount in exchange for having your father, your fiancé's father and ushers rent their tuxedos at that shop.

225. What should the groom wear for an informal wedding?

The customary attire for the groom at an informal wedding is a business suit with a white dress shirt and tie.

226. What should the groom wear for a semi-formal daytime wedding?

The customary attire for the groom at a semi-formal daytime wedding is a formal suit with a white dress shirt, cummerbund or vest, and a four-in-hand or bow tie.

227. What should the groom wear for a semi-formal evening wedding?

The customary attire for the groom at a semi-formal evening wedding is a formal suit or dinner jacket with matching trousers, a white shirt, cummerbund or vest, black bow tie, and cufflinks and studs.

228. What should the groom wear for a formal daytime wedding?

The customary attire for the groom at a formal daytime

wedding is a cutaway or stroller jacket with a waistcoat, striped trousers, a white wing-collared shirt, striped tie, and cufflinks and studs.

229. What should the groom wear for a formal evening wedding?

The customary attire for the groom at a formal evening wedding is a black dinner jacket with matching trousers, a waistcoat, a white tuxedo shirt, bow tie, cummerbund or vest, and cufflinks.

230. What should the groom wear for a very formal daytime wedding?

The customary attire for the groom at a very formal daytime wedding is a cutaway coat with a wing-collared shirt, an ascot, striped trousers, cufflinks, and gloves.

231. What should the groom wear for a very formal evening wedding?

The customary attire for the groom at a very formal evening wedding is a black tailcoat with matching striped trousers, bow tie, a white wing-collared shirt, a waistcoat, patent leather shoes, cuff-links and studs, and gloves.

232. As the groom, is it appropriate to wear leather sandals at a Caribbean destination wedding?

Your footwear choice is up to you, but leather sandals are fine for a beach, daytime wedding, as long as you are wearing a casual suit made of linen or another summery material.

233. When should I reserve tuxedos?

Reserve tuxedos for yourself and your ushers several weeks before the wedding to ensure a wide selection and to allow enough time for alterations. Plan to pick up the tuxedos a few days before the wedding to allow time for last minute alterations in case they don't fit properly. Ask about the store's return policy and be sure you delegate to the appropriate person (usually your Best Man) the responsibility of returning all tuxedos within the time allotted. Ushers customarily pay for their own tuxedos.

❋ Groom's Attire

234. What should I do about tux rentals if I have groomsmen who live out of the state or country?

Out-of-town men in your wedding party can be sized at any tuxedo shop. They can send their measurements to you or directly to the shop where you are going to rent your tuxedos. Make sure one of their first stops when they get to town for the wedding is the tux shop to try on their tuxedos and make sure there are no last-minute alterations needed.

235. Who should return the groomsmen's tuxes after the wedding?

The Best Man should shoulder the responsibility of returning any rented tuxedos after the wedding.

236. What should the groom do on the wedding day?

Don't make any other plans for the wedding day. You don't want to be anxious about running out of time or being late to your own wedding. All last-minute errands and chores should be designated to a family member or member of your wedding party. Make sure you arrive dressed in plenty of time at the ceremony site. There is nothing that causes more anxiety than being late to your own wedding. Have your Best Man check with your ushers to make sure they know where to go and at what time to arrive. This is a day to enjoy and be happy.

CHAPTER 12

The Wedding Party

237. **How should I choose my Maid of Honor?**

Your Maid of Honor should be a close female friend or family member who is responsible and has the time and dedication to commit to helping you plan various important aspects of the wedding. She will have to plan the bachelorette party, organize other girls in the wedding party, and possibly carry out other duties like creating favors or calling vendors. Make sure the person you choose is willing and able to help you in any way you need.

238. **How should I choose the Best Man?**

Your Best Man should be a close friend or family member who is responsible and has the time and dedication to commit to helping you plan various important aspects of the wedding. He will have to plan the bachelor party, organize other men in the wedding party, and possibly carry out other duties like calling vendors and returning tuxes. Make sure the person you choose is willing and able to help you in any way you need.

239. **What are the flower girl's duties and whom should I pick to be the flower girl?**

The flower girl should be a young family member between the ages of 4 and 8. She carries a basket filled with flowers, rose or paper rose petals to strew as she walks down the aisle. She follows the ring bearer or Maid of Honor and precedes the bride during the processional.

240. **What are some things I should consider for having a flower girl?**

Discuss any restrictions regarding rose petal, flower, or paper tossing with your ceremony site. Select a basket that complements your guest book and ring bearer pillow.

241. **My flower girl is very young and I want to avoid giving her petals to toss. What else can she carry?**

If the flower girl is very young (less than 7 years), consider giving her a small bouquet instead of a flower basket. Have her parents sit at the edge of the aisle to guide her along.

242. **What is the ring bearer's job and whom should I choose to be the ring bearer?**

A young boy in your family, between the ages of 4 and

8, carries the bride and groom's rings or mock rings on a pillow. He follows the Maid of Honor and precedes the flower girl or bride in the processional.

243. What should I consider when having a ring bearer?

If the ring bearer is very young (less than 7 years), place mock rings on the pillow in place of the real rings to prevent losing them. If mock rings are used, instruct your ring bearer to put the pillow upside down during the recessional so your guests don't see them.

244. Is there an alternative to a ring pillow?

Consider using a beautiful box or other meaningful receptacle in place of a traditional ring pillow. Ideas might include a jewelry box from your mother, a large seashell to complement a beach theme, or a dish from a loved one's home.

245. Can I have my pet in the wedding?

Pets can absolutely participate in the wedding ceremony if your venue allows it. Many retailers sell mini tuxedos, ring pillows, and special wedding attire for pets. If the venue gives you the OK, ask a responsible family member or friend to be in charge of your pet. You don't want to have to worry in the event that the animal acts up, needs water, or has to relieve itself.

246. When should I select the bridal attendants' shoes, dresses and accessories?

Nine months before the wedding.

247. Do my bridesmaids have to wear matching dresses?

One dress may not look good on every girl in your wedding party. If you want, you can give your bridesmaids two or three styles from the same designer and let them choose the style they like best. Or, you can choose a specific color and let the ladies pick their own dresses. You may want to approve the dresses to be sure they coordinate and are of your liking.

248. What are the Maid of Honor's responsibilities?

· Helps bride select attire and address invitations.
· Plans bridal shower.

- Arrives at dressing site 2 hours before ceremony to assist bride in dressing.
- Arrives dressed at ceremony site 1 hour before the wedding for photographs.
- Arranges the bride's veil and train before the processional and recessional.
- Holds bride's bouquet and groom's ring, if no ring bearer, during the ceremony.
- Witnesses the signing of the marriage license.
- Keeps bride on schedule.
- Dances with Best Man during the bridal party dance.
- Helps bride change into her going away clothes.
- Mails wedding announcements after the wedding.
- Returns bridal slip, if rented.

249. What are the Best Man's responsibilities?
- Responsible for organizing ushers' activities.
- Organizes bachelor party for groom.
- Drives groom to ceremony site and sees that he is properly dressed before the wedding.
- Arrives dressed at ceremony site 1 hour before the wedding for photographs.
- Brings marriage license to wedding.
- Pays the clergyman, musicians, photographer, and any other service providers the day of the wedding.
- Holds the bride's ring for the groom, if no ring bearer, until needed by officiant.
- Witnesses the signing of the marriage license.
- Drives newlyweds to reception if no hired driver.
- Offers first toast at reception, usually before dinner.
- Keeps groom on schedule.
- Dances with Maid of Honor during the bridal party dance.
- May drive couple to airport or honeymoon suite.
- Oversees return of tuxedo rentals for groom and ushers, on time and in good condition.

250. What are the bridesmaids' responsibilities?
- Assist Maid/Matron of Honor in planning bridal shower.
- Assist bride with errands and addressing invitations.
- Participate in all pre-wedding parties.
- Arrive at dressing site 2 hours before ceremony.
- Arrive dressed at ceremony site 1 hour before the wedding for photographs.
- Walk behind ushers in order of height during the

processional, either in pairs or in single file.
- Sit next to ushers at the head table.
- Dance with ushers and other important guests.
- Encourage single women to participate in the bouquet-tossing ceremony.

251. What are the ushers' responsibilities?
- Help Best Man with bachelor party.
- Arrive dressed at ceremony site 1 hour before the wedding for photographs.
- Distribute wedding programs and maps to the reception as guests arrive.
- Seat guests at the ceremony as follows:
  - If female, offer the right arm.
  - If male, walk along his left side.
  - If couple, offer right arm to female; male follows a step or two behind.
- Seat bride's guests in left pews.
- Seat groom's guests in right pews.
- Maintain equal number of guests in left and right pews, if possible.
- If a group of guests arrive at the same time, seat the eldest woman first.
- Just prior to the processional, escort groom's mother to her seat; then escort bride's mother to her seat.
- Two ushers may roll carpet down the aisle after both mothers are seated.
- If pew ribbons are used, two ushers may loosen them one row at a time after the ceremony.
- Direct guests to the reception site.
- Dance with bridesmaids and other important guests.

252. What are the Mother of the Bride's responsibilities?
- Helps prepare guest list for bride and her family.
- Helps plan the wedding ceremony and reception.
- Helps bride select her bridal gown.
- Helps bride keep track of gifts received.
- Selects her own attire according to the formality and color of the wedding.
- Makes accommodations for bride's out of town guests.
- Arrives dressed at ceremony site 1 hour before the wedding for photographs.
- Is the last person to be seated right before the processional begins.

- Sits in the left front pew to the left of bride's father during the ceremony.
- May stand up to signal the start of the processional.
- Can witness the signing of the marriage license.
- Dances with the groom after the First Dance.
- Acts as hostess at the reception.

253. What are the responsibilities of the Father of the Bride?
- Helps prepare guest list for bride and her family.
- Selects attire that complements groom's attire.
- Rides to the ceremony with bride in limousine.
- Arrives dressed at ceremony site 1 hour before the wedding for photographs.
- After giving bride away, sits in the left front pew to the right of bride's mother.
- If divorced, sits in second or third row unless financing the wedding.
- When officiant asks, "Who gives this bride away?" answers, "Her mother and I do," or something similar.
- Can witness the signing of the marriage license.
- Dances with bride after First Dance.
- Acts as host at the reception.

254. What are the Mother of the Groom's responsibilities?
- Helps prepare guest list for groom and his family.
- Selects attire that complements Mother of the Bride's attire.
- Makes accommodations for groom's out-of-town guests.
- With groom's father, plans rehearsal dinner.
- Arrives dressed at ceremony site 1 hour before the wedding for photographs.
- May stand up to signal the start of the processional.
- Can witness the signing of the marriage license.

255. What are the Father of the Groom's responsibilities?
- Helps prepare guest list for groom and his family.
- Selects attire that complements groom's attire.
- With groom's mother, plans rehearsal dinner.
- Offers toast to bride at rehearsal dinner.
- Arrives dressed at ceremony site 1 hour before the wedding for photographs.
- Can witness the signing of the marriage license.

256. What are the flower girl's responsibilities?

- Attends rehearsal to practice but is not required to attend pre-wedding parties.
- Arrives dressed at ceremony site 45 minutes before the wedding for photos.
- Carries a basket filled with loose rose petals to strew along bride's path during processional, if allowed by ceremony site.
- If very young, may sit with her parents during ceremony.

257. What are the ring bearer's responsibilities?

- Attends rehearsal to practice but is not required to attend pre-wedding parties.
- Arrives at ceremony site 45 minutes before the wedding for photographs.
- Carries a white pillow with rings attached.
- If younger than 7 years, carries artificial rings.
- If very young, may sit with his parents during ceremony.
- If artificial rings are used, turns the ring pillow over at the end of the ceremony.

258. What can I do if one of my in-laws wants to help plan the wedding?

It is not uncommon for in-laws to feel starved for attention during wedding planning. The Mother of the Bride will especially want to feel she is included. An easy way to include your mother in wedding planning is to put her in charge of invitations and RSVPs. She can address and send out invitations and keep track of who RSVPs — all important tasks. If you want, you can also invite her along to look at ceremony and reception sites or to meet vendors — just be clear with vendors that you are the point of contact, and be clear with her that you value her opinion, but the decisions are ultimately yours.

✿ Notes

....
....
....
....
....
....
....
....
....
....
....
....
....
....
....
....
....
....
....
....
....
....
....
....
....
....
....

CHAPTER 13

Photography

259. When should I book the photographer?

Nine months before the wedding.

260. How much do photographers cost?

It depends upon the quality of the photographer and whether or not they charge a flat or hourly rate, but photographers' packages can range from $900 to $7,000. This is not an area in which you want to skimp, so if you have the budget for it, hire the best photographer you can.

261. How do I go about selecting a photographer for my wedding?

The photographs you have taken at your wedding are your memories of the big day, so it is important that you do not skimp in this area. Hiring a good photographer is one of the most important tasks in planning your wedding. Make sure you hire a photographer who specializes in weddings. Your photographer should be experienced in wedding procedures and familiar with your ceremony and reception sites. This will allow him or her to anticipate your next move and be in the proper place at the right time to capture all the special moments. Personal rapport is extremely important. The photographer may be an expert, but if you don't feel comfortable or at ease with him or her, your photography will reflect this. Comfort and compatibility with your photographer can make or break your wedding day and your photographs!

When comparing prices, consider the number, size and finish of the photographs and the type of album the photographer will use. Ask how many proofs you will get to choose from. The more proofs, the better the selection you will have. Some photographers do not work with proofs. Rather, they simply supply you with a finished album after the wedding. Doing this may reduce the cost of your album but will also reduce your selection of photographs.

Also, some churches do not allow photographs to be shot during the ceremony. Make sure your photographer understands the rules and regulations of your church before planning the ceremony shots.

262. What should I ask to see when I meet with a photographer?

Look at his or her work. See if the photographer captured the excitement and emotion of the bridal couple. Also, remember that the wedding album should unfold like a storybook — the story of your wedding. Be sure to discuss with your photographer the photos you want so that there is no misunderstanding. A good wedding photographer should have a list of suggested shots to choose from. Look at albums ready to be delivered, or proofs of weddings recently photographed by your photographer. Notice the photographer's preferred style. Some photographers are known for formal poses, while others specialize in more candid, creative shots. Some can do both.

263. Should I ask for references from photographers I interview?

When asked to provide references, many photographers will give you the names of people they know are happy with their work. Some may even give you names from weddings they shot several years ago. This may not indicate the photographer's current ability or reputation. So when asking for references, be sure to ask for recent weddings the photographer has performed. This will give you a good idea of his or her current work. Be sure to ask if the photographer was prompt, cordial, properly dressed and whether he or she performed the duties as expected.

264. Should I have my photographer shoot in black and white or color or a combination of both?

Black and white photography can be very dramatic and beautiful; however, the colorful aspects of your wedding, including your flowers, dresses, venue, and décor, won't be aptly captured. You should ask for a combination of black and white and color photos to capture the complete essence and ambience of your wedding.

265. What is the benefit of digital film?

Today, most photographers use digital format cameras. This can be great, because it makes it easy to switch between black and white and color without having to replace rolls of film or use multiple cameras. You may also get a lot more images to choose from, as photographers using a digital camera can shoot far more pictures and take more chances than a photographer shooting with film.

266. What should I get in writing from my photographer?

Make sure the photographer you interview is the one who will actually photograph your wedding. There are many companies with more than one photographer. Often these companies use the work of the best photographer to sell their packages and then send a less experienced photographer to the wedding. Don't get caught in this trap! Be sure you sign a contract with the photographer who will shoot your wedding. Also make sure you get pricing information, such as the cost of extra hours of shooting, in writing. Finally, when the photographer tells you how long it will take to get proofs, request this in writing.

267. What type of album should I choose for the bride and groom's album?

There are a large variety of wedding albums. They vary in size, color, material, construction and price. Find one that you like and will feel proud of showing to your friends and family. Some of the most popular manufacturers of wedding albums are Art Leather, Leather Craftsman and Renaissance. Make sure you review the differences between these albums before selecting one. You will also need to select the finish process of your photos. Ask your photographer to show you samples of various finishes. Some of the most popular finishes are glossy, luster, semi-matte, pebble finish, spray texture and oil.

268. What is the parents' album and what photographs go in it?

The parents' album is a smaller version of the bride and groom's album. It usually contains about twenty 5" x 7" photographs of the couple with their family members. If given as a gift to the families, the album can be personalized with the bride and groom's names and date of their wedding on the front cover.

269. Should I order extra prints?

Extra prints are photographs ordered in addition to the main album or parents' albums. These are usually purchased as gifts for the bridal party, close friends and family members. It is important to discuss the cost of extra prints with your photographer since prices vary considerably. Some photographers offer the main album at great bargains to get the job, but then charge a fortune on extra prints. Think about how many extra prints you would like to order and figure this into your budget before selecting a photographer.

270. What are proofs/previews of my photographs?

Proofs/previews are the preliminary prints from which the bride and groom select photographs for their album and their parents' albums. They are normally 5" x 5" in size. With the advent of digital technology, many photographers who shoot with digital cameras make your proofs available online. You (and your guests) can browse the available photographs on the Internet and select the ones you'd like to receive prints of. You can often view your photographs within a few days of the wedding!

271. What do I need to consider when selecting a photographer's package?

When selecting a package, ask how many proofs the photographer will take. The more proofs, the wider the selection you will have to choose from. For a wide selection, the photographer must take at least 2 to 3 times the number of prints that will go into your album. Digital technology makes this much easier. Ask the photographer how soon after the wedding you will get your proofs. Request this in writing. The proofs should be ready by the time you get back from your honeymoon. Also request to see your proofs before you make the final payment.

272. Should I order negatives with my photographs?

Negatives come in different sizes depending on the type of film and equipment used. For example, the larger the negative, the higher the quality of the photograph, especially when enlarged. Don't let a photographer convince you that there is no difference in quality between a 35 mm camera and a medium format camera. The quality of a digital camera's photograph depends on the resolution of the camera. The higher the resolution, the better the quality of the photograph, especially when you are making large prints. Digital cameras do not produce negatives. You can see the proofs on a computer.

273. What should I think about when considering purchasing the files or negatives of my wedding photographs?

Many photographers will not sell you the negatives or photo files since they hope to make a profit on selling extra prints after the wedding. Ask the photographers you interview how long they keep the negatives or files and whether they are included in your package. A professional photographer should keep the negatives or files at least five years. Make sure you get this in writing.

274. What are boudoir photos?

Boudoir photos are a set of sexy, intimate photos that you give to your fiancé as a gift. You can hire a professional boudoir photographer who will style and shoot you in a studio or in your home. The photos will be sexy, but tasteful, and can be made into an album to give to your groom before the wedding.

275. What is my engagement photograph?

Many couples are interested in a set of engagement photos to accompany their wedding-day photography. These make a nice keepsake for the couple, as well as a gift for friends and family. Consider hiring the same photographer for engagement photos as for the wedding; many will build the price into the total photography package.

276. What should I consider when taking my engagement photos?

Decide whether you want candid shots, posed portrait shots, or a combination of both. Many couples prefer to have engagement photos taken outside and not in a studio; ask your photographer if he or she can scout locations. Engagement shoots can include more than one wardrobe change; bring outfits with bright colors and do not wear prints or white, which do not photograph as nicely. Ask your photographer to take some classic bridal portraits (shots of just bride).

277. What is a formal bridal portrait?

If you intend to announce your marriage in the newspaper the day after your wedding, you will need to have a formal bridal portrait taken several weeks before the wedding. This is a photograph of the bride taken before the wedding in the photographer's studio. This photograph, along with an announcement, can be sent to your local newspaper.

278. **What do I need to consider when getting my formal bridal portrait taken?**
Some fine bridal salons provide an attractive background where the bride may arrange to have her formal bridal photograph taken after the final fitting of her gown.
This will save you the hassle of bringing your gown and headpiece to the photographer's studio and dressing up once again. Consider having your trial makeup and hairstyling appointment the same day that your formal portrait is taken.

279. **How much does a parents' album cost?**
It can range from $100 to $600.

280. **How much do proofs/previews usually cost?**
It depends upon the photographer and what he or she offers, but they can range from $100 to $600.

281. **How expensive are negatives/digital files?**
It depends upon the package you've ordered from your photographer, as well as whether or not you're purchasing all of your wedding negatives, but the prices can range from $100 to $800.

282. **How much do engagement photographs cost?**
They can range anywhere from $75 to $300, depending on the photographer you use and how many pictures you have taken.

283. **How much do formal bridal portraits cost?**
They can cost about $75 to $300, depending upon the photographer you use.

284. **How can I save money when choosing a photographer?**
Consider hiring a professional photographer for the formal shots of your ceremony only. You can then place disposable cameras on each table at the reception and let your guests take candid shots. This will save you a considerable amount of money in photography. You can also lower the price of your album by paying a professional photographer to shoot your wedding, and then putting the photographs into the album yourself. This is a very time-consuming task, so your photographer may reduce the price of his or her

package if you opt to do this. To really save money, select a photographer who charges a flat fee to shoot the wedding and allows you to purchase the film. Compare at least three photographers for quality, value and price. Photographers who shoot weddings "on the side" are usually less expensive, but the quality of their photographs may not be as good. Select less 8" x 10"s for your album and more 4" x 6"s, and choose a moderately priced album. Ask for specials and package deals.

285. How do I tell the photographers we met with but did not choose that we have selected someone else to shoot our wedding?

While it is not obligatory to notify the vendors you do not choose of your decision, it is courteous and saves you and them time. Oftentimes, a photographer or other vendor will ask questions about why you opted for another company or vendor; you can give your reasons if you choose, or you can politely decline to say.

286. Should I rely on guests to take candid shots and skip the formal photography at my reception to cut costs?

If you opt not to hire a professional for your reception, you can rely on guests to take candid shots with their personal cameras and have them upload them to an online photo gallery you set up with Snapfish, Picasa, Flickr or other sites.

287. How can I save money on the parents' album?

Try to negotiate at least one free parents' album with the purchase of the bride and groom's album.

288. How can I save money on extra prints?

If you can wait, consider not ordering any reprints during the first few years after the wedding. A few years later, contact the photographer and ask if he or she will sell you the negatives/files. Most photographers will be glad to sell them at a bargain price at a later date. You can then make as many prints as you wish for a fraction of the cost.

289. How can I save money on proofs/previews?

Ask your photographer to use your proofs as part of your album package to save developing costs.

290. How can I save money on my engagement photographs?

Find a beautiful outdoor spot in your town and have a friend or family member take photos of you and your fiancé laughing, hugging and having fun. Your friends and family will enjoy seeing your excitement over the engagement.

291. How can I save money on my formal bridal portrait?

If you don't mind announcing your marriage several weeks after the wedding, consider having your formal portrait taken the day of your wedding. This will save you the studio costs, the hassle of getting dressed for the photo, and the photograph will be more natural since the bridal bouquet will be the one you carry down the aisle. Also, brides are always most beautiful on their wedding day!

292. What are some questions I should ask the photographer before booking him or her?

- What is the name & phone number of the photographer?
- What is the website and e-mail of the photographer?
- What is the address of the photographer?
- How many years of experience do you have as a photographer?
- What percentage of your business is dedicated to weddings?
- Approximately how many weddings have you photographed?
- Are you the person who will photograph my wedding?
- Will you bring an assistant with you to my wedding?
- How do you typically dress for weddings?
- Do you have a professional studio?
- What type of equipment do you use?
- Do you bring backup equipment with you to weddings?
- Do you visit the ceremony/reception sites prior to the wedding?
- Do you have liability insurance?
- Are you skilled in diffused lighting & soft focus?
- Can you take studio portraits?
- Can you retouch digital files?
- Can negatives/digital files be purchased? If so, what is the cost?
- What is the cost of the package I am interested in?
- What is your payment policy?
- What is your cancellation policy?
- Do you offer a money-back guarantee?

- Do you use proofs?
- How many proofs will I get?
- When will I get my proofs?
- When will I get my album?
- What is the cost of an engagement portrait?
- What is the cost of a formal bridal portrait?
- What is the cost of a parent album?
- What is the cost of a 5" x 7" reprint?
- What is the cost of an 8" x 10" reprint?
- What is the cost of an 11" x 14" reprint?
- What is the cost per additional hour of shooting at the wedding?

293. **What pictures should the photographer take of my wedding?**

It is important that you give your photographer a list of the pictures you want taken at your wedding. This will ensure that you are able to capture the moments that are most important to you. We've compiled a list of some of the pictures you may want to capture on your wedding day:

- Bride leaving her house
- Wedding rings with the invitation
- Bride getting dressed for the ceremony
- Bride looking at her bridal bouquet
- Maid of Honor putting garter on bride's leg
- Groom and Best Man before ceremony
- Bride by herself
- Bride with her mother
- Bride with her father
- Bride with mother and father
- Bride with her entire family
- Bride with her Maid of Honor
- Bride with her bridesmaids
- Bride with the flower girl and/or ring bearer
- Bride's mother putting on her corsage
- Groom leaving his house
- Groom putting on his boutonniere
- Groom with his mother
- Groom with his father
- Groom with mother and father
- Groom with his entire family
- Groom with his Best Man
- Groom with his ushers
- Groom shaking hands with his Best Man

- Groom with the bride's father
- Bride and her father getting out of the limousine
- Special members of the family being seated
- Groom waiting for the bride before the processional
- Bride and her father just before the processional
- Bride and groom saying their vows
- Bride and groom exchanging rings
- Groom kissing the bride at the altar
- The recessional
- Entrance of newlyweds and wedding party into the reception site
- Receiving line
- Guests signing the guest book
- Toasts
- First Dance
- Bride and her father dancing
- Groom and his mother dancing
- Bride dancing with groom's father
- Groom dancing with bride's mother
- Wedding party and guests dancing
- Cake table
- Cake-cutting ceremony
- Couple feeding each other cake
- Buffet table and its decoration
- Bouquet-tossing ceremony
- Garter-tossing ceremony
- Musicians
- The wedding party table
- The family tables
- Candid shots of your guests
- Bride and groom saying goodbye to their parents
- Bride and groom looking back, waving goodbye in the getaway car

✿ Notes

....
....
....
....
....
....
....
....
....
....
....
....
....
....
....
....
....
....
....
....
....
....
....
....

CHAPTER 14

Videography

294. What is videography?

Videography is a way to capture your wedding through video. You can hire a videographer who will videotape the entire day, capturing all the special moments on film. Unlike photographs, videography captures the mood of the wedding day in motion and sound. You have the option of selecting one, two, or three cameras. The more cameras used, the more action captured and the more expensive. An experienced videographer, however, can do a good job with just one camera.

295. How do I choose a videographer?

You will need to choose the type of video you want — do you want the footage edited down to a 30 minute film, or do you want an "as it happened" replay? You may wish to have both of these so you can see all the details, but have a shorter version that flows nicely as well. Remember, a short format video requires a lot of time in the editing room and will cost considerably more. Your personal film can take as much as 15-30 hours to put together! Be sure to hire a videographer who specializes in weddings, and ask to see samples of his or her work. Pay particular attention to details such as special effects, titles, and background music. Find out what's included in the cost of your package so there are no surprises at the end! As in photography, there are many companies with more than one videographer. These companies may use the work of their best videographer to sell their packages and then send a less experienced videographer to the wedding. Again, don't get caught in this trap! Be sure to interview the videographer who will shoot your wedding so you can get a good idea of his or her style and personality. Ask to see his or her own work.

296. How much do videographers cost?

It depends upon what the videographer charges, but they can range from $600 to $4,000.

297. What are titles and should I get them on my wedding video?

Titles and subtitles can be edited into your video before or after the filming. Titles are important since twenty years from now you may not remember the exact time of your wedding or the names of your bridal party members. Some videographers charge more for titling. Make sure you discuss this with your videographer and get in writing exactly what titles will be included. Titles may include the date, time and location of the wedding, the bride and groom's names, and names of special family members and/or the bridal party. Titles may also include special thanks to those who helped with the wedding. You can send these people a copy of your video after the wedding, which would be a very appropriate and inexpensive gift!

298. How much do titles for my wedding video cost?
Titles can cost from $50 to $300.

299. How can I save money on titles for my wedding video?
Consider asking for limited titles, such as only the names of the bride and groom and the date and time of the wedding.

300. What if the videographer charges for extra hours?
Find out how much your videographer would charge to stay longer than contracted in case your reception lasts longer than expected. Don't forget to get this in writing. Avoid paying extra hours beyond what's included in your selected package. You can do this by calculating the number of hours you think you'll need and negotiating that into your package price. Consider taping the ceremony only.

301. What is a photo montage?
A photo montage is a series of photographs set to music on video. The number of photographs depends on the length of the songs and the amount of time allotted for each photograph. A typical song usually allows for approximately 30 to 40 photographs. Photo montages are a great way to display and reproduce your photographs. Copies of this video can be made for considerably less than the cost of reproducing photographs.

302. What kind of pictures should I put in my photo montage?
Photo montages can include photos of you and your fiancé growing up, the rehearsal, the wedding day, the honeymoon, or any combination thereof. Send copies of your photo montage video to close friends and family members as a memento of your wedding.

303. How can I save money on a videographer?
Compare videographers' quality, value and price. There

is a wide range, and the most expensive is not necessarily the best. One camera is the most cost effective and may be all you need. Consider hiring a company that offers both videography and photography. You may save overall. Ask a family member or close friend to videotape your wedding. However, realize that without professional equipment and expertise the final product may not be quite the same.

304. How can I save money on a photo montage?

Digital technology has made this easy. With easy-to-use software you can create a beautiful, professional-looking photo montage that can be saved onto a recordable CD and transferred onto video or DVD in a studio. If you own a DVD-recorder, you can make your own copies.

305. What if I want extra copies of my wedding video?

A professional videographer can reproduce your video much better than you can. Ask your videographer how much he or she charges. You'll certainly want to give your parents a copy! Borrow a DVD burner from a friend and make copies yourself. Before considering this, be sure to ask your videographer if that is acceptable — many contracts prohibit this and doing so could be copyright infringement, as with copying any tape.

306. What questions should I ask a videographer before hiring him or her?

· What is the name & phone number of the videographer?
· What is the website and e-mail address of the videographer?
· What is the address of the videographer?
· How many years of experience do you have as a videographer?
· Approximately how many weddings have you recorded?
· Are you the person who will record my wedding?
· Will you bring an assistant with you to my wedding?
· What type of equipment do you use?
· Do you have a wireless microphone?
· What format do you use (Digital, VHS, Super VHS, 8mm)?
· Do you bring backup equipment with you?
· Do you visit the ceremony and reception sites before the wedding?
· Do you edit the footage after the event? Who keeps the

raw footage?
- When will I receive the final product?
- What is the cost of the desired package?
- What does it include?
- Can you make a photo montage? If so, what is your price?
- What do you charge for extra hours?
- What is your payment policy?
- What is your cancellation policy?
- Do you offer a money-back guarantee?

✿ Notes

....
....
....
....
....
....
....
....
....
....
....
....
....
....
....
....
....
....
....
....
....
....
....
....
....

CHAPTER 15

Stationery
& Invitations

307. When should I start writing out my guest list?

Begin creating your guest list as soon as possible. Ask both sets of parents for a list of people they would like to invite. You and your fiancé should make your own lists. Make certain that all names are spelled correctly and that all addresses are current. Determine if you wish to include children; if so, add their names to your list. All children over the age of 16 should receive their own invitation.

308. What percentage of my guest list can I expect to say they can attend?

For a traditional (non-destination) wedding, if you invite over 200 guests, estimate that about 25 percent of your guests will be unable to attend. If you are inviting fewer than 200 guests, consider that 15 to 20 percent will RSVP that they are unable to attend. However, you should always plan for every person on your list to RSVP "Yes," to be on the safe side.

309. How can I categorize my initial guest list so it is easy to pare down if need be?

Group your guests into three different categories: those who must be invited; those who should be invited; and those who it would be nice to invite. This will help you decide who you definitely want to attend your wedding.

310. We are over-budget and need to trim our guest list. What are some ways to do this?

Start by eliminating people who have been included on your guest list out of courtesy — this means people who you went to school with or grew up with but don't stay in touch with, friends of your parents (unless your parents are paying for the wedding), coworkers, and people who invited you to their wedding. You should never feel obligated to invite anyone. Also consider making your reception "adults-only"; the cost per plate for kids, who eat much less, can be nearly as much as the cost for adults.

311. Should we allow all our friends and family to bring guests to our wedding out of courtesy?

Allowing everyone on your guest list a "plus one" can get very expensive. Only married friends and family, your attendants, and those in a long-term committed relationship should be told to bring a guest.

312. Should I have an "A list" and "B list" for my guest list?

Many couples will create a B list of people to invite in the event that people from the original guest list are unable to attend. Plan to send those B invitations out several weeks before the wedding to give those guests time to RSVP.

313. How should we address it if a friend asks to bring a date whom we didn't invite?

While it is bad manners to ask to bring a date if one was not indicated on your invitation, it may happen. The couple can easily decline by explaining that their budget does not allow for extra guests beyond their list.

314. Should we invite any ex-girlfriends or ex-boyfriends to the wedding?

The rule of thumb is that you both must be friends with and comfortable with inviting that person to the wedding. If you are not both totally comfortable, do not send an invitation.

315. What kind of stationery do I need to purchase for my wedding?

We've compiled a list of the different kinds of stationery you will need for your wedding:

- Invitations
- Envelopes
- Response Cards/Envelopes with Stamps
- Reception Cards
- Ceremony Cards
- Pew Cards
- Seating/Place Cards
- Rain Cards
- Maps
- Ceremony Programs
- Announcements
- Thank-You Notes
- Personalized Napkins
- Personalized Matchbooks

316. When should I order my invitations?

Order your invitations at least 4 months before the wedding. Allow an additional month for engraved invitations.
The bride's parents traditionally issue invitations; but if the groom's parents are assuming some of the wedding expenses, the invitations should be in their names also. Mail

all invitations at the same time, 6 to 8 weeks before the wedding.

317. When should I buy stamps for my invitations and response cards?

Don't order stamps until you have had the post office weigh your completed invitation. It may exceed the size and weight for one stamp. Order commemorative stamps that fit the occasion.

318. What are my options when choosing invitations?

There are three types of invitations: traditional/formal, contemporary, and informal. The traditional/formal wedding invitation is white, soft cream, or ivory with raised black lettering. The printing is done on the top page of a double sheet of thick quality paper; the inside is left blank. The contemporary invitation is typically an individualized presentation that makes a statement about the bride and groom. Informal invitations are often printed on the front of a single, heavyweight card and may be handwritten or preprinted.

319. What is engraving in regards to invitations?

Engraving is the most expensive, traditional and formal type of printing. It also takes the longest to complete. In engraved printing, stationery is pressed onto a copper plate, which makes the letters rise slightly from the page.

320. What is thermography?

Thermography is a process that fuses powder and ink to create a raised letter. This takes less time than engraving and is less expensive because copper plates do not have to be engraved.

321. What is offset printing?

Offset printing, the least expensive, is the quickest to produce and offers a variety of styles and colors. It is also the least formal.

322. What do I need to consider when choosing invitations?

If all your guests are to be invited to both the ceremony and the reception, a combined invitation may be sent without separate enclosure cards. Order one invitation for each married or cohabiting couple who you plan to invite. The officiant and his or her spouse as well as your attendants should each receive an invitation.

323. What are some modern trends in invitations?

Invitations with embellishments, such as rhinestones or crystals are popular. Graphic prints lend a sophisticated, vintage feel. Monogramming is also trendy. Have a custom logo designed with your initials and use it to brand invitations, as well as the menu, favors, and even the cake.

324. How many invitations should I order?

Order approximately 20 percent more stationery than your actual guest count. Allow a minimum of two weeks to address and mail the invitations, longer if using a calligrapher or if your guest list is very large. You may also want to consider ordering invitations to the rehearsal dinner, as these should be in the same style as the wedding invitation.

325. What are response cards?

Response cards are enclosed with the invitation to determine the number of people who will be attending your wedding. They are the smallest card size accepted by the postal service and should be printed in the same style as the invitation. An invitation to only the wedding ceremony does not usually include a request for a reply. Response cards should be used when it is necessary to have an exact head count for meals or special seating arrangements. Response cards are widely accepted today. If included, these cards should be easy for your guests to understand and use. Include a self-addressed and stamped return envelope to make it easy for your guests to return the response cards.

326. What should I consider when placing an order for response cards?

You should not include a line that reads "number of persons" on your response cards because only those whose names appear on the inner and outer envelopes are invited. Each couple, each single person, and all children over the age of 16 should receive their own invitation. Indicate on the inner envelope if they may bring an escort or guest. The omitting of children's names from the inner envelope infers that the children are not invited.

327. What is a reception card?

If the guest list for the ceremony is larger than that for the reception, a separate card with the date, time and location for the reception should be enclosed with the ceremony invitation for those guests also invited to the reception. Reception cards should be placed in front of the invitation, facing the back flap and the person inserting them. They should be printed on the same quality paper and in the same style as the invitation itself.

328. What are ceremony cards?

If the guest list for the reception is larger than the guest list for the ceremony, a special insertion card with the date, time and location for the ceremony should be enclosed with the reception invitation for those guests also invited to the ceremony. Ceremony cards should be placed in front of the invitation, facing the back flap and the person inserting them. They should be printed on the same quality paper and in the same style as the invitation itself.

329. What are rain cards?

These cards are enclosed when guests are invited to an outdoor ceremony and/or reception, informing them of an alternate location in case of bad weather. As with other enclosures, rain cards should be placed in front of the invitation, facing the back flap and the person inserting them. They should be printed on the same quality paper and in the same style as the invitation itself.

330. Should I include maps in my invitations?

Maps to the ceremony and/or reception are becoming frequent inserts in wedding invitations. They need to be drawn and printed in the same style as the invitation and are usually on a small, heavier card. If they are not printed in the same style or on the same type of paper as the invitation, they should be mailed separately. Maps should include both written and visual instructions, keeping in mind the fact that guests may be coming from different locations. Order extra maps to hand out at the ceremony if the reception is at a different location.

331. What are ceremony programs?

Ceremony programs are printed documents showing the sequence of events during the ceremony. These programs add a personal touch to your wedding and are a convenient way of letting guests know who your attendants, officiant, and ceremony musicians are. Ceremony programs can be handed out by the ushers, or they can be placed at the back of the church for guests to take as they enter.

332. What are announcements?

Announcements are not obligatory but serve a useful purpose. They may be sent to friends who are not invited to the wedding because the number of guests must be limited, or because they live too far away. They may also be sent to acquaintances who, while not particularly close to the family, might still wish to know about the marriage. Announcements are also appropriate for friends and acquaintances who are not expected to attend and for whom you do not want to give an obligation of sending a gift. They should include the day, month, year, city, and state where the ceremony took place.

333. What do I need to consider when sending out announcements?

Announcements should never be sent to anyone who has received an invitation to the ceremony or the reception. They are printed on the same paper and in the same style as the invitation. They should be addressed before the wedding and mailed the day of or the day after the ceremony.

334. What do I need to consider when ordering thank-you notes?

Regardless of whether the bride has thanked the donor in person or not, she must write a thank-you note for every gift received. Order thank-you notes along with your other stationery at least four months before your wedding. You should order some with your maiden initials for thank-you notes sent before the ceremony, and the rest with your married initials for notes sent after the wedding and for future use. Send thank-you notes within two weeks of receiving a gift that arrives before the wedding, and within two months after the honeymoon for gifts received on or after your wedding day. Be sure to mention the gift you received in the body of the note and let the person know how much you like it and what you plan to do with it.

335. What is calligraphy?

Calligraphy is a form of elegant handwriting often used to address invitations for formal occasions. Traditional wedding invitations should be addressed in black or blue fountain pen. You may address the invitations yourself, hire a professional calligrapher, or have your invitations addressed using calligraphy by computer. Make sure you use the same method or person to address both the inner and outer envelopes.

336. How do I word my invitations when the bride's parents are sponsoring the wedding?

Mr. and Mrs. Alexander Waterman Smith
request the honor of your presence
at the marriage of their daughter
Carol Ann
to
Mr. William James Clark
on Saturday, the fifth of August
two thousand six
at two o'clock in the afternoon
Saint James by-the-Sea
La Jolla, California

337. How do I word my invitations when the groom's parents are sponsoring the wedding?

Mr. and Mrs. Michael Burdell Clark
request the honor of your presence
at the marriage of
Miss Carol Ann Smith
to their son
Mr. William James Clark

338. How do I word my invitations when both the bride and groom's parents are sponsoring the wedding:

Mr. and Mrs. Alexander Waterman Smith
and
Mr. and Mrs. Michael Burdell Clark
request the honor of your presence
at the marriage of their children
Miss Carol Ann Smith
to

Mr. William James Clark

OR

Mr. and Mrs. Alexander Waterman Smith
request the honor of your presence
at the marriage of their daughter
Carol Ann Smith
to
William James Clark
son of Mr. and Mrs. Michael Burdell Clark

339. How do I word my invitations when we are sponsoring our own wedding?

The honor of your presence is requested
at the marriage of
Miss Carol Ann Smith
and
Mr. William James Clark

OR

Miss Carol Ann Smith
and
Mr. William James Clark
request the honor of your presence
at their marriage

340. How do I word my invitations when the bride's mother is sponsoring the wedding and is not remarried?

Mrs. Julie Hurden Smith
requests the honor of your presence
at the marriage of her daughter
Carol Ann

341. How do I word my invitations when the bride's mother is sponsoring the wedding and is remarried?

Mrs. Julie Hurden Booker
requests the honor of your presence
at the marriage of her daughter
Carol Ann Smith

OR

Mr. and Mrs. John Thomas Booker
request the honor of your presence
at the marriage of Mrs. Booker's daughter
Carol Ann Smith

342. How do I word my invitations when the bride's father is sponsoring the wedding and is not remarried?

Mr. Alexander Waterman Smith
requests the honor of your presence
at the marriage of his daughter
Carol Ann

343. How do I word my invitations when the bride's father is sponsoring the wedding and is remarried?

Mr. and Mrs. Alexander Waterman Smith
request the honor of your presence
at the marriage of Mr. Smith's daughter
Carol Ann

344. How do I word my invitations when a close friend or relative is sponsoring the wedding?

Mr. and Mrs. Brandt Elliott Lawson
request the honor of your presence
at the marriage of their granddaughter
Carol Ann Smith

345. How do I word an invitation to a military ceremony?

In military ceremonies, the rank determines the placement of names:

a) Any title lower than sergeant should be omitted. Only the branch of service should be included under that person's name:

> Mr. and Mrs. Alexander Waterman Smith
> request the honor of your presence
> at the marriage of their daughter
> Carol Ann
> United States Army
> to
> William James Clark

b) Junior officers' titles are placed below their names and are followed by their branch of service:

> Mr. and Mrs. Alexander Waterman Smith
> request the honor of your presence
> at the marriage of their daughter
> Carol Ann
> to
> William James Clark
> First Lieutenant, United States Army

c) If the rank is higher than lieutenant, titles are placed before names, and the branch of service is placed on the following line:

> Mr. and Mrs. Alexander Waterman Smith
> request the honor of your presence
> at the marriage of their daughter
> Carol Ann
> to
> Captain William James Clark
> United States Navy

346. How do I word a less formal/more contemporary invitation?

> Mr. and Mrs. Alexander Waterman Smith
> would like you to
> join with their daughter
> Carol Ann
> and

William James Clark
in the celebration of their marriage

347. How do I word my response cards?

Here are examples of ways to word your response cards:

M_____
(The M may be eliminated from the line, especially if many
Drs. are invited)
____ accepts
____ regrets
Saturday the fifth of July
Oceanside Country Club

OR

The favor of your reply is requested
by the twenty-second of May
M_____
will _____ attend

348. How do I word my reception cards?

Here are some examples of wording for reception cards:

Mr. and Mrs. Alexander Waterman Smith
request the pleasure of your company
Saturday, the third of July
at three o'clock
Oceanside Country Club
2020 Waterview Lane
Oceanside, California

Sample of a less formal reception card:

Reception immediately following the ceremony
Oceanside Country Club
2020 Waterview Lane
Oceanside, California

349. How do I word my ceremony program?

Below is an example of a ceremony program:

The Marriage of
Carol Ann Smith and William James Clark
the eleventh of March, 2008
San Diego, California

OUR CEREMONY

Prelude: All I Ask of You, by Andrew Lloyd Webber
Processional: Canon in D Major, by Pachelbel
Rite of Marriage
Welcome guests
Statement of intentions
Marriage vows
Exchange of rings
Blessing of bride and groom
Pronouncement of marriage
Presentation of the bride and groom
Recessional: Trumpet Voluntary, by Jeromiah Clarke

OUR WEDDING PARTY

Maid of Honor: Susan Smith, Sister of Bride
Best Man: Brandt Clark, Brother of Groom
Bridesmaids: Janet Anderson, Friend of Bride
Lisa Bennett, Friend of Bride
Ushers: Mark Gleason, Friend of Groom
Tommy Olson, Friend of Groom
Officiant: Father Henry Thomas

OUR RECEPTION

Please join us after the ceremony
in the celebration of our marriage at:
La Valencia Hotel
1132 Prospect Street
La Jolla, CA

350. When should we mail our Save the Date cards?
Four to six months before the wedding.

351. When should we address the invitations?
Four to six months before the wedding.

352. When should we mail invitations?
Six to eight weeks before the wedding.

353. How much do invitations usually cost?

It depends upon the type of invitation you want to purchase, but invitations can cost from $0.75 to $8 per invitation.

354. How much do response cards cost?

They can range from $0.40 to $1 each.

355. How much do ceremony cards cost?

They can cost from $0.40 to $1 each.

356. How much do pew cards cost?

Pew cards can cost from $0.25 to $1 each.

357. How much do rain cards cost?

Rain cards can cost from $0.25 to $1 each.

358. How much do ceremony programs cost?

They can cost from $0.75 to $3 each.

359. How much do thank-you notes cost?

They can cost from $0.40 to $0.75 each.

360. How can I save money on my invitations?

Thermography looks like engraving and is a fraction of the cost. Choose paper stock that is reasonable and yet achieves your overall look. Select invitations that can be mailed using just one stamp. Order at least 25 extra invitations in case you soil some or add people to your list. To reorder this small number of invitations later would cost nearly three times the amount you'll spend up front.

361. How can I save money on reception cards?

If all people invited to the ceremony are also invited to the reception, include the reception information on the invitation and eliminate the reception card altogether. This will save printing and postage costs.

362. How can I save money on pew cards?

Include the pew card with the invitation to special guests and just say "Within the Ribbon." After you have received all your RSVPs, you will know how many pews need to be reserved. This will save you the cost of mailing the pew cards separately.

363. How can I save money on maps?

If you are comfortable with computers, you can purchase software that allows you to draw your own maps. Print a map to both the ceremony and reception on the same sheet of paper, perhaps one on each side. This will save you the cost of mailing two maps. Or have your ushers hand out maps to the reception after the ceremony.

364. How can I save money on calligraphy?

You may want to consider taking a short course to learn the art of calligraphy so that you can address your own invitations. If you have a computer with a laser printer, you can address the invitations yourself using one of many beautiful calligraphy fonts.

365. What questions should I ask the stationery provider when picking out my invitations?

Here are some important questions to ask the stationery provider. Be sure to get everything in writing:

- What is the name and phone number of the stationery provider?
- What is the website and e-mail of the stationery provider?
- What is the address of the stationery provider?
- How many years of experience do you have?
- What lines of stationery do you carry?
- What types of printing process do you offer?
- How soon in advance does the order have to be placed?
- What is the turnaround time?
- What is the cost of the desired invitation?
- What is the cost of the desired announcement?
- What is the cost of the desired response card?
- What is the cost of the desired reception card?
- What is the cost of the desired thank-you note?
- What is the cost of the desired wedding program?
- What is the cost of addressing the envelopes in calligraphy?
- What is your payment policy?
- What is your cancellation policy?

366. What are the guidelines for addressing invitations?

We recommend that you start addressing your envelopes at least three months before your wedding, and preferably four months if you are using calligraphy or if your guest list is above 200. You may want to ask your Maid of Honor or bridesmaids to help you with this time-consuming task, as this is traditionally part of their responsibilities. Organize a luncheon or late afternoon get-together with hors d'oeuvres and make a party out of it! If you are working with a wedding consultant, he or she can also help you address invitations. There are typically two envelopes that need to be addressed for wedding invitations: an inner envelope and an outer envelope. The inner envelope is placed unsealed inside the outer envelope, with the flap away from the person inserting it. The invitation and all enclosures are placed inside the inner envelope facing the back flap. The inner envelope contains the name (or names) of the person (or people) who are invited to the ceremony and/or reception. The address is not included on the inner envelope. The outer envelope contains the name (or names) and address of the person (or people) to whom the inner envelope belongs.

367. How do I address my invitations?

Below is an example of the various ways you can address your invitations, based on the recipients. (Note: First names and addresses are NOT included on the inner envelopes. Outer envelopes DO include first names and addresses.)

Husband and Wife:
Inner: Mr. and Mrs. Smith (with same surname)
Outer: Mr. and Mrs. Thomas Smith (use middle name, if known)
Inner: Ms. Banks and Mr. Smith (with different surnames)
Outer: Ms. Anita Banks (wife first)
Mr. Thomas Smith (wife's name & title above husband's)
Inner: Dr. Smith and Mr. Smith (wife has professional title)
Outer: Dr. Anita Smith
Mr. Thomas Smith (wife's name & title above husband's)
Inner: Mr. and Mrs. Smith (with children under 16)
John, Mary, and Glen (in order of age, parents names above children's)
Outer: Mr. and Mrs. Thomas Smith

Single Woman (regardless of age):
Inner: Miss/Ms. Smith
Outer: Miss/Ms. Beverly Smith

Single Woman and Guest:
Inner: Miss/Ms. Smith

Outer: Miss/Ms. Beverly Smith
Mr. Jones (or "and Guest")

Single Man:
Inner: Mr. Jones (Master for a young boy)
Outer: Mr. William Jones

Single Man and Guest:
Inner: Mr. Jones
Miss/Ms. Smith (or "and Guest")
Outer: Mr. William Jones

Unmarried Couple Living Together:
Inner: Mr. Knight and Ms. Orlandi
(names listed alphabetically)
Outer: Mr. Michael Knight
Ms. Paula Orlandi

Two Sisters (over 16):
Inner: The Misses Smith
Outer: The Misses Mary and Jane Smith (in order of age)

Two Brothers (over 16):
Inner: The Messrs. Smith
Outer: The Messrs. John and Glen Smith (in order of age)

Brothers & Sisters (over 16):
Inner: Mary, Jane, John & Glen
(name the girls first, in order of age)
Outer: The Misses Smith
The Messrs. Smith (name the girls first)

A Brother and Sister (over 16):
Inner: Jane and John (name the girl first)
Outer: Miss Jane Smith and Mr. John Smith

Widow:
Inner: Mrs. Smith
Outer: Mrs. William Smith

Divorcee:
Inner: Mrs. Smith
Outer: Mrs. Jones Smith (maiden name and former husband's surname)

❋ Notes

....

....

....

....

....

....

....

....

....

....

....

....

....

....

....

....

....

....

....

....

....

....

....

....

CHAPTER 16

Reception

368. Where can I have my reception?

Some of the more popular options you have when selecting a reception site include private homes, gardens, hotels, clubs, restaurants, halls, parks, museums, yachts, and wineries. When comparing the cost of different locations, consider the rental fee, food, beverages, parking, gratuity, set-up charges and the cost of rental equipment needed such as tables, chairs, canopies, and so forth. If you are planning an outdoor reception, be sure to have a backup site in case of rain.

369. How do I choose a reception site?

The selection of a reception site will depend on its availability, price, proximity to the ceremony site, and the number of people it will accommodate. There are two basic types of reception sites. The first type charges a per person fee which includes the facility, food, tables, silverware, china, and so forth. Examples: hotels, restaurants and catered yachts. The second type charges a room rental fee and you are responsible for providing the food, beverages, linens, and possibly tables and chairs. Examples: clubs, halls, parks, museums, and private homes. The advantage of the first type is that most everything is done for you. The disadvantage, however, is that your choices of food, china, and linen are limited. Usually you are not permitted to bring in an outside caterer and must select from a predetermined menu.

370. How much does a reception cost?

The cost of a reception can range anywhere from $300 to $5,000.

371. What percentage of my budget should go towards the reception?

The cost of the reception is approximately 35 percent of the total cost of your wedding.

372. What should I be wary of when booking a reception site?

Keep in mind that some hotels are known for double booking. A bride may reserve the largest or most elegant room in a hotel for her reception, only to find out later that the hotel took the liberty to book a more profitable event in the room she had reserved and moved her reception over to a smaller or less elegant room.

373. Should we get the time of our reception and the name of the room we are booking in writing?

Definitely put your rental hours and the name of your room in your contract. Be careful of hotels that book events too close together, as well. You don't want your guests to wait outside while your room is being set up for the reception. And you don't want to be forced out before you are ready to leave because the hotel needs to arrange the room for the next reception.

374. What services are included at the reception site?

Check with the reception site coordinator to see if the following services are included with the cost of the site:

- Waiters
- Bartenders
- Set Up
- Clean Up
- Security
- Hors d'oeuvres
- Buffet Meal
- Seated Meal
- Cocktails
- Champagne
- Wine
- Beer
- Punch
- Soft Drinks
- Coffee/Tea
- Cake

375. What questions should I ask the coordinator of a reception site?

Here's a list of some useful questions you should ask the site coordinator when looking at reception sites for your wedding:

- What is the name of the reception site?
- What is the website of the reception site?
- What is the address of the reception site?
- What is the name and phone number of my contact person?
- What dates and times are available?
- What is the maximum number of guests for a seated reception?
- What is the maximum number of guests for a cocktail

reception?
- What is the reception site fee?
- What is the price range for a seated lunch?
- What is the price range for a buffet lunch?
- What is the price range for a seated dinner?
- What is the price range for a buffet dinner?
- What is the corkage fee?
- What is the cake-cutting fee?
- What is the ratio of servers to guests?
- How much time will be allotted for my reception?
- What music restrictions are there, if any?
- What alcohol restrictions are there, if any?
- Are there any restrictions for rice or rose petal-tossing?
- What room and table decorations are available?
- Is a changing room available?
- Is there handicap accessibility?
- Is a dance floor included in the site fee?
- Are tables, chairs, and linens included in the site fee?
- Are outside caterers allowed?
- Are kitchen facilities available for outside caterers?
- Does the facility have full liability insurance?
- What "perks" or giveaways are offered?
- How many parking spaces are available for my wedding party?
- How many parking spaces are available for my guests?
- What is the cost for parking, if any?
- What is the cost for sleeping rooms, if available?
- What is the payment policy?
- What is the cancellation policy?
- Are credit cards accepted?

376. **What are favors?**

Party favors are little gift items given to your guests as mementos of your wedding. They add a very special touch to your wedding and can become keepsakes for your guests. White matchboxes engraved with the couple's names and wedding date; cocktail napkins marked in the same way; individually wrapped and marked chocolates, almonds, or fine candy are all popular party favors. Wine or champagne bottles marked with the bride and groom's names and wedding date on a personalized label are also very popular. These come in different sizes and can be purchased by the case. If you can afford it, you may also consider porcelain or ceramic party favors. These can be custom-fired with your name and wedding date on them. A new idea that's gaining in popularity among environmentally conscientious couples is to present each guest with a tiny shoot of a tree to be planted in honor of the bride and groom.

377. What should I consider when ordering favors?

Personalized favors need to be ordered several weeks in advance. Inevitably, favors will get left behind by some guests; guests are most likely to keep their favors if there are of the edible variety.

378. If cost is an issue, can I skip favors?

If you want to save money on ordering favors, try giving away flowers or table centerpieces to guests as favors.

379. Should I order napkins and/or matchbooks for my wedding favors?

Napkins and matchbooks may also be ordered from your stationer. These are placed around the reception room as decorative items and mementos of the event. Napkins and matchbooks can be printed in your wedding colors, or simply white with gold or silver lettering. Include both of your names and the wedding date. You may consider including a phrase or thought, or a small graphic design above your names.

380. How much do napkins and/or matchbooks cost?

These can cost from $0.50 to $1.50 each.

381. How much should I spend on favors?

Party favors can cost anywhere from $1 to $5 per person.

382. What kind of decorations should I have at my wedding reception?

Decorations can enhance your wedding by unifying all of the components of your ceremony and reception. Decorations can range anywhere from floral arrangements, twinkling lights, and centerpieces, to more personal touches made to seating cards, menus, favors and more. Most items are purchased or arranged based on the look and feel the couple wants for their wedding. For example, if the theme is Asian-inspired, paper lanterns and take-out boxes can create beautiful "Japanese style" ambience.

383. What should I consider when creating a centerpiece?

Table centerpieces lend style and elegance to your reception. Each of the tables at your reception, including the head table, should be decorated with a centerpiece. Select a table centerpiece that complements your colors and/or setting. The centerpiece for the head table should be larger or more elaborate than for the other tables. Make sure that your centerpiece is kept low enough so as not to hinder conversation among guests seated across from each other. Consider using a centerpiece that your guests can take home as a memento of your wedding.

384. What kind of flowers should I have for my table centerpieces?

Flowers are, of course, a popular choice for table centerpieces. Floral centerpieces should mimic the color scheme and floral theme throughout the day. For contemporary weddings, trends include low table arrangements with large blooms, including statement-making flowers, such as protea and chrysanthemum, or grouping multiple small vases together as a centerpiece. Calla lilies or long-stemmed blooms are also perfect for more contemporary ceremonies. To invoke a classic bit of symbolism place blue and white irises at the bride and groom's table to signify that marriage will have both vibrant and pales times.

385. Do I have to use flowers in my centerpieces?

Non-floral elements like feathers, fruit, pods, pepper berries, shells, lace, and stones can be used to create beautiful centerpieces. Something as simple as filling a vase with lemons or green apples adds a vibrant touch to a table. Or, an arrangement of shells makes a very nice centerpiece for a seaside reception. If you hold your wedding around the time of a major holiday, many venues with have holiday decorations available that you may want to use, such as pinecone centerpieces or greenery.

386. How much do table centerpieces cost?

They can cost from $20 to $100 each.

387. How can I save money on my table centerpieces?

Consider making your own table centerpieces using materials that are inexpensive like mason jars, candles, stones, fruit, and succulents. Non-floral items will always make for a less-expensive option. Or transport floral arrangements from the ceremony site to your reception and reuse them.

388. Should I have a candy buffet at my reception?
You can make a lovely candy buffet that acts as both décor and favors by arranging glass vases, bowls, and jars with various types of treats. Provide small boxes or vellum or clear bags so guests can take home a sample of candy.

389. How much candy should I buy for my candy buffet?
Select 5 to 10 kinds of candy. Get several pounds of each or one-quarter to one-half a pound of candy per person at your wedding.

390. What should I consider when creating my own candy buffet?
Include a metal scoop in each jar so guests don't use their hands. Also, put a note on any candy that contains nuts in case guests have allergies.

391. Should I use balloons to decorate my reception site?
Balloons are often used to decorate a reception site. A popular idea is to release balloons at the church or reception. This adds a festive, exciting, and memorable touch to your wedding. Balloons can be used to create an arch backdrop for the wedding cake or inexpensive centerpieces for the tables. Color coordinate your balloons to match your color scheme. Balloons should be delivered and set-up well in advance — at least before the photographer shows up. If you are planning to release balloons at the church or reception, check with your city. Releasing balloons in some cities might be illegal. Also make sure there are no wires where balloons can get entangled. If they do, you could be held responsible for damages or cleanup expenses.

392. How much do balloons cost?
They can cost from $75 to $500.

393. Are disposable cameras a good idea at my reception?
A great way to inexpensively obtain many candid photographs of your wedding day is to place a disposable 35 mm camera loaded with film on each table at your reception and have your guests take shots of the event. Tell your DJ, musician, or wedding coordinator to encourage your guests

to take photographs with the disposables.

394. How many disposable cameras should I provide?

If you are planning a large reception, consider buying cameras with only 12 exposures. Otherwise, you may end up with too many photographs. For example, if 200 guests attend your reception and you seat 8 guests per table, you will need to purchase 25 cameras. If each camera has 36 exposures, you will end up with 825 photographs. If the cameras have only 12 exposures, you will end up with 300 photographs, which is a much more reasonable quantity!

395. What is the cake knife?

Your cake knife should complement your overall style; this item will bring you happy memories of your wedding day every time you use it. The cake knife is used to cut the cake at the reception. The bride usually cuts the first two slices of the wedding cake with the groom's hand placed over hers. The groom feeds the bride first, then the bride feeds the groom. This tradition makes beautiful wedding photographs.

396. What are the toasting glasses?

You will need toasting glasses to toast each other after cutting the cake. They are usually decorated with ribbons or flowers and kept near the cake. This tradition also makes beautiful wedding photographs.

397. What should I consider when selecting a cake knife or toasting glasses?

Consider having your initials and wedding date engraved on your wedding knife as a memento. Consider purchasing crystal or silver toasting glasses as a keepsake of your wedding. Have your florist decorate your knife and toasting glasses with flowers or ribbons.

398. How much do a cake knife and toasting glasses cost?

Cake knives can cost $15 to $120, and toasting glasses can cost from $10 to $100.

399. What leg should I wear the garter on?

You can wear the garter on either leg. Just wear it above the knee.

400. What are some additional fees I should expect at my reception?

Some reception sites and caterers charge an extra fee for bartending and for setting up the bar. The bartending fee could be and often is waived if you meet a minimum requirement on beverages consumed. Try to negotiate this with your caterer prior to hiring him or her. Many reception sites and caterers make money by marking up the food and alcohol they sell. You may wish to provide your own alcohol for several reasons. First, it is more cost effective. Second, you may want to serve an exotic wine or champagne that the reception site or caterer does not offer. In either case, and if your reception site or caterer allows it, be prepared to pay a corkage fee. This is the fee for each bottle brought into the reception site and opened by a member of their staff. You need to consider whether the expenses saved after paying the corkage fee justify the hassle and liability of bringing in your own alcohol. In addition to corkage and cake-cutting fees, some facilities also charge extra to pour coffee with the wedding cake. Again, when comparing the cost of various reception sites, don't forget to add up all the extra miscellaneous costs, such as the fee for pouring coffee. It is customary to pay a gratuity fee to your caterer. The average gratuity is 15% to 20% of your food and beverage bill. Gratuities can even go as high as 25%. Ask about these costs up front and select your caterer or reception site accordingly.

401. How can I save money on my reception?

Since the cost of the reception is approximately 35% of the total cost of your wedding, you can save the most money by limiting your guest list. If you hire a wedding consultant, he or she may be able to cut your cake and save you the cake-cutting fee. Check this out with your facility or caterer. Reception sites that charge a room rental fee may waive this fee if you meet minimum requirements on food and beverages consumed. Try to negotiate this before you book the facility. Consider a brunch or early afternoon wedding so the reception will fall between meals, allowing you to serve hors d'oeuvres instead of a full meal. Consider serving hors d'oeuvres "buffet style." Your guests will eat less this way than if waiters and waitresses are constantly serving them hors d'oeuvres. Or tray-pass hors d'oeuvres during cocktail hour and choose a lighter meal. Compare two or three caterers; there is a wide price range between caterers for the same food. Compare the total cost of catering (main entree plus hors d'oeuvres) when selecting a caterer.

402. How much do seating/place cards cost?
Seating/place cards can cost from $0.25 to $1 each.

403. When should I arrange the seating list and/or the reception room layout?
Two to six weeks before the wedding.

404. What are seating/place cards?
Seating/place cards are used to let guests know where they should be seated at the reception and are a good way of putting people together so they feel most comfortable. Place cards should be laid out alphabetically on a table at the entrance to the reception. Each card should correspond to a table — either by number, color, or other identifying factor. Each table should be marked accordingly.

405. What are my options for seating/place cards?
Select a traditional or contemporary design for your place cards, depending on the style of your wedding. Place cards may have the bride and groom's names, the wedding date, the guest's name, and the table number, color, or other identifying factor.

406. What are some unique alternatives to traditional place cards?
For a vineyard wedding, cut a slit in a wine cork and use it as a place card holder. Cover a corkboard with pretty fabric and pin place cards to the boards. Thread place cards with ribbon and hang them from a small tree or clothesline. Instead of traditional cards, use a white-out pen to write guests' names on smooth river stones; a large bag can be purchased at a home-improvement store.

407. What is the proper formation for the receiving line?
From left to right, this is the proper order people should stand in the receiving line:
· Bride's Mother
· Bride's Father
· Groom's Mother

- Groom's Father
- Bride
- Groom
- Maid of Honor
- Bridesmaids

408. What is the purpose of the receiving line?

The receiving line is for guests to give their blessings to the couple and their parents.

409. What is the proper seating for the head table at the reception?

From left to right, this is the proper seating formation for the head table, if you have one at your reception:

- Bridesmaid
- Usher
- Bridesmaid
- Best Man
- Bride
- Groom
- Maid of Honor
- Usher
- Bridesmaid
- Usher

410. What is the proper seating for the parents' table at the reception?

The proper seating formation for the parents' table at the reception is as follows (assuming the table is round):

- Officiant
- Groom's Mother
- Groom's Father
- Bride's Mother
- Bride's Father
- Other Relatives

411. What should I serve during the toast at my reception?

Traditionally, at least champagne or sparkling punch should be served to toast the couple.

412. When should the toasting begin at the reception?

The toast begins after the receiving line breaks up at a cocktail reception or before dinner during a dinner reception. Toasts can also be offered after the main course or after the cake is served.

413. Who is the first person to offer a toast at the reception?
It is customary for the Best Man to offer a toast at the reception to introduce himself, the wedding party, and the newly married couple. This is followed by the groom thanking his Best Man and then toasting his bride and both sets of parents. After the groom's toast, anybody else can offer a toast. Typically, the father of the bride and the Maid of Honor offer a toast.

414. What should be included in the groom's toast?
Your toast could be to express thanks to everybody involved in planning the wedding, to give thanks to those who traveled long distances to come to your wedding, or to give any other kind of information. It can be serious, such as expressing how much you love your new wife; or it can be funny, such as describing how your fiancée played "hard to get" when you two first met. During the toast, everyone rises except those who are being toasted. And no one should drink from their cup until after the toast. After you finish your toast, raise your glass toward the person or persons being toasted. Your toast should sound sincere and not overly rehearsed. However, it is a good idea to practice it beforehand. If you are anxious about speaking in public, you may want to join your local Toastmaster's Club. This is an organization that helps people develop confidence in public speaking.

415. How long should the groom's toast be?
Your toast should not be so short that it sounds rude, or so long that your guests get bored.

416. What are rental items and why should I consider them?
Not all items need to be purchased for the ceremony and reception. There are many items that you have the option of renting, such as a tent, canopy, chairs and linens for the reception. This allows you to host a reception in your own home, or in less traditional locations, such as an art museum, a local park or at the beach. Be sure to take into account the cost for all these rental items when creating your budget.

417. Should I rent a tent and/or canopy for my wedding?
A large tent or canopy may be required for receptions held

outdoors to protect you and your guests from the sun or rain. Usually rented through party rental suppliers, tents and canopies can be expensive due to the labor involved in delivery and set-up. Tents and canopies come in different sizes and colors. Depending on the shape of your reception area, you may need to rent several smaller canopies rather than one large one. Contact several party rental suppliers to discuss the options. Consider this cost when making a decision between an outdoor and an indoor reception. In cooler weather, heaters may also be necessary. To save money, shop early and compare prices with several party rental suppliers.

418. Should I rent a dance floor for my wedding?

A dance floor will be provided by most hotels and clubs. However, if your reception site does not have a dance floor, you may need to rent one through your caterer or a party rental supplier. When comparing prices of dance floors, include the delivery and set-up fees.

419. How do I go about renting tables and chairs for my wedding?

You will have to provide tables and chairs for your guests if your reception site or caterer doesn't provide them as part of their package. For a full meal, you will have to provide tables and seating for all guests. For a cocktail reception, you only need to provide tables and chairs for approximately 30 to 50 percent of your guests. Ask your caterer or reception site manager for advice. There are various types of tables and chairs to choose from. The most commonly used chairs for wedding receptions are typically white wooden or plastic chairs. The most common tables for receptions are round tables that seat 8 guests. The most common head table arrangement is several rectangular tables placed end-to-end to seat your entire wedding party on one side, facing your guests. Contact various party rental suppliers to find out what types of chairs and tables they carry as well as their price ranges. When comparing prices of renting tables and chairs, include the cost of delivery and set-up.

420. Should I rent linens and tableware for my wedding?

You will also need to provide linens and tableware for your reception if your reception site or caterer does not provide them as part of their package. For a sit-down reception where the meal is served by waiters and waitresses, tables are usually set with a cloth (usually white, but may be color coordinated with the wedding), a centerpiece, and complete place settings. At a less formal buffet reception where guests serve themselves, tables are covered with a cloth but place settings are not mandatory. The necessary plates and silverware may be located at the buffet table, next to the food. Linens and tableware depend on the formality of your reception. When comparing prices of linens and tableware, include the cost of delivery and set-up.

421. Do I need to rent heaters for my outdoor wedding?

You may need to rent heaters if your ceremony or reception will be held outdoors and if the temperature could drop below 65 degrees. There are electric and gas heaters, both of which come in different sizes. Gas heaters are more popular since they do not have unsightly and unsafe electric cords.

422. Do I need to rent lanterns for my wedding?

Lanterns are often used at evening receptions. Many choices are available, from fire lanterns to electric ones. Consider the formality of the reception and choose the proper lighting to complement your decorations.

423. How much does renting a tent and/or canopy cost?

It can cost from $300 to $5,000 or more, depending on how many tents you needs and the suppliers you are renting from.

424. How much does renting a dance floor cost?

It can cost from $100 to $600, depending on how large you want the dance floor to be.

425. How much does it cost to rent tables and chairs for my wedding?

It can cost from $3 to $10 per person to rent tables and chairs.

426. How much does it cost to rent tableware and linens for my wedding?

It can cost from $3 to $25 per person to rent linens and tableware.

427. How much do heaters cost?
They can cost from $25 to $75 per heater to rent.

428. How much does it cost to rent lanterns?
It can cost from $6 to $60 per lamp.

429. How can I save money when renting tables and chairs for my wedding?
Attempt to negotiate free delivery and set-up with party rental suppliers in exchange for giving them your business.

430. What kind of questions should I ask the rental supplier I am considering renting items from?
- What is the name of the party rental supplier?
- What is the address of the party rental supplier?
- What is the website and e-mail of the party rental supplier?
- What is the name and phone number of my contact person?
- How many years have you been in business?
- What are your hours of operation?
- Do you have liability insurance?
- What is the cost per item needed?
- What is the cost of pick-up and delivery?
- What is the cost of setting up the items rented?
- When would the items be delivered?
- When would the items be picked up after the event?
- What is your payment policy?
- What is your cancellation policy?

431. When should I meet with all my service providers to confirm the details of the wedding day?
Two to six weeks before the wedding.

✽ Notes

....

....

....

....

....

....

....

....

....

....

....

....

....

....

....

....

....

....

....

....

....

....

....

....

CHAPTER 17

Caterers

Caterers

432. Should I hire a caterer?

If your reception is going to be in a facility that does not provide food, you will need to hire an outside caterer. The caterer will be responsible for preparing, cooking, and serving the food. The caterer will also be responsible for beverages and for cleaning up after the event. Before signing a contract, make sure you understand all the services the caterer will provide. Your contract should state the amount and type of food and beverages that will be served, the way in which they will be served, the number of servers who will be available, and the cost per food item or person.

433. How do we select our menu?

The menu will be determined by your tastes and the season. Let the caterer know what type of cuisine and dishes you have in mind. You can also ask your caterer what his or her specialties are, and you may want to include those. If your reception is going to be at a hotel, restaurant or other facility that provides food, you will need to select a meal to serve your guests. Most of these facilities will have a predetermined menu from which to select your meal. Generally, you will want to serve a red meat option, a white meat or fish options, and a vegetarian option for your main course.

434. What options do I have with catering?

Food can be served either buffet style or as a sit-down meal. It should be chosen according to the time of day, year, and formality of the wedding. Although there are many main dishes to choose from, chicken and beef are the most popular selections for a large event. Ask your facility manager or caterer for their specialty. If you have a special type of food you would like to serve at your reception, select a facility or caterer who specializes in preparing it.

435. Does my caterer need to bring cooking, heating, and refrigeration equipment to my wedding?

Check to see if the location for your reception provides refrigeration and cooking equipment. If not, make sure your caterer is fully self-supported with portable refrigeration and heating equipment. A competent caterer will prepare much of the food in his or her own kitchen and should provide an adequate staff of cooks, servers, and bartenders. Be careful about using mayonnaise, cream sauces, or custard fillings

— you don't want to risk any food spoiling.

436. What questions should I ask caterers?
- What is the name of the caterer?
- What is the website and e-mail of the caterer?
- What is the address of the caterer?
- What is the name and phone number of my contact person?
- How many years have you been in business?
- What percentage of your business is dedicated to wedding receptions?
- Do you have liability insurance/license to serve alcohol?
- When is the final head-count needed?
- What is your ratio of servers to guests?
- How do your servers dress for wedding receptions?
- What is your price range for a seated lunch/buffet lunch?
- What is your price range for a seated/buffet dinner?
- How much gratuity is expected?
- What is your specialty?
- What is your cake-cutting fee?
- What is your bartending fee?
- What is your fee to clean-up after the reception?
- What is your payment/cancellation policy?
- Do you accept credit cards?

437. We had tastings with several caterers; should I notify the caterers we did not choose of our decision to go with another company?
You are not obliged to notify the vendors you do not choose of your decision, but it is courteous and saves you (and them) time. A vendor may ask questions about why you opted for another company, and you can give your reasons if you choose, or you can politely decline to say.

438. When should I finalize my beverage and food menu for the reception?
Six to eight weeks before the wedding.

439. How can I save money on catering?
One way to save money is to give only 85 to 95 percent of your final guest count to your caterer or facility manager, depending on how certain you are that all of your guests who have responded will come. Chances are that several of your guests will not show up. But if they do, your caterer should

still have enough food for all of them. This is especially true with buffet style receptions, in which case the facility or caterer will charge extra for each additional guest. However, if you give a complete count of your guests to your caterer and some of them don't show up, you will still have to pay for their plates. If offering a buffet meal, have the catering staff serve the food onto guests' plates rather than allowing guests to serve themselves. This will help to regulate the amount of food consumed. Select food that is not too time-consuming to prepare, or food that does not have expensive ingredients. Also, consider a brunch or early afternoon wedding so the reception will fall between meals, allowing you to serve hors d'oeuvres instead of a full meal. Or tray pass hors d'oeuvres during cocktail hour and choose a lighter meal.

440. Should I serve hors d'oeuvres at my reception?
At receptions where a full meal is to be served, hors d'oeuvres may be offered to guests during the first hour of the reception. However, at a tea or cocktail reception, hors d'oeuvres will be the "main course."

441. What types of hors d'oeuvres should I serve at my reception?
There are many options for hors d'oeuvres, depending on the formality of your reception and the type of food to be served at the meal. Popular items are foods that can easily be picked up and eaten with one hand. Hors d'oeuvres may be set out on tables "buffet style" for guests to help themselves, or they may be passed around on trays by waiters and waitresses. When selecting hors d'oeuvres for your reception, consider whether heating or refrigeration will be available and choose your food accordingly. When planning your menu, consider the time of day. You should select lighter hors d'oeuvres for a midday reception and heavier hors d'oeuvres for an evening reception.

442. Should I provide meals for my vendors?
It is considered a courtesy to feed your photographer, videographer, and all other "service providers" at the reception. Check options and prices with your caterer or reception site manager. Make sure you allocate a place for your service providers to eat. You may want them to eat with your guests, or you may prefer setting a place outside

the main room for them to eat. Your service providers may be more comfortable with the latter. You don't need to feed your service providers the same meal as your guests. You can order sandwiches or another less expensive meal for them. If the meal is a buffet, there should be enough food left after all your guests have been served for your service providers to eat. Tell them they are welcome to eat after all your guests have been served.

443. Is there gratuity for a caterer?

It is customary to pay a gratuity fee to your caterer. The average gratuity is 15% to 20% of your food and beverage bill. Gratuities can range up to 25%. Ask about these costs up front and select your caterer or reception site accordingly.

CHAPTER 18

Alcohol & The Bar

444. What types of drinks should I serve at my reception?

White and red wines, scotch, vodka, gin, rum, and beer are the most popular alcoholic beverages. Sodas and fruit punch are popular nonalcoholic beverages served at receptions. And of course, don't forget coffee or tea.

445. What are my options for serving alcohol?

There are a number of options and variations for serving alcoholic beverages: a full open bar where you pay for your guests to drink as much as they wish; an open bar for the first hour, followed by a cash bar where guests pay for their own drinks; cash bar only; beer and wine only; nonalcoholic beverages only; or any combination thereof.

446. How should I determine what alcohol to serve?

In selecting the type of alcohol to serve, consider the age and preference of your guests, the type of food that will be served, and the time of day your guests will be drinking. Never serve liquor without some type of food.

447. How do I tell my guests I am having a cash bar?

If you plan to have a no-host or "cash" bar, you should notify your guests so they know to bring cash with them. A simple line that says "No-Host Bar" on the reception card or on your wedding website should suffice.

448. Can I serve a custom cocktail?

It is a nice idea to serve a custom cocktail; plus, if you serve only beer and wine and a custom drink, you can save as much as 50 percent on bar costs. Serve a cocktail that is special to you as a couple. Did you have mojitos on your first date? Does your family have a tradition of drinking a special drink that signifies your heritage and culture? You might give the drink recipe and a special glass as your party favors.

449. Can I purchase my own liquor if my reception site doesn't offer it?

If you plan to serve alcoholic beverages at a reception site that does not provide liquor, make sure your caterer has a license to serve alcohol and that your reception site allows alcoholic beverages. If you plan to order your own alcohol, do so three or four weeks before the event. You may want to find a retailer that lets you return unopened cases or bottles, to help cut costs.

450. How can I figure out how much alcohol I need?

On average, you should allow 1 drink per person per hour at the reception. A bottle of champagne will usually serve six glasses. If you are hosting an open bar at a hotel or restaurant, ask the catering manager how they charge for liquor: by consumption or by number of bottles opened. Get this in writing before the event and then ask for a full consumption report after the event.

Use the following chart to plan your beverage needs:

Beverages	Amount based on 100 guests
Bourbon	3 Fifths
Gin	3 Fifths
Rum	2 Fifths
Scotch	4 Quarts
Vodka	5 Quarts
White Wine	2 Cases
Red Wine	1 Case
Champagne	3 Cases
Mixers	2 Cases each: Club Soda, Seltzer, Beer Water, Tonic Water, Ginger Ale, Cola

451. What should I be wary of with the bar?

The hosts of a party can be held legally responsible for the conduct and safety of their guests. Keep this in mind when planning the quantity and type of beverages to serve. If you are hosting an open bar, speak to the bartender ahead of time and let him or her know to watch out for guests who may be too drunk. You don't want guests to be over-served. Also make sure the bartender never serves underage guests and questions any guest he or she thinks may be under 21.

452. How much should I spend on alcohol?

Beverages at your reception can range anywhere from $8 to $35 per person depending on the beverages and brands you choose to serve and the type of bar you choose.

453. How can I save money on the bar?

To keep beverage costs down, serve punch, wine, or nonalcoholic drinks only. If your caterer allows it, consider buying liquor from a wholesaler who will let you return unopened bottles. Or host beer, wine, and soft drinks only and have mixed drinks available on a cash basis. The bartending fee is often waived if you meet the minimum requirements on beverages consumed. Omit waiters and waitresses. People tend to drink almost twice as much if there are waiters and waitresses constantly asking them if they would like another drink and then bringing drinks to them.

454. How can I save money on the champagne toast?

For the toast, tray pass champagne only to those guests who want it, not to everyone. Many people will make a toast with whatever they are currently drinking. Consider serving sparkling cider in place of champagne.

455. What is a bartending fee?

Some reception sites and caterers charge an extra fee for bartending, pouring coffee, and setting up the bar. The bartending fee could be and often is waived if you meet a minimum requirement on beverages consumed. Try to negotiate this with your caterer prior to hiring him or her.

456. What is a bar set-up fee?

You may be charged an extra fee setting up the bar. Often, if you meet a minimum requirement on beverages consumed the reception site or caterer will waive this fee, so be sure to try to negotiate this prior to hiring anyone.

457. What is a corkage fee?

Many reception sites and caterers make money by marking up the food and alcohol they sell. You may wish to provide your own alcohol for several reasons. First, it is more cost effective. Second, you may want to serve an exotic wine or champagne that the reception site or caterer does not offer. In either case, and if your reception site or caterer allows it, be prepared to pay a corkage fee. This is the fee for each bottle brought into the reception site and opened by a member of their staff. You need to consider whether the expenses saved after paying the corkage fee justify the hassle and liability of bringing in your own alcohol. The corkage fee can cost anywhere from $5 to $20 per bottle.

458. How much is the bartender's fee?

Bartender's fees can range from $75 to $500.

459. How much is the bar set-up fee?

Bar set-up fees can range from $75 to $500.

460. How much is the corkage fee?

The corkage fee can cost anywhere from $5 to $20 per bottle.

461. How much is the fee to pour coffee?

The fee to pour coffee ranges from $0.25 to $1 per person.

CHAPTER 19

Reception
Music

462. What is reception music?

Music is a major part of your reception, and should be planned carefully. Music helps create the atmosphere of your wedding. Special songs will make your reception unique. When you select music for your reception, keep in mind the age and musical preference of your guests, your budget, and any restrictions that the reception site may have.

463. What are my music options?

Deciding how you want your music played during your ceremony and reception is just as important as choosing the right type of music. Your options are just as varied as the music itself. These options include vocalists, trios and quartets, live bands, DJs, and recorded music.

464. What are the different parts of the reception that I can select specific music for?

Cocktail Hour
Newlyweds' Entrance/Receiving Line
During Dinner
Toasts
First Dance
Family Dances
Bouquet Toss
Garter Removal and Toss
Cake Cutting
Money Dance
Ethnic Dances
Last Dance

465. Do I need a wedding music timeline?

Because music is such an essential part of your wedding, it is important to set up a planning timeline. Following this timeline will allow you to pick the best music professionals at the best prices, rather than being forced to make last minute decisions you will later regret. This timeline assumes that you have 9 to 12 months to plan your wedding, but it can be adjusted to fit your schedule.

Nine Months to One Year Before the Wedding
1. Book the location of your ceremony and reception
2. Decide on genres of music (classical, popular, jazz, etc.)
3. Begin comparing musicians

Six to Nine Months Before the Wedding
1. Make a final decision on your music professional
2. Carefully review and sign music professional contract
3. Begin making your music selections

Three to Four Months Before the Wedding
1. Make final decisions on music choices for special dances, recessional and processional, unity candle ceremony, etc.
2. Purchase any needed sheet music or CDs (be sure to give yourself enough time to special order items if needed)
3. Write out a script and schedule of announcements you want your DJ or MC to make

Four to Six Weeks Before the Wedding
1. Meet with music professional and go over your final selections and special requests/instructions
2. Re-confirm all details of the music for the wedding, including address of ceremony and reception, final payment, and music choices
3. Give sheet music or CDs to music professional

One Week Before the Wedding
1. Make a final phone call to music professional to confirm all details
2. Give music professional's tip to your wedding coordinator, Maid of Honor, or Best Man (whomever will be in charge of tipping at your reception)
3. Make any final payments as specified in your contract

466. **Should I hire a DJ to play the music at my reception?**
A DJ is a popular choice for providing music at many weddings. A DJ will provide an extensive library of recorded music to play throughout your wedding. With a DJ, you have many more options for music throughout your ceremony and reception than you do when you hire musicians. A good DJ will have recordings of everything from classical music for your ceremony, to the most popular First Dance songs, to all-time party favorites. With a DJ, you also have more control over volume and can choose any music that you can find already recorded. A DJ can also ensure that your party flows smoothly by watching the reactions of your guests to certain music. In this way, your DJ can change the play list to reflect what people like throughout the party. When looking

at a DJ's song list, make sure that the music is varied from different genres and eras. If you are having your ceremony and reception at a religious site, be sure to let your DJ know what can and cannot be played. DJs charge by the hour and typically you must hire them for a minimum number of hours. The hourly rate ranges from $50 to $300, with a typical commitment of two to five hours.

467. What should I consider when hiring a DJ to play music at my reception?

A great DJ can make a party, just as a below-average one can ruin it, so it is important that you choose carefully. If you open up your phone book to "DJ", you will find an almost endless list of people available in your area. The key to finding a good DJ is to find an experienced professional with an extensive song list. While DJs don't have demo tapes, many will provide a video that will give you an idea of their style. Along with the DJ's personal style, you will want to evaluate their play list. Look for a wide variety of music, from different genres, as well as different eras. Inquire into the DJ's level of commitment; is the DJ doing this to earn extra money on the weekends or are weddings the DJ's primary business? A higher level of commitment often means a higher level of professionalism as the DJ relies on referrals.

468. Can my DJ also be my Master of Ceremonies?

If you want your musician to act as a Master of Ceremonies or MC, make sure he or she has a complete timeline for your reception in order to announce the various events such as the toasts, First Dance, and cutting of the cake.

469. Should I hire a live band to perform the music at my wedding?

Many couples hire live bands to perform at their weddings. A live band can be as small as four musicians playing the guitar, drums, piano and bass, to a full Big Band complete with a horn section. Bands go a long way in creating an atmosphere for a wedding, especially at the reception. Hiring a band that will play all jazz numbers helps to make your wedding completely different than a wedding that has all Big Band music. A band playing dance standards from the Forties and Fifties also creates a more formal feel to your wedding. You might want to consider hiring a local rock band, maybe one that you and your fiancé saw perform on one of your early dates. A good live band will keep your guests on their feet and having fun throughout your reception. The cost goes up with the number of musicians in the band so you may want to look for smaller groups. Also, it is harder to control the volume of a large live band, so check with your reception site to see how late loud music can be played. Consider if you want loud music at all. If you have many older guests or want your guests to be able to spend time talking to one another, a live rock band may not be the best choice. Live bands are hired on an hourly or per event charge and can run from $400 to $5,000.

470. What should I consider when hiring a band to play music at my reception?

There are as many types of bands as there are types of music, so narrowing down your search can be a little difficult. Begin by deciding when you want the band to play. Will they need to provide music for the ceremony or just the reception?

Next, consider the size of your reception venue. A large band will overwhelm a small room, while a small band may not have enough volume to engage everyone in a larger setting.

Finally, consider what types of music you are most interested in. A jazz band may not be familiar with today's pop hits, while a band that plays traditional wedding favorites may not perform a unique, personal favorite up to your standards. Also, be sure to inquire about equipment needs. A band that has a lot of equipment and needs multiple electrical outlets may have a problem performing outdoors.

471. Should I have a soloist to perform the music at my reception?

A soloist is a single musician performing live music. Soloists often perform as part of the wedding ceremony and may also be used to provide background music for the cocktail hour or beginning of the reception. Be sure that the soloist can perform your musical choices. Many classical pieces and some popular songs were written for specific instruments. You will need to check on the availability of sheet music before deciding on a soloist. Also, you might want to ask your soloist to perform the specific piece you are most interested in before hiring him or her. Soloists are hired by the hour and typically charge $50 to $400 an hour.

472. Should I use recorded music at my reception?

Some couples choose to use recorded music without hiring a DJ. If you are choosing music that is already in your personal music collection, this can be a big money saver. It will require you to put together a list of what is to be played and when during the ceremony. It will also require that whomever you put in charge of the music understands exactly what you want. Be sure that the person who will be playing the music is present at the rehearsal and use that time to run through your musical selections as well. Using recorded music that someone plays over a sound system works best if you can burn a CD of the music you want in the order you want it. Also, be sure that all the music is appropriate for your reception site, is the correct length, and that your site has an adequate sound system that you can use. This can cost from $5 to $50, depending on whether or not you need to purchase recordings of songs you want.

473. Should I save money on a DJ by having an "iPod wedding"?

An iPod wedding just means that you create a playlist of all your reception music and put it on an mP3 player. This can save money, but just beware of the pitfalls, which include dead batteries, scratchy sound systems, and uncomfortable lulls in the music. If you plan to have an iPod wedding you will need to ask a trusted, technologically savvy friend to man the mP3 player. You will need this person to act as MC — to play the right songs at the right times and make sure no one changes songs during the reception. You will also need to make sure your reception site has a good sound system and that your MC becomes familiar with how to hook it up and work it properly. Make sure your MC has backup CDs, as well as all the cords to charge the mP3 player or computer. In general, an iPod wedding is best for small receptions.

474. What questions should I ask when hiring a music professional to play at my wedding?

What are the particulars?

Start by getting the exact name of the band or DJ service, their address and phone number. If you find someone who is perfect, you want to be sure you can get a hold of him or her again. Also, having the exact name will make checking into their references much easier.

How many years of professional experience do you have?
Experience goes a long way in the professional music
business. Professionals who have been performing
at weddings for a long period of time are more likely
to have seen it all and will stay calm and collected should
anything not go according to plan. Professional
experience also provides a track record for you to check
into.

What percentage of your business is dedicated to weddings?
Many musicians moonlight in addition to their day jobs,
and so they may not have performed at many weddings.
Performing for a wedding is different from performing in
a professional orchestra, being a high school band teacher,
or even performing at other types of functions. You want
your music professional to specialize in weddings as much as
possible.

Are you the person who will be performing at my wedding?
Make sure that the people you interview, listen to demo
tapes from or personally audition are the same people who
will be performing at your wedding. Of course emergencies
sometimes arise, but you want to be sure that the wedding
performance will be of the same caliber as the audition.
The best way to ensure this is by having the same music
professionals.

What instruments do you play?
Make sure that any musician you are interested in hiring
plays the instrument you are most interested in. Many
musicians play multiple instruments, but specialize in one
particular type, so check to make sure that the instrument
you will want him or her to play is the one he or she is the
most proficient with.

What type of music do you specialize in?
If you have a specific theme or atmosphere you are hoping to
create at your wedding, this question is especially important.
You want your DJ or musicians to specialize in the music you
are most interested in. Hiring a band that does '80s cover
tunes to perform jazz standards is a recipe for disaster.

What are your hourly fees?
Ask this question during your initial contact with any

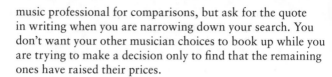

music professional for comparisons, but ask for the quote in writing when you are narrowing down your search. You don't want your other musician choices to book up while you are trying to make a decision only to find that the remaining ones have raised their prices.

Do you have an hourly minimum requirement?
Since most wedding ceremony and receptions last for many hours, minimums may not matter. However, if you are hiring a musician to perform only at your ceremony, you may want to be sure that the hourly minimum requirement will not run much longer than your ceremony. Some ceremonies are as short as thirty minutes, so if your musician has a two-hour minimum, you may be paying them for time they are not actually performing.

What is the cost of a soloist/duet/trio/quartet?
Some musicians will be able to work within your budget by changing the number of musicians they perform with.

What is your cost for additional hours?
If your reception is in full swing, or if your ceremony starts a little later than originally planned, you want to be sure your musicians will be able to stay for the duration. You will also want to establish the cost for additional time BEFORE the situation arises.

Do you have a cordless microphone?
When it is time for toasts at the reception, you will want to have a cordless microphone. This will allow the person giving the toast to stand in front of your guests without having to go on stage. Most band leaders or DJs will allow you to use their cordless microphone, but be sure to check that they have one and that you can use it during the reception.

What equipment will you bring? Do you have back-up equipment/musicians?
Check to make sure that any music professional you are interested in hiring has all his or her own equipment, including items such as extension cords and power strips. Also, ensure that your music professional will have back-up equipment to use if there are any equipment failures. Equally important are back-up professionals. If the DJ, or someone in

the band, is ill or has an emergency, who will come in their place?

Will you play recorded music during your break?
Your DJ can easily play recorded music during any breaks, but you want to be sure that any musicians you hire can do the same. Be sure that they have the equipment to play recorded music, and ask if you need to provide the recorded music or if they will bring it with them.

Do you have liability insurance?
Some musicians will require a bride and groom to sign a contract that will make them responsible for any damage done to their equipment during the wedding. Because this leaves the bride and groom open to the possibility of having to pay large sums in damages, or even to lawsuits, you may want to make sure that the music professional you are interested in hiring carries his or her own insurance. Check to see what the insurance will cover as well, since you may want to augment it with your own wedding insurance.

What is your payment/cancellation policy?
Payment and cancellation policies vary so find one that meets your needs. You may also want to ask your music professionals if they can work within your budget. Perhaps they could take a larger down payment, but give you longer time to pay the balance due.

475. How should I ask my musician or DJ to dress for my wedding?

You want your music professionals to come to your wedding properly attired. That can mean tuxedos and formal dresses, Zoot suits from the 1940s, or Renaissance inspired costumes. If your wedding has a theme, check to see if the musicians are willing to dress accordingly. Be prepared to pay the costs of costume rental if you are asking for something unusual.

476. Who is responsible for my musicians' food and where will they eat?

Often, music professionals expect to be served the same meal that your guests will be eating. You will need to include them in your guest count if this is the case, so take that into consideration. If you prefer, you may be able to make arrangements to serve them a simpler meal, such as sandwiches or hamburgers. Also, decide beforehand where you want your musicians to eat.

477. **How many breaks should my DJ be allowed and for how long?**

Your music professional will need to take a few breaks some time during your wedding. Just be sure they are not expecting an excessive amount of break time. You may want to arrange for recorded music to be played while he or she is on a break.

478. **What are the key points in a standard contract that I need when hiring my music professional?**

· The date, time and location of the wedding.
· The exact time that the music professional will start and end.
· The hourly rate of the music professional, the minimum required time and the hourly rate for any additional time that might become necessary.
· The name of the DJ, or each musician who will perform. Clearly state who will be performing in case of illness or emergency cancellation - and how to get a hold of that person.
· A list of all equipment the band or DJ will bring. Be sure it is spelled out if you have agreed to bring anything as well.
· A description of the DJ's or MC's duties - including any pre-wedding meetings to go over your musical program.
· The number and duration of breaks, and if recorded music will be played during those breaks.
· A description of what the DJ or band will be wearing (appropriate, acceptable attire).
· A list of special songs to be played. If you have asked the band to learn new songs be sure you specify that they will be rehearsed prior to the wedding.
· A clear description of the payment and cancellation policy.
· A statement that the bride or groom will not be held responsible for damages done to equipment by guests or any other third party.

479. Should we write out a music program for our ceremony and reception?

It is very important to write a program for both your ceremony and reception to share with your music professional. In the program, clearly indicate which songs you want played/performed for each part of the ceremony, the approximate time you expect the music to begin, and if you are having an MC or DJ host the reception, what you want announced before each part. Providing a program will ensure that everything runs smoothly and that the perfect song is playing for every moment of your wedding.

480. What type of music should I play during the cocktail hour of my reception?

The cocktail hour may or may not be an extension of your postlude, depending on how and where you have your reception. If your guests have traveled to a new location, you may want to change the style of your music to reflect a more party-like atmosphere. You may want to choose background music that can be played as your guests mingle around the bar and cocktail area. Smooth jazz, instrumental versions of pop songs, string quartets playing classical pieces, or a band playing low-key jazz standards are all good choices for the cocktail hour.

481. What type of music should I play during the newlyweds' entrance at my reception?

The entrance of the bride and groom to the reception is the first time that you will be introduced to your family and friends as husband and wife. This is a grand entrance, so choose music that fits the moment. There are numerous choices for classical music that will create a feeling of celebration. For less formal receptions, you may want to choose popular rock or R&B songs. Because the song will most likely not play long (you will soon change to the music for your First Dance) you have the freedom to choose a song that has a great chorus, even if you do not want the rest of the song played.

482. What type of music should I play during dinner at my reception?

If you are serving a meal during the reception, you should decide what type of music to play while your guests dine. Follow the same rule of thumb that you would for the cocktail hour; in other words, background music that sets the mood for your reception. If you have hired a harpist or string quartet for your ceremony, consider having them perform throughout the dinner hour as well. Smooth Jazz, New Age and Easy Listening are all good choices. If a DJ is providing your music, be sure they keep music at an appropriate volume.

483. What type of music should I play for the First Dance at my reception?

The First Dance is probably the most romantic moment of your reception and choosing the right song can be the easiest or most difficult musical choice you will have to make. If you and your spouse have a song that has special meaning for you, this is the perfect time to play it. If you do not have something already picked out, you will want to choose a song that conveys the feelings and thoughts you have about each other and your marriage. Start by using the list of First Dance songs found in this section. You may want to listen to a radio station that specializes in love songs or ballads, or ask your wedding consultant, DJ or bandleader for more suggestions. The key to picking the perfect First Dance song is to listen to as many different songs as possible and work with your fiancé to narrow down the list to a few favorites. If you and your fiancé have specific musical tastes, or favorite genres, that may be a great way to start the selection process. The most important thing to keep in mind is this: your First Dance is a special dance that celebrates your marriage, so choose music that you both love!

484. What song should we play during our First Dance?

We have compiled a list of songs that are popular selections to play during your First Dance:
· A Whole New World - Peabo Bryson & Regina Belle
· After All - Cher
· All My Life - K-Ci & Jojo
· Always - Atlantic Starr
· Always - Sarah Vaughn & Billy Eckstein
· Amazed - Lonestar
· Annie's Song - John Denver
· As Time Goes By - Tony Bennett
· At Last - Etta James
· Beautiful - Gordon Lightfoot
· Because You Loved Me - Celine Dion

- Best Thing That Ever Happened To Me - Gladys Knight & The Pips
- Can You Feel The Love Tonight - Elton John
- Can't Help Falling In Love - Elvis Presley
- Chances Are - Johnny Mathis
- Close To You - Carpenters
- Crazy - Patsy Cline
- Crazy For You - Madonna
- Don't Know Much - Linda Ronstadt & Aaron Neville
- Dreaming Of You - Selena
- Endless Love - Lionel Richie (With Diana Ross)
- Eternal Flame - Bangles
- Every Breath You Take - Police
- (Everything I Do) I Do It For You - Bryan Adams
- For You I Will - Monica
- Forever And Ever, Amen - Randy Travis
- From This Moment On - Shania Twain & Brian White
- Grow Old With Me - Party Doll & Mary Chapin Carpenter
- Have I Told You Lately - Rod Stewart
- Have You Ever Really Loved A Woman - Bryan Adams
- Hold Me - Teddy Pendergrass
- I Do, Cherish You - Mark Wills
- I Don't Want To Miss A Thing - Aerosmith
- I Finally Found - Barbra Streisand & Bryan Adams
- I Get A Kick Out Of You - Frank Sinatra
- I Give My Heart - John Berry
- I Honestly Love You - Olivia Newton-John
- I Only Have Eyes For You - The Flamingo
- I Swear - All-4-One
- If - Bread
- I'll Stand By You - The Pretenders
- In My Life - Beatles
- In Your Eyes - Peter Gabriel
- It Had To Be You - Harry Connick Jr.
- It's Your Love - Faith Hill & Tim Mcgraw
- Just The Way You Are - Billy Joel
- Lady - Kenny Rogers
- Let's Stay Together - Al Green
- Love, Me - Collin Raye
- Me And You - Kenny Chesney
- Nobody Loves Me Like You Do - Anne Murray
- The One - Elton John
- Our Love Is Here To Stay - Billie Holiday

- Perhaps Love - Placido Domingo & John Denver
- Say You Say Me - Lionel Richie
- Sentimental Journey - Doris Day
- She's Got A Way - Billy Joel
- Some Enchanted Evening - Original Cast Of South Pacific
- Spend My Life With You - Eric Benet (With Tamia)
- Take My Breath Away - Berlin
- To Love Somebody - Michael Bolton
- To Make You Feel My Love - Garth Brooks
- Tonight And Forever - Carly Simon
- True Companion - Marc Cohn
- Truly Madly Deeply - Savage Garden
- Unchained Melody - Righteous Brothers
- Unexpected Song - Bernadette Peters
- Valentine - Martina Mcbride & Jim Brickman
- The Way You Look Tonight - Tony Bennett
- The Wedding Song (There Is Love) - Petula Clark
- We've Only Just Begun - Carpenters
- When A Man Loves A Woman - Michael Bolton
- When I Fall In Love - Nat King Cole
- When I Said I Do - Clint Black
- Wonderful Tonight - Eric Clapton
- You And I - Crystal Gayle And Eddie Rabbit
- You Are So Beautiful - Joe Cocker
- You Decorated My Life - Kenny Rogers
- You're Still The One - Shania Twain
- You're The Inspiration - Chicago

485. **How do we select the songs to play during the family dances at our reception?**

After you and your new spouse have had your First Dance, it is customary to invite other family members to share a dance with the bride and the groom. Traditionally there is a bride and father-of-the-bride dance, and a groom and mother-of-the-groom dance. You can have these dances simultaneously or separately, depending on your preference and the formality of your reception. The music for these dances can be a favorite song of one of the parents, a meaningful popular song, or the instrumental version of a song that has special meaning about one of the parents, such as a lullaby your father or mother used to sing. This dance is an opportunity to give your parents special recognition and to thank them for their love and support through the years, so choose something they will like and appreciate. You may also want to consider having more family dances to include step-parents, grandparents and even mentors who are special to you and your fiancé. You do not have to dance with the same family member through the whole song. If there are others you wish to recognize with a special dance, change partners mid-way through the music.

486. What song should we play during the Father-Daughter dance at our reception?

We have compiled a list of songs that are popular selections to play during the Father-Daughter dance:

- A Smile Like Yours - Natalie Cole
- All I Have - Beth Neilsen Chapman
- Butterfly Kisses - Bob Carlisle
- Can You Feel The Love Tonight - Elton John
- Child Of Mine - Carole King
- Daddy's Girl - Peter Cetera
- Daddy's Hands - Holly Dunn
- Father-Daughter Harmony - Phil Keaggy
- Father's Eyes - Amy Grant
- Hero - Mariah Carey
- In My Life - John Lennon
- Isn't She Lovely - Stevie Wonder
- Lullaby - Billy Joel
- Me And My Father - Cosy Sheridan
- My Father - Nina Simone
- My Funny Valentine - Chet Baker
- My Girl - The Temptations
- Thank Heaven For Little Girls - Maurice Chevalier
- Through The Years - Kenny Rogers
- Unforgettable - Natalie Cole & Nat King Cole
- The Way You Look Tonight - Frank Sinatra
- What A Wonderful World - Louis Armstrong
- Your Smiling Face - James Taylor

487. What song should we play during the Mother-Son dance at our Reception?

We have compiled a list of songs that are popular selections to play during the Mother-Son dance:

- All The Things You Are - Tony Bennett
- Because You Loved Me - Celine Dion
- Blessed - Elton John
- Dearly Beloved - Dinah Shore
- For All We Know - Carpenters

- Have I Told You Lately That I Love You - Bing Crosby & Andrews Sisters
- I Am Your Child - Barry Manilow
- I Had A Good Mother And Father - Kate Wolf
- I Wish You Love - Natalie Cole
- In This Life - Bette Midler
- Long Ago - Gail Marten
- Make Someone Happy - Jimmy Durante
- Moon River - Andy Williams
- Stand By Me - Ben E King
- Sunrise, Sunset - Original Cast of Fiddler On The Roof
- 'Til The End Of Time - Perry Como
- Wind Beneath My Wings - Bette Midler
- You Are The Sunshine Of My Life - Stevie Wonder
- You Light Up My Life - Debby Boone
- You've Got A Friend - James Taylor

488. How do we select songs to play during the toasts at our reception?

Another highlight of your reception will be the toasts. Traditionally the Best Man and the Maid of Honor will toast the bride and groom at the beginning of the reception. They may toast just before the meal is served, during the actual meal, or shortly after the First Dance. You can choose to have music playing softly in the background for your toasts, acting as a soundtrack to the speeches. You might want to have instrumental versions of songs that celebrate friendship, such as "That's What Friends Are For" or "Stand By Me." Or you may choose to have a favorite piece of classical music performed. If you went to school with the Maid of Honor or Best Man, consider having your school song playing, or your sorority or fraternity's song. Whatever music you choose, be sure it is played at a low enough volume so your guests can easily hear the toasts.

489. What songs should we play during the toasts at our reception?

- All The Man That I Need - Whitney Houston
- Doin' It All For My Baby - Huey Lewis & The News
- Enjoy It! - Maurice Chevalier
- Everything Is Beautiful - Foster & Allen
- Friends - Elton John
- The Greatest Love Of All - Whitney Houston
- I Pledge My Love - Peaches & Herb

- Shower The People - James Taylor
- That's What Friends Are For - Dionne Warwick
- These Are The Days -10,000 Maniacs
- Sacred Emotion - Donny Osmond
- Your Song - Elton John

490. How do we select the song to play during the bouquet toss at our reception?

A popular tradition at many receptions is the bouquet toss. This is when the single women at the wedding get together while the bride tosses her bouquet over her shoulder toward the group. The woman who catches the bouquet is said to be the next to marry. This tradition is meant to be fun, so choose music that keeps with the theme. Upbeat tempos and lively songs are the perfect choice for the bouquet toss.

491. What song should we play during the bouquet toss at our reception?

- All The Man That I Need - Whitney Houston
- Doin' It All For My Baby - Huey Lewis & The News
- Enjoy It! - Maurice Chevalier
- Everything Is Beautiful - Foster & Allen
- Friends - Elton John
- The Greatest Love Of All - Whitney Houston
- I Pledge My Love - Peaches & Herb
- Shower The People - James Taylor
- That's What Friends Are For - Dionne Warwick
- These Are The Days -10,000 Maniacs
- Sacred Emotion - Donny Osmond
- Your Song - Elton John

492. How do we select the music to be played during our reception that will have guests dancing?

It may seem like you have covered all the bases by choosing songs for all the special moments throughout your reception, but you also have to consider what will be played during the rest of the party. There are many factors to keep in mind while choosing the play list for your reception: how formal your wedding is, whether you have a band or a DJ, the location of the reception, and the age of your guests. While you should feel free to choose music that you and your spouse enjoy, you will find that your guests will enjoy your reception more if you play a variety of musical genres. Play pieces from different eras, such as swing, big band, Motown and '80s rock. If you are having a very formal reception you may want to stay with a musical theme, such as jazz standards or waltzes. For less formal receptions, get your guests up and dancing with party favorites like the Chicken Dance, the Bunny Hop, a Conga line and the Macarena. Try to keep in mind that older guests, parents and children may not appreciate lyrics that can be considered offensive. Some church and temple halls will not allow certain music to be played even at the reception, so be sure to check and then pass along any restrictions to your DJ or band leader.

493. **What songs should we play during our reception to have our guests enjoying themselves?**

We have compiled a list of "can't miss" party songs that are popular selections to play during your reception:

- Alley Cat - Various Artists
- Born To Hand Jive - Original Broadway Cast Of Grease
- The Bunny Hop - Brave Combo
- Celebration - Kool & The Gang
- The Chicken Dance - Brave Combo
- Electric Boogie - Marcia Griffiths
- The Hokey Pokey - Brave Combo
- Hot, Hot, Hot - Buster Poindexter
- The Hustle - Various
- Ice, Ice, Baby - Vanilla Ice
- Macarena - Los Del Rio
- Tequila - The Champs
- The Twist - Chubby Checker
- Theme From New York, New York - Mel Torme
- Stayin' Alive - Bee Gees
- YMCA - Village People

494. **How do we select the song to play during the garter removal and toss at our reception?**

The tradition of the garter toss started as a way to prove that a couple had consummated their marriage. The couple's consummation would be witnessed and as proof, the garter would be brought out of the wedding chamber and shown to the guests. Today the groom removes the garter and tosses it over his shoulder to a group of single men. The garter toss is also a fun tradition that deserves a great song.

495. What song should we play during the garter removal and toss at our reception?

- Another One Bites The Dust - Queen
- Baby, I Love Your Way - Big Mountain
- Can I Steal A Little Love - Frank Sinatra
- Heaven - Bryan Adams
- Heaven Must Be Missing An Angel - Tavares
- Ebb Tide - Tom Jones
- Fever - Peggy Lee
- If I Ever Fall In Love - Shai
- Kiss - Prince
- Let's Get It On - Marvin Gaye
- Love Is Alive - Gary Wright
- Makin' Whoopee - Dr. John
- Oh, Pretty Woman - Roy Orbison
- Oh Yeah - Yello
- Shameless - Garth Brooks
- Stand By Your Man - Tammy Wynette
- The Stripper - David Rose
- Sweet Nothin's - Brenda Lee
- Theme From Mission Impossible - Larry Mullen/Adam Clayton
- Wild Thing - Tone-Loc
- You Sexy Thing - Hot Chocolate
- (You've Got) Personality - Mitch Ryder

496. How do we select the song to play during the cake cutting at our reception?

The wedding cake goes back as far as the ancient Romans who used a cake made of wheat flour, water and salt during marriage ceremonies. The wedding cake has come a long way since then and now the cake cutting is a traditional part of most receptions. The first cut is made by both the bride and the groom. Together, they hold the cake-cutting knife and cut the first slice. This act is meant to symbolize the bride and groom's shared future. The cake cutting is often set to music, and in fact your DJ or MC will signal to your guests that the cake cutting is going to take place by changing music. Once again, keep in mind how formal your reception is when picking the music for this tradition. As with the other parts of your wedding, this is a celebratory moment so have fun with the music!

497. What song should we play during the cake cutting at our reception?
   · All I Do Is Dream Of You - Dean Martin
   · Appetite For Love - Sy Klopps
   · Can't Smile Without You - Carpenters
   · Chapel Of Love - Bette Midler
   · Completely - Michael Bolton
   · For Your Sweet Love - Rick Nelson
   · He's Sure The Boy I Love - Darlene Love
   · How Sweet It Is (To Be Loved By You) - James Taylor
   · I Got You Babe - Sonny And Cher
   · I Love You Too Much - Andrews Sisters
   · I Only Have Eyes For You - Doris Day
   · If You Say My Eyes Are Beautiful - Whitney Houston
   · Joy To The World - Three Dog Night
   · Look Heart, No Hands - Randy Travis
   · Love And Marriage - Frank Sinatra
   · Oh Happy Day - Joan Baez
   · Recipe For Love - Harry Connick Jr.
   · Recipe For My Love - Danny Jennsen
   · Sugar, Sugar - Archies
   · Somewhere Out There - Linda Ronstadt w/James Ingram
   · This Guy's In Love With You - Herb Albert

498. How do we select the song to play during the Money or Dollar Dance at our reception?
   The Money Dance, or Dollar Dance, is a tradition that is alive and well. Originally a Polish tradition, this dance has made its way into American weddings in various parts of the country. It is a way for the bride and groom to make a little extra money for their honeymoon or for starting their new life together. The dance is traditionally started with the bride and the Best Man. While they dance, the Best Man pins a dollar to the bride's dress, or places it in a small satin purse the bride carries. Guests are then invited to "pay" for dances with the bride by pinning dollars on her or placing them in her purse. While there is no obligation for the guests to take part in this tradition, many guests do find the Money Dance a fun way to help the couple pay their expenses. The musical choices for a Money Dance are varied. You can choose music that is simply fun to dance to or go with songs that have a money theme.

499. What song should we play during the Money or Dollar Dance at our reception?
- 10 Cents A Dance - Nancye Hayes
- Betcha Nickel - Ella Fitzgerald
- Coins And Promises - Margaret Becker
- For Love Of Money - O'jay
- Got A Penny - Nat King Cole
- I Need Some Money - John Lee Hooker
- The Magic Penny - Cathy Fink
- Material Girl - Madonna
- Money Blues - Louie Armstrong
- Money Honey - Elvis Presley
- Money, Money, Money - Abba
- Money (That's What I Want) - Beatles
- Money (Tired Of Working) - Steve Bassett
- Pennies From Heaven - Billie Holiday
- Penny For Your Thoughts - Tavares
- Private Dancer - Tina Turner
- She Works Hard For Her Money - Donna Summer
- Three Coins In A Fountain - The Four Aces

500. How do we select the songs to play during the ethnic dances at our reception?

Your wedding is the perfect time to celebrate your culture and heritage. Whether you and your fiancé share the same heritage, or your marriage is a melding of different ethnicities, you can highlight and honor your cultures through music. Some cultures have traditional songs and dances that are played at all weddings; for others, simply playing ethnic music is enough to pay homage to your heritage. Jewish, Irish and Polish weddings have traditional songs and dances. For other cultures that do not have a specific wedding song or dance, have your band or DJ play some traditional music. Be prepared to provide a CD or sheet music, because many musicians will not have a variety of ethnic music to choose from.

501. What songs should we play during the ethnic dances at our reception?
- 4 Wedding Polkas - Trebunia Family Band : Polish
- Bashana - Shlomit : Jewish
- Haste To The Wedding - Maggie Sansone : Irish
- Dame Tu Amore Guantanamera - Yakare : Latin
- Did Your Mother Come From Ireland - Bing Crosby : Irish

- Dodi Li - Various: Jewish
- Granada - Jose Carreras : Latin
- Hava Nagila - Danny Albert : Jewish
- If You Love Me Polka - Various : Polish
- Mala Femmena - Al Ciaola : Italian
- Mexican Hat Dance - Erich Kunzel : Latin
- My Wild Irish Rose - The Irish Tenors : Irish
- Neopolitan Song - Bruna Bertone : Italian
- Ose Shalom - David & The High Spirits : Jewish
- O Sole Mio - Roberto Alagna : Italian
- Raisins And Almonds - Mandy Patinkin : Jewish
- Sabbath Prayer - Uri Cain : Jewish
- Tarantella - Various : Italian
- To Life - Original Broadway Cast Of Fiddler On The Roof : Jewish
- Tzena Tzena - The Barry Sisters : Jewish
- When Irish Eyes Are Smiling - Bing Crosby : Irish
- Zorba The Greek - Various : Greek

502. How do we select the song to play during the Last Dance at our reception?

Before making your exit and starting your new life together, you and you new spouse may want to have one final dance. This is the perfect time to get one more romantic moment in, especially if you have been dancing with other friends and family throughout the reception. If you and your spouse had trouble agreeing on a First Dance song, you may want to have one song played for the First Dance and one for the Last Dance. Once again, this is a chance to celebrate your love, so choose a song that has special meaning to you and your fiancé. You may want to start the last dance with just you and your new spouse and then have your DJ or bandleader invite everyone to join you.

503. What song should we play during the last dance at our reception?

- A Little More Time On You - Alabama W/ N' Sync
- All I Ever Need Is You - Ray Charles
- All Through The Night - Cyndi Lauper
- The Dance - Garth Brooks
- Dedicated To The One I Love - Mamas & The Papas
- Don't Say Goodnight - Isley Brothers
- Dreaming My Dreams With You - Collin Raye
- Dream Weaver - Gary Wright

- Goodnight Sweetheart - David Kersh
- Goodnight Sweetheart - The Flamingos
- I Cross My Heart - George Strait
- (I Love You) For Sentimental Reasons - Ella Fitzgerald
- (I've Had) The Time Of My Life - Bill Medley & Jennifer Warren
- Just To See Her - Smokey Robinson
- Last Dance - Donna Summer
- Love Will Find A Way - Pablo Cruise
- On The Wings Of Love - Jeffrey Osborne
- One In A Million You - Larry Graham
- Save The Best For Last - Vanessa Williams
- She Believes In Me - Kenny Rogers
- You're Still The One - Shania Twain
- The Vows Go Unbroken - Kenny Rogers

504. **How can I save money on reception music?**

You will probably get a better price if you hire a band or DJ directly than if you hire them through an entertainment agency. Check the music department of local colleges and universities for names of student musicians and DJs. You may be able to hire a student for a fraction of the price of a professional musician or DJ. A DJ is typically less expensive than a live musician, saving $200 to $1,000. Some facilities have contracts with certain DJs, and you may be able to save money by hiring one of them.

✿ Notes

....

....

....

....

....

....

....

....

....

....

....

....

....

....

....

....

....

....

....

....

....

....

....

CHAPTER 20

Cakes & Bakeries

505. How do I decide what type of wedding cake to order?

When ordering your cake, you will have to decide not only on a flavor, but also on a size, shape and color. Size is determined by the number of guests. You can choose from one large tier to two, three, or more smaller tiers. The cake can be round, square or heart-shaped. The most common flavors are chocolate, carrot, lemon, rum, and "white" cakes. You can be creative by adding a filling to your cake, such as custard, strawberry, or chocolate. Price, workmanship, quality, and taste vary considerably from baker to baker. In addition to flavor, size, and cost, consider decoration and spoilage (sugar keeps longer than cream frostings).

506. Can we have multiple cake flavors if we can't agree on one?

It is normal to have tiers of different flavors if you can't agree on one flavor. Just make sure there is a label on your cake table to let guests know what is what.

507. Where should I order my wedding cake?

Some hotels and restaurants may be able to provide a wedding cake; however, you will probably be better off ordering your cake from a bakery that specializes in wedding cakes.

508. Should we schedule cake tastings?

Ask to see photographs of other wedding cakes your baker has created, and by all means, ask for a tasting! The baker should provide you will a selection of popular flavors and fillings so you can be sure you're getting your perfect cake. Also, visiting the bakery in person gives you a sense of the quality and workmanship.

509. What should we do if we or our guests have special dietary requests, such as a gluten-free or vegan cake?

Not every standard bakery can handle this type of request. You will want to find a bakery that can do a special order for a kosher, vegan, diary-free, sugar-free, wheat-free or gluten-free cake. You might also contact a local vegan or kosher restaurant in your area to see what they recommend or if they take special orders.

510. When should we pick the wedding cake?
Two to four months before the wedding.

511. How much wedding cake should I order?
Talk to your baker about how much cake to order; you may only need to order cake for 75 percent of your RSVP list, for instance.

512. What are some alternatives to a traditional wedding cake?
Cupcakes are a growing trend that can also save money. Individual cakes, tarts, or fruit pies are a nice alternative to a cake for a smaller wedding. Finally, if you have friends and family who bake, consider asking them for help creating your cake-alternative. A dessert bar filled with fudge, cupcakes, cookies, and other desserts is a nice option.

513. What is the groom's cake?
The groom's cake is an old Southern tradition whereby a small cake is cut up and distributed to guests in little white boxes engraved with the bride and groom's names. Today the groom's cake, if offered, is cut and served along with the wedding cake. The cake can be designed to represent the groom's interests, such as a favorite sports team or pastime.

514. When during the reception should we cut the cake?
The cake cutting and photos come toward the end of the reception, following the bouquet toss and garter toss.

515. What is behind the tradition of saving the top tier of the cake?
When determining the size of the cake, don't forget that you'll be saving the top tier for your first anniversary. This tradition dates back to the 19th century; modernly, the newlyweds preserve their cake top to be eaten on their first anniversary, as a reminder of their beautiful wedding day. This top tier should be removed before the cake is cut, wrapped in several layers of plastic wrap or put inside a plastic container, and kept frozen until the anniversary.

516. After the bride and groom cut the first slice of cake, who cuts the rest?
The bride and groom should cut pieces of cake for their parents. Then the caterer usually cuts and distributes the

cake, but any friend or family member can be asked.

517. What is the cake delivery and set-up fee?

This is the fee charged by bakers to deliver and set up your wedding cake at the reception site. It usually includes a deposit on the cake pillars and plate, which will be refunded upon their return to the baker.

518. What is the cake cutting fee?

Most reception sites and caterers charge a fee for each slice of cake they cut if the cake is brought in from an outside bakery. This fee will probably shock you. It is simply their way of enticing you to order the cake through them. And unfortunately, many caterers will not allow a member of your party to cut the cake.

519. What is the cake top?

The bride's cake is often topped and surrounded with fresh flowers, but traditional "cake tops" (figurines set atop the wedding cake) are also very popular. Some options are bells, love birds, a bridal couple or replica of two wedding rings are popular choices for cake tops and can be saved as mementos of your wedding day.

520. What do I need to be aware of when selecting a cake top?

Some porcelain and other heavier cake tops need to be anchored down into the cake. If you're planning to use a cake top other than flowers, be sure to discuss this with your baker.

521. How much does a wedding cake cost?

It depends upon the bakery and the size of your cake, but they can range from $2 to $12 a piece.

522. How much does a groom's cake cost?

They can range from $1 to $2 a piece.

523. How much does the cake delivery and set-up fee cost?

It can range from $40 to $100.

524. How much does the cake cutting fee cost?

It can range from $0.75 to $2.50 a person.

525. How much do cake tops cost?
They can cost anywhere from $20 to $150.

526. What kind of questions should I ask the bakery when interviewing them about my wedding cake?
- What is the name of the bakery?
- What is the bakery's website and e-mail?
- What is the address of the bakery?
- What is the name and phone number of my contact person?
- How many years have you been making wedding cakes?
- What are your wedding cake specialties?
- Do you offer free tastings of your wedding cakes?
- Are your wedding cakes fresh or frozen?
- How far in advance should I order my cake?
- Can you make a groom's cake?
- Do you lend, rent or sell cake knives?
- What is the cost per serving of my desired cake?
- What is your cake pillar and plate rental fee, if any?
- Is this fee refundable upon the return of these items?
- When must these items be returned?
- What is your cake delivery and set-up fee?
- What is your payment policy?
- What is your cancellation policy?

527. How can I save money on my wedding cake?
Some bakers have set-up and delivery fees, some don't. Check for individuals who bake from their home. They are usually more reasonable, but you should check with your local health department before hiring one of these at-home bakers. Also, some caterers have contracts with bakeries and can pass on savings to you. Some bakeries require a deposit on columns and plates; other bakeries use disposable columns and plates, saving you the rental fee and the hassle of returning these items.

528. How can I save money on a groom's cake?
Because of its cost and the labor involved in cutting and distributing the cake, very few people offer this delightful custom any more. However, there is the possibility that you or a family member can bake it.

529. How can I save money on the cake delivery and set-up fee?
Have a friend or family member get a quick lesson on how to

set up your cake. Have them pick it up and set it up the day of your wedding, then have the florist decorate the cake and/ or cake table with flowers and greenery. Make sure this is a trustworthy friend, and one who has an impeccable driving record; you do not want your cake to topple over in the car on the way to the reception.

530. How can I save money on the cake-cutting fee?
Many hotels and restaurants include a dessert in the cost of their meal packages. If you forego this dessert and substitute your cake as the dessert, they may be willing to waive the cake-cutting fee. Be sure to ask them.

531. How can I save money on a cake top?
Borrow a cake top from a friend or a family member as "something borrowed," an age-old wedding tradition. Or use fresh flowers instead of purchasing a cake topper.

532. How can I save money on a cake knife and toasting glasses?
Borrow your cake knife or toasting glasses from a friend or family member as "something borrowed," an age-old wedding tradition. Use the reception facility's glasses and knife, and decorate them with flowers or ribbon.

CHAPTER 21

Flowers

✿ Flowers

533. How should I pick the flowers for my wedding?

Flowers add beauty, fragrance and color to your wedding.
Like everything else, flowers should fit your overall style and
color scheme. The purpose of flowers at the main altar is
to direct the guests' visual attention toward the front of the
church and to the bridal couple. Therefore, they must be seen
by guests seated toward the back. You may also want to use
flowers, candles, or ribbons to mark the aisle pews and add
color.

534. When should I book my florist?

Six to nine months before the wedding.

535. When should I make my final floral selections?

Two to six weeks before the wedding.

536. What are my options for my bridal bouquet?

The bridal bouquet is one of the most important elements
of the bride's attire and deserves special attention. Start by
selecting the color and shape of the bouquet. The bridal
bouquet should be carried low enough so that all the
intricate details of your gown are visible. There are many
colors, scents, sizes, shapes and styles of bouquets to choose
from. Popular styles are the cascade, cluster, contemporary
and hand-tied garden bouquets. Using scented flowers in
your bouquet will evoke memories of your wedding day
whenever you smell them in the future. Popular fragrant
flowers for bouquets are gardenias, freesia, stephanotis,
bouvardia, and narcissus. Select flowers that are in season to
assure availability.

537. What should I consider when selecting flowers for my bridal bouquet?

Your flowers should complement the season, your gown,
your color scheme, your attendants' attire, and the style
and formality of your wedding. If you have a favorite
flower, build your bouquet around it and include it in all
your arrangements. Whatever flowers you select, final
arrangements should be made well in advance of your
wedding date to ensure availability. Confirm your final order
and delivery time a few days before the wedding. Have the
flowers delivered before the photographer arrives so that you
can include them in your pre-ceremony photos.

538. Are there certain flowers that are symbolic for weddings?

Some flowers carry centuries of symbolism. Consider stephanotis — tradition regards it as the bridal good-luck flower! Pimpernel signifies change; white flowers radiate innocence; forget-me-nots indicate true love; and ivy stands for friendship, fidelity, and matrimony — the three essentials for a happy marriage. No flower, however, has as much symbolism for brides as the orange blossom, having at least 700 years of nuptial history. Its unusual ability to simultaneously bear flowers and produce fruit symbolizes the fusion of beauty, personality, and fertility.

539. How should I determine the size and style of my bouquet?

In determining the size of your bouquet, consider your gown and your overall stature. Carry a smaller bouquet if you're petite or if your gown is fairly ornate. A long, cascading bouquet complements a fairly simple gown or a tall or larger bride. Arm bouquets look best when resting naturally in the crook of your arm. For a natural, fresh-picked look, have your florist put together a cluster of flowers tied together with a ribbon. For a Victorian appeal, carry a nosegay or a basket filled with flowers. Or carry a Bible or other family heirloom decorated with just a few flowers. For a contemporary look, you may want to consider carrying an arrangement of calla lilies or other long-stemmed flower over your arm. For a dramatic statement, carry a single stem of your favorite flower.

540. What flowers are popular for a traditional all-white bouquet?

The traditional bridal bouquet is made of white flowers. Stephanotis, gardenias, white roses, orchids and lilies of the valley are popular choices for an all-white bouquet.

541. What flowers are popular for a colorful bouquet?

If you prefer a colorful bouquet, you may want to consider using roses, tulips, stock, peonies, freesia, and gerbera, which come in a wide variety of colors and create a full, vibrant bouquet.

542. What do I need to beware of when selecting flowers for my bridal bouquet?

If your bouquet includes delicate flowers that will not

withstand hours of heat or a lack of water, make sure your florist uses a bouquet holder to keep them fresh. If you want to carry fresh-cut stems without a bouquet holder, make sure the flowers you select are hardy enough to go without water for the duration of your ceremony and reception.

543. **Should I have my bridal bouquet preserved?**
The bridal bouquet can be preserved to make a beautiful memento of the wedding. Have your bouquet dried, mounted, and framed to hang on your wall or to display on an easel in a quiet corner of your home. You can also have an artist paint your bouquet.

544. **How much does it cost to have my bridal bouquet preserved?**
Bouquet preservation can cost from $100 to $500.

545. **What is the tossing bouquet?**
If you want to preserve your bridal bouquet, consider having your florist make a smaller, less expensive bouquet specifically for tossing. This will be the bouquet you toss to your single, female friends toward the end of the reception. Tradition has it that the woman who catches the bouquet is the next to be married. Have your florist include a few sprigs of fresh ivy in the tossing bouquet to symbolize friendship and fidelity.

546. **What kind of flowers should I use for the Maid of Honor's bouquet?**
The Maid of Honor's bouquet can be somewhat larger or of a different color than the rest of the bridesmaids' bouquets. This will help to set her apart from the others.

547. **What kind of flowers should I use for the bridesmaids' bouquets?**
The bridesmaids' bouquets should complement the bridal bouquet but are generally smaller in size. The size and color should coordinate with the bridesmaids' dresses and the overall style of the wedding. Bridesmaids' bouquets are usually identical, but don't have to be. To personalize your bridesmaids' bouquets, insert a different flower in each of their bouquets to make a statement. For example, if one of your bridesmaids has been sad, give her a lily of the valley to symbolize the return of happiness. To tell a friend that

you admire her, insert yellow jasmine. A pansy will let your friend know that you are thinking of her. Choose a bouquet style (cascade, cluster, contemporary, hand-tied) that complements the formality of your wedding and the height of your attendants. If your bridesmaids will be wearing floral print dresses, select flowers that complement the floral print.

548. Do the ladies in my wedding party keep their bouquets?

You can ask the wedding party to decorate their table or the cake table with their bouquets, but they should be allowed to take them home with them after the wedding if they wish.

549. What kind of flowers should I use for the Maid of Honor and bridesmaids' hairpieces?

For a garden wedding, have your Maid of Honor and bridesmaids wear garlands of flowers in their hair. Provide your Maid of Honor with a slightly different color or variety of flower to set her apart from the others. You may consider using artificial flowers for the hairpieces as long as they are in keeping with the flowers carried by members of the bridal party. Since it is not always easy to find good artificial blooms, other types of hairpieces may be more satisfactory, durable, and attractive. Flowers used for the hairpiece must be a sturdy and long-lived variety.

550. What kind of flowers should I use for the flower girl's hairpiece?

Flower girls often wear a wreath of flowers as a hairpiece. This is another place where artificial flowers may be used, but they must be in keeping with the flowers carried by members of the bridal party. If the flowers used for the hairpiece are not a sturdy and long-lived variety, a ribbon, bow, or hat might be a better choice.

551. What is the bride's going away corsage?

You may want to consider wearing a corsage on your going-away outfit. This makes for pretty photos as you and your new husband leave the reception for your honeymoon. Have your florist create a corsage that echoes the beauty of your bouquet. Put a protective shield under lilies when using them as a corsage, as their anthers will easily stain fabric. Be careful when using Alstroemeria as a corsage, as its sap can be harmful if it enters the human bloodstream.

552. What are the family members' corsages?

The groom is responsible for providing flowers for his mother, the bride's mother, and the grandmothers. The officiant, if female, may also be given a corsage to reflect her important role in the ceremony. The corsages don't have to be identical, but they should be coordinated with the color of their dresses. The groom may order flowers that can be pinned to a pocketbook or worn around a wrist. He should ask which style the women prefer, and if a particular color is needed to coordinate with their dresses. The groom may also want to consider ordering corsages for other close family members, such as sisters and aunts. This will add a little to your floral expenses but will make these female family members feel more included in your wedding and will let guests know that they are related to the bride and groom.

553. What flowers are popular for family members' corsages?

Gardenias, camellias, white orchids, or cymbidium orchids are excellent choices for corsages, as they go well with any outfit. Beware: Put a protective shield under lilies when using them as corsages, as their anthers will easily stain fabric. Be careful when using Alstroemeria as corsages, as its sap can be harmful if it enters the human bloodstream.

554. Should I purchase family member corsages for step-parents or divorced parents' partners if I am not close with them?

You should provide corsages only for those who you consider family.

555. On which wrist should the corsages be worn?

Corsages and boutonnieres traditionally go on the left side.

556. What kind of flowers should I use for the groom's boutonniere?

The groom wears his boutonniere on the left lapel, nearest to his heart. Boutonnieres are generally a single blossom such as a rosebud, stephanotis, freesia or a miniature carnation. If a rosebud is used for the wedding party, have the groom wear two rosebuds, or add a sprig of baby's breath to differentiate him from the groomsmen. Consider using a small cluster of flowers instead of a single bloom for the groom's boutonniere.

557. What should I use for the ushers' boutonnieres?

The groom gives each man in his wedding party a boutonniere to wear on his left lapel. The officiant, if male, may also be given a boutonniere to reflect his important role in the ceremony. The ring bearer may or may not wear a boutonniere, depending on his outfit. A boutonniere is more appropriate on a tuxedo than on knickers and knee socks. Generally, a single blossom such as a rosebud, freesia, or miniature carnation is used as a boutonniere. The groom should also consider ordering boutonnieres for other close family members such as fathers, grandfathers, and brothers. This will make these male family members feel more included in your wedding and will let guests know that they are related to the bride and groom.

558. What kind of flowers should I use for the main altar?

The purpose of flowers at the main altar is to direct the guests' visual attention toward the front of the church or synagogue and to the bridal couple. Therefore, they must be seen by guests seated in the back. The flowers for the ceremony site can be as elaborate or as simple as you wish. Your officiant's advice, or that of the altar guild or florist, can be most helpful in choosing flowers for the altar and chancel. If your ceremony is outside, decorate the arch, gazebo, or other structure serving as the altar with flowers or greenery. In a Jewish ceremony, vows are said under a chuppah, which is placed at the altar and covered with greenery and fresh flowers.

559. What do I need to consider when choosing flowers for the main altar?

In choosing floral accents, consider the decor of your ceremony site. Some churches and synagogues are ornate enough and don't need extra flowers. Too many arrangements would get lost in the architectural splendor. Select a few dramatic showpieces that will complement the existing decor. Be sure to ask if there are any restrictions on flowers at the church or synagogue. Remember, decorations should be determined by the size and style of the building, the formality of the wedding, the preferences of the bride, the cost, and the regulations of the particular site.

560. How can I decorate the altar candelabra?

In a candlelight ceremony, the candelabra may be decorated

with flowers or greenery for a dramatic effect. Ivy may be twined around the candelabra, or flowers may be strung to them.

561. How can I decorate the aisle pews with flowers?
Flowers, candles or ribbons are often used to mark the aisle pews and add color. A cluster of flowers, a cascade of greens, or a cascade of flowers and ribbons are all popular choices. Candles with adorning greenery add an elegant touch.
Use hardy flowers that can tolerate being handled as pew ornaments. Gardenias and camellias, for example, are too sensitive to last long. Avoid using Allium in your aisle pew decorations as they have an odor of onions.

562. How should I decorate my reception site with flowers?
Flowers add beauty, fragrance, and color to your reception. Flowers for the reception, like everything else, should fit your overall style and color scheme. Flowers can help transform a stark reception hall into a warm, inviting and colorful room. Consider renting indoor plants or small trees to give your reception a garden-like atmosphere. Decorate them with twinkling lights to achieve a magical effect.

563. How should I decorate the head table with flowers?
The head table is where the wedding party will sit during the reception. This important table should be decorated with a larger or more dramatic centerpiece than the guest tables. Consider using a different color or style of arrangement to set the head table apart from the other tables. Avoid using highly fragrant flowers, such as narcissus, on tables where food is being served or eaten, as their fragrance may conflict with other aromas.

564. How should I decorate the guest tables with flowers?
At a reception where guests are seated, a small flower arrangement may be placed on each table. The arrangements should complement the table linens and the size of the table, and should be kept low enough so as not to hinder conversation among guests seated across from each other. Avoid using highly fragrant flowers, like narcissus, on tables where food is being served or eaten, as their fragrance may conflict with other aromas.

565. I would like specific guests to get our floral centerpieces after the wedding; how can I designate this without offending other guests?

Place a note that says "Please do not remove the centerpieces" next to each one.

566. How should I decorate the buffet table with flowers?

If buffet tables are used, have some type of floral arrangement on the tables to add color and beauty to your display of food. Whole fruits and bunches of berries offer a variety of design possibilities. Figs add a festive touch. Pineapples are a sign of hospitality. Vegetables offer an endless array of options to decorate with. Herbs are yet another option in decorating. A mixture of rosemary and mint combined with scented geraniums makes a very unique table decoration. Depending on the size of the table, place one or two arrangements at each side. Avoid placing certain flowers, such as carnations, snapdragons, or the star of Bethlehem, next to buffet displays of fruits or vegetables, as they are extremely sensitive to the gasses emitted by these foods.

567. How should I decorate the cake table with flowers?

As the cake table is often in a central location at the reception, it should be decorated with flowers that go along with your theme or color scheme. To save money, have your bridesmaids place their bouquets on the cake table during the reception, or decorate the cake top only and surround the base with greenery and a few loose flowers.

568. How can I decorate my wedding cake with flowers?

Flowers are a beautiful addition to a wedding cake and are commonly seen spilling out between the cake tiers. Use only nonpoisonous flowers, and have your florist — not the caterer — design the floral decorations for your cake. A florist will be able to blend the cake decorations into your overall floral theme.

569. Can I decorate my cake knife with flowers?

Decorate your cake knife with a satin ribbon and flowers. Consider engraving the cake knife with your names and wedding date.

570. Can I decorate my toasting glasses with flowers?

Tie small flowers with ribbon onto the stems of your champagne glasses. These wedding accessories deserve a special floral touch since they will most likely be included in your special photographs. Consider engraving your toasting glasses with your names and wedding date.

571. Can I use succulents in place of flowers to decorate my wedding?

Succulents are good for weddings for many reasons; for one, they are very hardy, so you won't have to worry about wilting flowers. However, they also blend beautifully with traditional wedding flowers. The results are dramatic, organic, and modern. Also, they are fairly inexpensive and can be bought in bulk at any nursery. Succulents are especially great for beach, outdoor, rustic, and Southwestern-style weddings. Use them in bouquets, boutonnieres, centerpieces, favors, placecard holders, and more.

572. Will my florist deliver my flowers to my ceremony and reception sites?

Most florists charge a fee to deliver flowers to the ceremony and reception sites and to arrange them onsite. Make sure your florist knows where your sites are and what time to arrive for set-up.

573. How much does the bridal bouquet cost?

It can range from $75 to $500, depending on what kind of flowers you use and how big your bouquet is.

574. How much does the Maid of Honor's bouquet cost?

Depending on the type of flowers used and the size of the bouquet, the Maid of Honor's bouquet can cost from $25 to $100.

575. How much do bridesmaids' bouquets usually cost?

Depending on the type of flowers used and the sizes of the bouquets, bridesmaids' bouquets can cost from $25 to $100 each.

576. How much do the Maid of Honor and bridesmaids' hairpieces cost?

They can range from $8 to $100, depending on the kind of flowers you use.

577. How much does the flower girl's hairpiece cost?

The flower girl's wreath or hairpiece can cost from $8 to $75, depending on the type of flowers used.

578. How much does the bride's going away corsage usually cost?

The bride's going away corsage typically costs from $10 to $50, depending upon the type of flower you use.

579. How much do the family members' corsages cost?

They can cost from $10 to $35 each, depending upon the type of flowers used.

580. How much does the groom's boutonniere usually cost?

The groom's boutonniere can cost from $4 to $25.

581. How much do ushers' boutonnieres cost?

They can cost from $3 to $15, depending upon the type of flowers you choose.

582. How much do flowers for my ceremony site cost?

They can cost from $300 to $3,000, depending on the type and amount of flowers you use. Many ceremony sites will have natural beauty and won't need as many floral arrangements. Many couples choose just a few larger arrangements for the ceremony site.

583. How much does it cost to decorate my reception site with flowers?

It can cost from $300 to $3,000 or more, depending upon the type of flowers you use and the amount of decorating you do.

584. How much does it cost to decorate the altar candelabra with flowers?

It can cost from $50 to $200.

585. How much does it cost to decorate the aisle pews with flowers?

It can cost from $20 to $100, depending upon the type of flowers you use and the number of pews you decorate.

586. How much does it cost to decorate the head table with flowers?

It can cost from $100 to $600, depending on the type of flowers used and the extent of the decorations.

587. How much does it cost to decorate my guest tables with flowers?

It can cost from $100 to $500 or more, depending upon the type of flowers used and the number of guests and guest tables you have at your reception.

588. How much does it cost to decorate the buffet table with flowers?

It can cost from $50 to $500 or more.

589. How much does it cost to decorate the cake table with flowers?

It can cost from $30 to $300 or more.

590. How much does it cost to decorate the wedding cake with flowers?

It can cost from $20 to $100 or more, depending upon the type of flowers used and the size of the wedding cake.

591. How much does the tossing bouquet cost?

It can cost from $20 to $100.

592. How much does it cost to decorate my toasting glasses with flowers?

It can cost from $10 to $35, depending on the type of flowers you use.

593. How much does it cost for floral delivery and set-up?

It can cost from $25 to $200 or more, depending on the amount of floral decorations you have.

594. How can I save money on the flower girl's basket?

To try and save money on a flower girl's basket, ask your florist if you can borrow a basket and attach a pretty white bow to it.

595. How can I save money on flowers for my bridal bouquet?

The cost of some flowers may be significantly higher during their off-season. Try to select flowers that are in bloom and plentiful at the time of your wedding. Avoid exotic, out-of-season flowers. Allow your florist to emphasize your colors using more reasonable, seasonal flowers to achieve your overall look. If you have a favorite flower that is costly or out of season, consider using silk for that one flower. Avoid scheduling your wedding near holidays such as Valentine's Day and Mother's Day when the price of flowers is higher. Because every attendant will carry or wear flowers, consider keeping the size of your wedding party down to accommodate your floral budget.

596. **How can I save money on the tossing bouquet?**
Use the floral cake top or guest book table "tickler bouquet" as the tossing bouquet. Or omit the tossing bouquet altogether and simply toss your bridal bouquet.

597. **How can I save money on the bridesmaids' bouquets?**
Have your attendants carry a single stemmed rose, lily or other suitable flower for an elegant look that also saves money.

598. **How can I save money on my bride's going away corsage?**
Ask your florist if he or she can design your bridal bouquet in such a way that the center flowers may be removed and worn as a corsage. Or omit this corsage altogether.

599. **How can I save money on the family members' corsages?**
Ask your florist to recommend reasonable flowers for corsages. Dendrobium orchids are reasonable and make lovely corsages.

600. **How can I save money on the groom's boutonniere?**
You can save money by using mini-carnations for the groom's boutonniere, instead of roses. You can also create the boutonnieres out of non-floral elements such as feathers or fabric.

601. **How can I save money on flowers for the main altar?**
Decorate the ceremony site with greenery only. Candlelight and greenery are elegant in and of themselves. Use greenery and flowers from your garden. Have your ceremony outside in a beautiful garden or by the water, surrounded by nature.

602. How can I save money on decorating the aisle pews with flowers?

It is not necessary to decorate all of the aisle pews, or any at all. To save money, decorate only the reserved family pews. Or decorate every second or third pew.

603. How can I save money when decorating my reception site with flowers?

You can save money by taking flowers from the ceremony to the reception site for decorations. However, you must coordinate this move carefully to avoid having your guests arrive at an undecorated reception room. Use greenery rather than flowers to fill large areas. Trees and garlands of ivy can give a dramatic impact for little money. Use greenery and flowers from your garden. Have your reception outside in a beautiful garden or by the water, surrounded by natural beauty.

604. How can I save money on decorating the head table with flowers?

You can decorate the head table with the bridal or bridesmaids' bouquets to save money.

605. How can I save money on decorating my guest tables with flowers?

To keep the cost down and for less formal receptions, use small potted flowering plants placed in baskets or pots, or consider using dried or silk arrangements that you can make yourself and give later as gifts. Or place a wreath of greenery entwined with colored ribbon in the center of each table. Use a different colored ribbon at each table and assign your guests to tables by ribbon color instead of number.

606. What kind of questions should I ask the florist when picking out the flowers for my wedding?

- What is the name of the florist?
- What is the website and e-mail of the florist?
- What is the address of the florist?
- What is the name and phone number of my contact person?
- How many years of professional floral experience do you have?
- What percentage of your business is dedicated to weddings?

- Do you have access to out-of-season flowers?
- Will you visit my wedding sites to make floral recommendations?
- Can you preserve my bridal bouquet?
- Do you rent vases and candleholders?
- Can you provide silk flowers?
- What is the cost of my desired bridal bouquet?
- What is the cost of my desired bridesmaids' bouquets?
- What is the cost of my desired boutonnieres?
- What is the cost of my desired corsages?
- Do you have liability insurance?
- What are your delivery/set-up fees?
- What is your payment/cancellation policy?
- What are your business hours?

607. What type of flower is Allium?

There are two types of Allium: the giant Allium and the miniature Allium. The giant variety is a fluffy looking, bubble-shaped purple flower that is 4-10 inches in diameter and sits on a stem that is at least 2 feet long. The smaller Allium is egg-shaped with flowers that are only 1-2 inches across and sit atop a stem that is half the size of its giant brother. These flowers, which come from the mountains in ancient China, are excellent for banquet table arrangements because of their striking appearance. Warning: it is best to use these flowers on a table from which you are offering food such as hors d'oeuvres, because they do have an odor of onions. But if you place these flowers in water 24 hours before the wedding, much of the odor will be eliminated. Historically, these flowers are used at weddings because onions were a sign of good luck and health. The smaller varieties are available throughout most of the year, but the giant Allium are only available in the late spring and early summer. They will keep for about 10 days.

608. What type of flower is Alstroemeria?

Native to South America, Alstroemeria is named for the Swedish jurist Clas Alstroemer. This automatically makes the flower appropriate for weddings since marriage is an official act. Also known as a Peruvian Lily, there are more than 50 varieties within the Alstroemeria assortment in popular colors and shades. Alstroemeria are available year-round in hues of pink, salmon, orange, red, lavender and yellow. During the winter, spring and fall, they may be purchased in white. The whitest varieties currently available are "Bianca," "Paloma" and "Casablanca." The orchid-like "Casablanca" has large, beautiful white flowers with less striping on the petals. The flowers typically are multicolored clusters on a stalk. They are excellent and economical for wedding table arrangements because one stem contains many clusters, which makes the table arrangement look like it contains lots of flowers. The Alstroemeria's worldwide popularity is attributed to its versatility and long life. It is ideal for use in mixed bouquets, arrangements, corsages, and on its own or by the bunch in a vase. With proper care, Alstroemeria will last from 2-3 weeks. A word of warning: Alstroemeria contains a chemical that may cause dermatitis in susceptible people, and sap from the Alstroemeria can be harmful if it enters the human bloodstream. So handle these cut flowers with care!

609. What type of flower is Amaryllis?

Amaryllis, botanically known as Hippeastrum, is sometimes called the Belladonna Lily. It is a bulb flower that originated in South AfricIts unusual star shaped flowers sit majestically atop a large, hollow stem. Shaded in colors of crimson, pink and white, this flower makes an excellent focal point for a table arrangement or an altar arrangement. Amaryllis first becomes available in the late summer and is readily available until year's end. The flower is odorless. If you are getting married at Christmas time, we recommend using a few "Christmas Gift" white Amaryllis within your flower decor. The flower will remain open for five days.

610. What type of flower is the Anemone?

The Anemone has many names in many different parts of the country. It is sometimes called a windflower, sometimes a poppy, and also a lily of the field. The Anemone was first discovered in China in the early 1900s by Italian explorers who brought the flower back with them because they were so impressed by its texture and regal coloration. In Italy these flowers were made into a crown and worn by the bride at weddings. The Anemone's vibrant purple, pink, red, blue and white flowers often come with a contrasting center. They stand on a long, bending stem, which makes it useful in incorporating the flower into hair ornaments. The average Anemone will keep for a week. It has no scent. A word of caution: do not mix this flower with Narcissus; the Anemone is sensitive to the gasses emitted from Narcissus' stem.

611. What type of flower is the Aster?

The Aster is a long-lasting perennial with American roots. It was first discovered by the early settlers and was originally called "The Ancestor Flower." It acquired this name because it was passed along from one generation to another. This gives its place at a wedding particular significance as family members witness a major step in their next generation. The white "Monte Cassino" aster is a bushy, double flower variety with a diameter of 2-4 inches. There are also single flowered varieties, notably the "Pink Star," "Blue Star," and "White Star," which are becoming increasingly popular. These flowers are generally available year-round and are excellent in both bouquets and table arrangements to add fullness to the design. One of the sparser varieties is the "Climax," which is available only in late September and October. Asters will frequently last up to one week after the wedding.

612. What type of flower is Baby's Breath?

Baby's Breath is botanically named Gypsophila and contains hundreds of tiny white or pink flowers covering a multitude of intertwining stems. This wonderful filler flower is perfect as a backdrop to any arrangement or bouquet. Because the flowers are less than 1/4 inch in diameter, they set off the top note flower in a bridal bouquet. It is also possible to dye them other colors to match your wedding decor without harming them. Baby's Breath, sometimes referred to as "gyp," is available year-round. Baby's Breath is an excellent flower to use at weddings because Gypsophila is derived from the Greek word Philein, which means "to love." The plant was first discovered in the Mediterranean. Shortly thereafter, species were discovered as far away as Siberia. The Dutch and Israelis have been growing this long-lasting flower for the last 200 years. It has a life span of up to 3 weeks and has no scent.

613. What type of flower is a Bachelor's Button?

What more appropriate flower for a wedding than a Bachelor's Button? Botanically it is called Centaurea. It is one of the rare, strikingly blue flowers. It is appropriately used at weddings since the groom is no longer a bachelor and no longer blue. Ushers frequently wear this flower in their lapels. In many parts of the U.S., this flower is more commonly known as a cornflower, so called because it was originally a weed found in cornfields. The flower has been actively grown as a commercial product since the mid-1400s. Lately the Dutch have produced different colors of this 2-inch diameter flower. You can purchase the variety in pure white, scarlet, and pink from early spring into early winter. The normal keeping period of a Bachelor's Button is about 5 days.

614. What type of flower is the Billy Button?

Craspedia globosa originated in the Outback of Australia. Its common name is "drumsticks," but native Aussies gave it the nickname Billy Buttons. The Billy Button is a globular flower that grows atop an unbranched and leafless stem. The stems are approximately 6 inches long and its pom pom like flower gives it the look of a drumstick used to beat a bass drum. The flowers are yellow and are used to add interest to a table arrangement. If properly cared for, they will last up to two weeks.

615. What type of flower is the Bird of Paradise?

The Bird of Paradise is the common name for Strelitzia. The flower was named after King George III of England's wife, Charlotte von Mecklenburg-Strelitz. The royal lady was admired for her elegance and color, so it was most appropriate that this elegant, colorful flower be named in her honor. Strelitzia originated in South Africa. The flower sits atop a 3-foot stalk. It is two-toned: orange and blue. It received its common Bird of Paradise name because it actually gives the appearance of a beautiful bird perched on a stalk. Available year-round, the Bird of Paradise is used primarily at weddings to project a note of elegance in table decorations. It is best to use this unscented flower sparingly in floral design so as not to detract from its impact. It will last about 2 weeks.

616. What type of flower is Bouvardia?

A fragrant bloom often used for weddings, Bouvardia seems to have everything going for it. It has a characteristic scent, making it especially appealing for bouquet work and small arrangements. It has an incredibly long vase life of three weeks and is available year-round. The flowers are delicate and grow in clusters. Each tubular Bouvardia blossom is star shaped. The flower is formed by a cluster of these regularly shaped stars and is set off by simple leaves, which make an excellent frame for the blossoms. Each flower in the cluster is about 1 inch in diameter. The Bouvardia blossom comes in shades of white, pink, salmon and red. Historically, the Bouvardia was known for its curative abilities. It was named in honor of Dr. Charles Bouvard, who was the physician to King Louis XII. He created hundreds of different medicines using the flower. The King thought this flower was responsible for his long life. Symbolically, Bouvardia is welcome at weddings as brides and grooms are toasted for a long life. This extremely fragrant variety will last in excess of 2 weeks.

617. What type of flower is the Calla Lily?

Although the Calla lily isn't really a lily, it shares many of the lily's qualities. It first became popular in the U.S. when Katherine Hepburn said, "The Calla lilies are in bloom again…" in Stage Door. The elegant Ms. Hepburn has long been associated with this traditional, long-lasting and elegant flower, which is grown primarily in England and Holland. Calla lilies, botanically named Zantedeschia, are named after an Italian botanist Zantedeschi, who discovered them in South Africa. They were given the name "calla" from the Greek word "Kallos," meaning beautiful. Sitting regally above its 2-3 foot stalk, the Calla is an extremely decorative flower. Its trumpet-like shape captivates the eye and is frequently used in wedding receptions and at the church to herald the bride. Calla lilies are available year-round in white, yellow, red and pink coloration. Although they are dominating in appearance, their scent is insignificant.

618. What type of flower is the Carnation?

Even the most demanding bride will be satisfied by the vast selection of Carnations available. No other flower offers a better selection of colors, shades and types. The botanical name for Carnation is Dianthus. Appropriately, this name translates from the Greek as "divine flower." It is the perfect flower for such a divine event as a wedding ceremony or reception. Available year-round in every size, from standard to giant to mini-spray Carnations, they are extremely popular. First discovered on the west coast of Europe, Carnations truly bloomed as a favorite when they were brought to America in the early 1900s. Fascinated by its exceedingly large variety, Americans adopted the flower as their own, and Europeans soon began referring to it as the "American Carnation." Through breeding techniques, the variations of this sweet smelling flower were so great that their numbers swelled by the dozens each year. Available in either full-size or miniature varieties, Carnations are grown in large numbers in California, Holland and South America and are available year-round. Because of their abundance, except for rare varieties, they will be affordable on any wedding budget. Each stem contains multiple flowers which makes them even more attractive from an economic as well as a visual standpoint. Carnations are commonly used to frame the walkway in the church, as a bridal canopy, as boutonnieres, and in floral arrangements. One note of caution: avoid placing Carnation arrangements next to buffet displays of fruit or vegetables, as the flower is quite sensitive to the gasses they emit.

619. What type of flower is the Chrysanthemum?

The Chrysanthemum, or Mum, is one of the most abundant and popular flowers in the world. One can trace its origin to the western part of Russia. The botanical and the common name are identical and come from the Latin word meaning "yellow flower." Although yellow Chrysanthemum are among the most common color, they are available in many different colors as well as color combinations. The giant version of the flower is also referred to as a Pom Pom and is the flower of choice at football games. Available year-round in a multitude of shapes and sizes, the Chrysanthemum is a preferred flower at weddings. A white variety, the "Marguerite," was used by French, Italian and English royalty at weddings to signify that the choice of bride by the groom was purely correct. In the U.S., two varieties with special meaning names, the "Happy" and the "Funshine," are frequently chosen for table decorations and wedding aisle arrangements. The shapes of the Mum vary from puff-ball to daisy-like, tubular, and spider-like varieties. Even though many different colored Mums can be obtained from a florist, the hearty nature of Chrysanthemum makes it possible for the flowers to be successfully dyed to match a particular wedding color scheme. Except for Mums that are dyed, arrangements usually last 2 to 3 weeks after the final toast to the bride and groom.

620. What type of flower is the Celosia?

The Celosia is known by many names in many lands. It is sometimes called a Crested Cockscomb; sometimes a Burnt Plume; a Plume Celosia; a Chinese Wool Flower or a Plumed Brain Flower... the latter because its ruffled flowers resemble the focal point of the mind. This flower was first used at weddings to symbolize the joining of one's mind to one's mate. The foliage comes in deep shades of orange, red, yellow, purple and creamy white. The flame varieties appear as compact spikes, while the cockscomb varieties have compact heads like the comb on a rooster's head. The coarse flowers sit atop a thick, fleshy stalk and become the focal point of any arrangement in which they are included. The heads of the flowers are 2-8 inches across and, when cut to size, they make an exciting and attractive decoration for the bride and groom's place setting. After the wedding, they can easily be dried and kept as a remembrance. These flowers first originated in Africa, but the first known cultivated varieties came from Japan. They are available from May until September. They have no scent and are best used at indoor functions since they have a tendency to react to atmospheric differences and spot easily.

621. What type of flower is the Daffodil?

Daffodil, although common, is unusual in that its common name and its scientific name, Narcissus, are equally well known by the general public. Legend has it that the name of the flower comes from a youth who was so in love with his own beauty that the gods turned him into this beautiful Narcissus flower. To this day, self-love is still referred to by the term "narcissistic." You can find Daffodils in white, pink and multi-colors; the overwhelming majority, however, are yellow. The flower is trumpet shaped with star-like petals projecting from the center. Its leaves are strap-shaped. You are best off getting your Daffodils from a greenhouse. An easy way to tell if your Daffodils are from a greenhouse is that greenhouse grown Narcissus are generally delivered with their leaves, while field grown are typically delivered without their leaves. In planning wedding arrangements, remember that this flower is quite fragrant so make sure it is placed in areas where it will not conflict with other aromas. The "Paper White" variety is very attractive, but be aware that this particular variety has an extremely pungent odor. Another word of caution: the stems tend to get slimy in water, but this can easily be counteracted with preservative. Daffodils generally last more than a week. Although some varieties are available between November and April, keep in mind that this sunny yellow bulb flower is least expensive during its growing season in the spring.

622. What type of flower is the Dahlia?

The Dahlia was first discovered in the plains of Mexico nearly 400 years ago, where it was called acoctli. Although quite beautiful in appearance, nothing was done to bring about its cultivation until 200 years later. At that time, botanical experts in Mexico sent a gift of Dahlia seeds to the royal gardens in Madrid where they were cultivated and given as a gift to the wife of the Mexican ambassador to the Spanish court. The flower was named in honor of a noted botanical author from Sweden, Dahl. Dahlias immediately became popular for use in royal functions, and members of the royal court sought them out to establish their position in society. Dahlias have a strong, spicy smell and are available in a broad range of shapes, from fluffy to cactus to pom-pom to peony flower. Most of the Dahlias today are cultivated in Holland, but Californians have recently become more interested in developing hybrids. Dahlias are increasingly available from July through November. Dahlias come in a variety of colors that include purple, lavender, red, yellow, pink and even bronze and white. The newest varieties include two-tone flowers. Dahlias measure 4-8 inches across and sit on stems that are 1-3 feet in length. When the Dahlia is in full bloom, it makes an excellent decorative hair piece or bridal bouquet adornment. Its average vase life is 1-2 weeks. These flowers are similar in appearance to Chrysanthemums and, when feasible, may be used in their place in arrangements.

623. What type of flower is Delphinium?

A summer wedding is the perfect time to feature Delphinium. Although most varieties are available year-round, all varieties are readily available from June through November. Also known as Larkspur, this multi-bloomed flower is regal yet soft in appearance. It has spike-shaped flower clusters of 1-2 inch disc shaped flowers towering in 8-20 inch spikes on stems 1 1/2 to 4 feet long. Useful alone in vases or for decoration, they will last at least one week. They are popularly used in Flemish-style bouquets. A perfect variety for an "old fashioned wedding" theme, Delphinium originated in Asia, although today they can be found in cultivation on most continents. Delphinium consolida was named by the Greeks after the god of the city of Delphi. In Greek, Consolida means "to strengthen" which adds meaning to a wedding where one hopes the matrimonial bond will strengthen the betrothed's commitment to each other. Pink, white and blue varieties are the most dominant and most traditional, although red and mixed types can also be obtained. One of the pink varieties, the "Princess Caroline," so named because it was used at Princess Caroline of Monaco's wedding, is characterized by outstanding uniformity in both color and length. Like other pure and hybrid varieties, these Delphinium have no scent.

624. What type of flower is Eucalyptus?

The common name "Eucalyptus" is the same as its botanical name. There are several varieties of Eucalyptus available in either a green-gray or blue-green color. All are very aromatic. "Silver Dollar" is the type of Eucalyptus traditionally used at weddings. Romantics believe that placing branches of this tree at a wedding will bring good fortune to the newlyweds. Eucalyptus originated in Australia. It is available year-round and makes an interesting setting for many other varieties of flowers. Today Eucalyptus is cultivated primarily in the United States and Israel. Eucalyptus oil was historically used in medication. It is considered good luck to have it at weddings as a symbol that the couple will enjoy good health together.

625. What type of flower is Freesia?

Freesia is one of the most popular flowers, possibly because it is so distinctive. The flower was named after a German doctor, F.F. Freese, who discovered it in Cape Colony in South Africa. Freesia have long, narrow sword-shaped leaves which grow in two rows. The flower stalk is branched with 8-14 flowers growing from the top of the stalk at a 90-degree angle, forming a comb. Some compare this comb of flowers to a wedding party, with the two largest blooms signifying the bride and groom and the remaining buds the attendants. A note of caution: handle Freesia delicately. Like a bride, they must be treated gently and with respect if they are to flourish. You can determine how fresh your Freesia is by the numbers of flowers along the comb that are open.

Remember, for a wedding it is best to have your flowers at their fullest bloom on that day. This is one flower that appreciates some sugar in its water. Freesia can last for more than 2 weeks. Freesia come in a wide palette of colors and are available throughout the year. White and yellow varieties predominate, although Freesia are also available in shades of blue, red, purple, orange and pink. Freesia are often added to other, larger flowers in long cascading bouquets. Its blooms can also be separated and wired to headpieces or used in tight cluster designs.

626. What type of flower is Gardenia?

If ever there was a flower suited for a wedding party corsage, it is the Gardenia. Its small and spotless white blooms appear to have been strategically placed against shiny leaves. This flower is dainty enough to complement any member of the bridal group's gown but impressive enough to make a statement. The fragrance of the Gardenia flower is jasmine-like and projects a pleasant but not overpowering scent. Some bridal parties also use potted Gardenia plants to set off the tables on which the reception seating arrangement cards are placed. The Gardenia was discovered in Asia by botanist Garden who brought them with him to England in the mid-1700s. Although these flowers are somewhat available in all parts of the world throughout the year, the great majority of the cut flowers are used in America. Since Gardenias are primarily used in small personal carrying arrangements at weddings and then either pressed or dried as memories, their keeping time is unimportant.

627. What type of flower is the Gerbera Daisy?

The Gerbera Daisy is sometimes known as the African Daisy or Transvaal Daisy because of its origination in South Africa, where it was discovered by Dutch botanist Gronovius in 1737. He named the Gerbera in honor of his Danish colleague Traugott Gerber. The flower is very similar in appearance to a field daisy but comes in a large variety of colors and sizes. The most popular colors are yellow, red, orange, pink, white and two tone. There are more than 41 different varieties available from Holland throughout the year. With their bright and splashy appearance, Gerbera are wonderful for informal weddings. Because of their broad range of sizes from standard to micro to mini, they are particularly attractive in table arrangements. One intriguing new standard variety is the "Fire Ball" which has a two foot stem, is almost 5 inches in diameter and appears to be an amazing mass of orange flames. Since Gerbera have a long vase life of 2 to 3 weeks, wedding party guests can enjoy them long after the wedding.

628. What type of flower is Gladiolus?

This flower adds majesty to any large arrangement at a wedding. Gladiolus are often used in tall fabric covered vases to line the bridal aisle to the altar. Since they have no scent, they make excellent decorative flowers to enhance the look of food serving areas at the reception. Experienced floral designers can also take individual blooms from the Gladiolus and create a camellia-like flower known as a "glamellia" for use as corsages and boutonnieres. The species was discovered growing wild in Africa. It was brought back to Europe in bulb form by amateur horticulturists and was later improved and domesticated by professional breeders. Today, the Gladiolus is known as a Glad in some parts of the USA and as a Sword Lily in other areas. The color palette of the flower and its gradations of shading are so varied that it can easily fit into any wedding color scheme. You can choose from reds, whites, yellows, pinks, violets, orange and purple varieties. The flowers grow in clusters up its sword-like stem, with the larger flowers appearing closer to the bottom. This makes it an excellent flower for table settings since the beauty of the flower can easily be enjoyed at eye level. Glads are available year-round but are most plentiful in the summer.

629. What type of flower is the Iris?

The Iris, in its undeveloped form, was discovered in Africa in the late-1800s. However, once it was brought to Holland and cross hybridized, it truly took a position in the world of flowers. That importance was recognized in the scientific name given to the flower Iris Hollandica. The name Iris itself translates into "rainbow," as strong multiple colors are among the flower's top notes of interest. The Iris has an unusual leaf-colored stem that runs up its entire 2-foot stem. Atop this stem is a single blossom which features turned back petals and a contrasting color comb. Dutch Iris will keep for an entire week. The most popular Iris is of a blazing dark blue color, however there is growing interest in the yellow, white and two-tone varieties. Make note of the strength of color in buying Iris. If the color is faint, it may indicate that the buds will have difficulty opening in time for the ceremony. There are many legends surrounding the significance of Iris at weddings. Perhaps the most interesting is that a blue Iris and a white Iris were placed in a bud vase at the bride's table to remind her that her marriage would have both vibrant and pale times. It is said that this started the traditional pledge that marriages are for better or for worse.

630. **What type of flower is the Liatris?**
The Liatris grows to as much as 16 inches and features a lavender-pink flower. The flower spike is tube-like and opens from the top down. Depending on where in the United States you are from, the Liatris is also called a Gayfeather, a Blazing Star, or a Button Snakeroot. The flower was originally grown in the eastern section of America but was formally cultivated in England around 1734. The vertical erectness of the Liatris and its long vase life of about 2 weeks make this flower popular for vase and floral arrangements at weddings. The Liatris is odorless and best used in modern floral arrangements.

631. **What type of flower are Lilies?**
No flower is more frequently used at weddings than this hybrid. These lilies were originally found in China and Japan. The first known use of lilies at weddings was by the Ming dynasty in China. Asiatics come in a wider color selection than the Orientals. These include yellow, pink, peach, ivory and white as well as combinations of these colors. The Asiatic is smaller than the Oriental lily, although each contains 3-7 flowers per stem. Two of the most popular lilies are the "Stargazer" and the "Casablanca." The "Stargazer" is noted for its red accent marks that highlight the white throat of this orchid-like flower. The "Casablanca" is a huge white flower that takes its name from the Spanish "Casa" (house) and "Blanca" (white). They are found throughout the world. Lilies are strongly scented. The Oriental hybrids are more heavily scented than the Asiatic varieties. One must be careful to keep them separate and apart from other fragrant flowers. They are versatile enough to be used in bouquets, floral arrangements, altar decorations and church aisle decorations. There are over 4,000 different lily varieties. Among the new popular

varieties used in American weddings is the "La Rive" which has a very soft pink coloration. White lilies are often used as a single flower placed upon a white wedding Bible. Because they vary so greatly in color and are available to some extent throughout the year, there is a lily for every bride. Warning: Put a protective shield under the lily when using them as corsages. The anthers that project from the center of the flower will easily stain fabric. It is safest to remove the anther prior to using them in this manner.

632. What type of flower is the Lily of the Valley?

Wedding Bells traditionally proclaim a marriage. Perhaps this explains why the Lily of the Valley is found at most weddings. It is popularly used in bridal bouquets and other arrangements because its flowers are reminiscent of wedding bells. Like a bride and groom, its oval basal leaves stand in pairs around a pendulous stalk. The flower cluster of 4-10 white, bell-shaped blooms sits atop the stalk much as church bells are at the top of the steeple. Botanically known as Convallaria majalis, this delicate looking perennial was first seen growing in Western Europe in May, 1420. This makes sense since May is the only month in which it blooms naturally. Today most of the supply is still from Western Europe, however current technology permits bridal parties to obtain it year round. If Lily of the Valley is to be used in vases, it is best to put the whole flower, including the roots, in the water. This will allow you to enjoy it for about 5 days.

633. What type of flower is Lisianthus?

Lisianthus is more commonly referred to as Eustoma. Part of its appeal is its large size. In fact, its very name means wide-open mouth. The 4 petaled blossom presents itself in a saucer shape with a single stamen and seed capsule apparent in its center. The ornamental flower sits atop a 30-32 inch stem with opposing oval leaves. Some are single flowered varieties, others double. The Eustoma found its way to Europe and the United States from Japan. It is available in dark purple, pink, white and two-tone. The flowers make a dramatic addition to arrangements. Since each flower is very large, just a few can add drama to entry way and table displays. While most varieties are available from May through December, some varieties, such as "Dark Blue Fuji," can be obtained year-round. Lisianthus can last from 3-4 weeks.

634. What type of flower is the Nerine?

The Nerine, also known as the Spider Lily, is primarily available in pink, although it is also available in red, orange and white. It is a bulbous plant which originated in the coastal regions of South AfricIts botanical name is after the Greek sea-god, Nereus. Legend has it that the bulb was placed aboard ships to be traded and that some of them were hijacked to the Isle of Guernsey where they proliferate today. The leaves of Nerine are about 10 inches long. The average 16-inch flower stalk bears a cluster of 6-10 trumpet-shaped blooms with rather undulating flower lobes. Each flower is 1-3 inches in diameter. As a complete flower, Nerine's height, erectness, and rather open, airy appearance make it a good choice for those wishing a more contemporary look to their wedding design. Individually, its flowers can be used for corsages for the wedding party. It is available year-round. The flowers last for more than one week. The most popular varieties are "Favoriet" and "Pink Triumph." Perhaps the Nerine is used to symbolize the triumph of the young girl winning her favorite guy.

635. What type of flower is the Orchid (Cattleya)?

The variety of orchid most commonly seen in the United States is a hybrid called Cattleya. Named after a British merchant, the Cattleya is a relatively expensive and fragile flower. For this reason, it has traditionally been reserved for very special occasions, such as weddings, where it is commonly used as the focal point for the bridal bouquet or as a corsage for the mother of the bride and the mother of the groom. Native to South America and grown worldwide today, this variety is available year-round in lavender, white, yellow and orange. The flower itself makes a statement. Its lip, with beautiful markings, is usually a darker color than the other petals. The flower grows on a stalk that is 4-6 inches in length, although most times the stem is cut and the flower is worn as a corsage. Since the flower itself is about 8 inches in diameter, it can be worn alone and still look impressive. Although orchids can last about a week, they are sensitive to damaging.

636. What type of flower is the Orchid (Cymbidium)?

There are many varieties of orchids. Some varieties, such as the Cymbidium and Dendrobian, are very versatile. Both are excellent for arrangements, corsages and bouquets.

Cymbidiums are particularly spectacular when used in a hand-tied bouquet or in a slight cascade for the bridal attendants. The regal Dendrobian works well when incorporated into the ceremony design. Cymbidium orchids are ancestors of the orchid hybrids. They come in both large and small flowered varieties. Large flowered varieties originated in Burma, India and the Himalayas while small flowered varieties are native to Taiwan and China. The Dendrobian orchid was originally discovered in Australia and eastern Indonesia. Cymbidiums stand 12-32 inches high. Large flowered varieties carry 8-18 flowers on the stem, each measuring 4-6 inches in diameter, while 2/3 of the stem of the small flowered varieties is crowded with flowers. Dendrobian orchid stalks are at least a foot long and each contains 8-12 flowers measuring 3 1/2 to almost 5 inches in diameter. This variety is butterfly shaped on a long stem. The flower is generally lavender or white. Available year-round, Cymbidium and Dendrobian orchids have no scent. In order to ensure a 2-5 week life for Cymbidiums, they should be kept out of the sun. Dendrobians are particularly sensitive to pollution. They last 8-12 days.

637. What type of flower is the Peony?

Peonies give spring weddings a unique, elegant look and aroma. The cultivation of peonies began in China more than 1,000 years ago; however, its name is derived from the doctor of the Greek gods and alludes to its medicinal qualities. There is only a six-week window, between May and June, during which Peonies can be purchased, although this time frame is expanding somewhat. Its limited availability period adds to its uniqueness in wedding centerpiece arrangements. Its soft yet elegant composition imparts dignity and femininity to wedding designs. Peonies retain their beauty for up to 2 weeks. Peonies are usually double flowered with a diameter of about 6 inches. The 30 varieties generally available are most popularly found in white, red and pink. By far the most popular peony is the pink "Sarah Bernhardt," which accounts for half of all peonies. Other popular varieties are the white "Shirley Temple," the bright pink "Dr. Arthur Fleming," and the red "Karl Rosenfield." The white "Duchesse de Nemours" variety has a strong fragrance. New early flowering varieties are being introduced in salmon-orange, orange-red and cream-white. These too are named for famous people.

638. What type of flower is the Pincushion?

The Pincushion Flower is so-named because its center
appears to be a pincushion filled with pins. A perennial
summer bloom, it contains 3 inch round flowers on 2
foot long stems. At one time the flower stems were weak,
impacting their usability, but this problem has been
overcome through breeding. Its botanical name, Scabiosa,
derives from the skin disease "scabies" for which it was
thought to be a remedy. Originally cultivated in the
Mediterranean regions, it requires a temperate climate or
summer temperatures. Perhaps part of its decorative appeal is
that it is available for only 3-4 months of the year. Scabiosa
is primarily purchased in shades of lavender blue, violet blue
and white, although it originally was found naturally in a
crimson color. The flower has a frilly looking petal that is
very feminine. It is frequently used in table arrangements
because of its pleasing shape and striking blue color. It has
no scent. Its vase life is 3-7 days.

639. What type of flower is Protea?

Brides and grooms are the king and queen of their night.
Perhaps this is well symbolized by using Protea in wedding
arrangements. The king Protea (cynaroides) and queen
Protea (magnifica) are large, with well-formed flower heads.
As with people, the king is often taller than his queen; the
king achieving 2-3 feet in length and the queen 1 1/2 to 2
feet. There are also smaller varieties. A Protea is a Honeypot
or Sugar bush. It is a woody plant which was originally
cultivated in Australia, Israel and southern parts of AfricIts
leaves are simple and alternate. The shape of the flower is
irregular with 4 external segments that grow alternately
with the petals. The flowers are somewhat arched inwards.
The center is double and surrounded by hairy bracts. Some
varieties are black topped. Some have a woolly appearance.
The long-lasting Protea makes a dramatic statement when
used in low table arrangements. They are most appropriately
used in contemporary wedding design. Protea's eye-catching
appeal will be wasted if your arrangement is elevated, as its
beauty lies in its compact form and coloration, which is best
appreciated at low levels.

640. What type of flower is Queen Anne's Lace?

The name says it all. Delicate and lacy, Queen Anne's
Lace looks like the lace used in bridal gown design. It is a

white, flat flower comprised of hundreds of small florets on a straight 1 1/2 to 3 foot stem. Actually, it is a summer wildflower that grows in the field, and most florists do not carry it. But do not gather it directly from a field as it may bear chiggers or other small critters. Once picked, it has a life span of only about 3 days. Apart from informal wildflower arrangements, it can also be used in the hair to complement the wedding gown.

641. What type of flower is Ranunculus?

A Ranunculus is like a very full peony. This early spring flower originated in the Persian Gulf and is sometimes called a Persian Buttercup or Iranian Peony. The Ranunculus name is from the latin rana, meaning "frog." It was so named because the flower grows best in swampy areas. This flower is extremely full and tightly packed with petals. It is available in multiple shades of orange, red, pink, yellow and white. Ranunculus are up to 4 inches across and sit on 10-18 inch stems. The flower was frequently used by Persian shahs to decorate the bridal suite. These brightly colored, unscented flowers will last more than a week with proper care.

642. What type of flower are Roses?

No flower symbolizes love more than the rose, making it the perfect wedding flower. Fittingly, among the more than 130 popular varieties are the "Bridal Pink," "Darling," "Kiss," "Flirt" and "Only Love." Many varieties are named for women, although women today often give roses to men as a symbol of their love. Perhaps due to their names, " Purple Prince" and "Idole" are popular choices for men. Rose varieties can be categorized as large flowered, medium flowered, small flowered or cluster. Some are heavily scented; some moderately; some lightly and some have no scent at all. Depending upon the variety, roses can last up to 3 weeks. The rose is from the family Rosaceae. It is naturally a prickly shrub with feathery leaves and showy flowers having five petals in the wild state but often being doubled or partly doubled under cultivation. The thorns on the stalks vary depending on the variety. The stalk length runs between 12 inches and 40 inches, depending upon variety and quality. The leaves are compound and may consist of five leaflets. They can be obtained in reds, pinks, salmon, orange, lavender, cream, white and two-tone colors. Some rose varieties were first seen in Asia; others in Central Europe, the Middle East and Asia Minor. They can easily be used for any phase of wedding design: altar and church decorations, corsages and boutonnieres, hand bouquets, and centerpieces. Roses can be used to complement any wedding decor. For example, the "Porcelina" rose, which is a large, ivory colored flower, can be used to create an elegant bridal bouquet, eliciting a formal atmosphere. The softly colored "Champagne" rose, singly wrapped in a napkin at each dinner plate, is a nice touch to symbolize your affection and appreciation for your guests. Warning: make sure to remove all thorns! So remember, when you want to have a perfect wedding, make sure to seal your vows with a kiss... a "Kiss" rose!

643. **What type of flower is Saponaria?**

The name of this flower is derived from the Latin word for soap because the sap of the plant is said to have a cleansing effect. It was originally used in weddings as a sign that the bride was cleansed or pure. Although first found in the Mediterranean region, Saponaria today is primarily field grown in The Netherlands. It is a very delicate, small flower on long, flowing stems. It is used as a filler in bouquets because of the abundance of flowers on each stalk. Deep pink is the most commonly used variety, but it is also available in pure white. Both its colors and its delicate scent make this flower popular for use in weddings. It is only available in June, July and August, but the flower can be forced indoors for weddings in late May.

644.

What type of flower is the Snapdragon?

The botanical name for Snapdragon is Antirrhinum majus. It originated in the Mediterranean region of France and Spain more than 400 years ago. It is now one of the most popular flowers around. The flowers sit in graduated clusters atop a spike that is between 8 and 12 inches in length and along a stem that can grow as long as 45 inches. Snapdragons are available in shades of red, orange, lavender, pink, salmon and white. They have no scent. Because of their abundance of color and their vertical shape, Snapdragons are extremely useful in vase arrangements. These flowers are readily available in May and June and then again in late summer until the end of October. Snapdragons can also be found in limited supply in late winter and early spring. Properly cared for, they can last about a week. Note of warning: these flowers require sufficient water supply at all times. They are also extremely sensitive to ethylene gas and should be kept far away from fruits and vegetables on food table displays. If kept too close, they will start to drop their buds on the table.

645. What type of flower is Speedwell?

The scientific name of Speedwell is Veronica longifoliIt's a very old plant and the first record of its cultivation was in Switzerland/France in the mid-1500s. The flower itself is primarily blue and grows cone-shaped sitting above heart-shaped leaves. It must be carefully cared for, otherwise it has the tendency to dry out and become limp. There are some pink and white varieties grown in Virginia. These flowers have the same tendency to dry out and must be carefully pre-treated. Speedwell is available only in the heat of the summer. The flower is primarily used in mixed bouquets and basic floral arrangements. The Veronica longifolia has a limited vase life of about 5 days.

646. What kind of flower is the Star of Bethlehem?

The Star of Bethlehem, botanically known as Ornithogalum, features white flowers with either a white-green or a black-grey center. A series of 2 dozen or more flowers sit pyramid shape atop a stem that is approximately 15 inches long. These flowers originated in Africa but were formally cultivated in Holland 450 years ago. The Star of Bethlehem was so named because it reminded the priests of flowers that were found in churches of the sacred city of Bethlehem. In medieval times this flower was used to signify the religious commitment of the bride to the groom. The Star of Bethlehem was a rarely used flower until about 50 years ago, when florists discovered that its flowers easily adapted to dying in a variety of shades. These flowers are strong, and will maintain their presence for up to a month. Although this flower is normally long lived, it is particularly sensitive to fruits and vegetables. Therefore it is advisable not to use it on tables that feature edibles. These flowers look particularly nice in small bud vases and are frequently used to decorate cocktail tables.

647. What type of flower is Statice?

Statice or limonium gives the appearance of a sea of color. Perhaps that is why it is also known as Sea Lavender. Statice used to be predominantly yellow, but today most varieties are seen in shades of blue. They are also available in purple, lavender, white, and pink. Statice originated in Turkestan and areas in the Mediterranean. Botanically, blue Sea Lavender is called Statice perezii. It was named after the Dutch baron P.J.R. de Perez who was Governor of the Dutch West Indies 1803-1859. This variety is distinguished by its smooth, bare foot stalk, comprised of multi-branching stems of small, star-shaped flower clusters. The other major variety consists primarily of purple flowers with a splash of white. Both are used as filler flowers in large arrangements and are the perfect addition to any natural-looking wedding design. Statice lasts about 2 weeks and dries well, so the bride can have a beautiful keepsake of her wedding. It is available year-round.

648. What type of flower is Stephanotis?

Pure white and fragrant, this traditional wedding flower has been used in bridal bouquets, corsages, and wedding decorations for centuries. Sometimes referred to as Madagascar Jasmine, it is delicately fragranced and has a pure white waxy color. Although it is relatively expensive and must be handled carefully to avoid bruising, Stephanotis is perfect for wedding use any time of the year. Originally from Madagascar and first introduced in England at the beginning of the 19th century, Stephanotis is actually an evergreen climbing shrub with long tendrils and shiny dark green leaves that average 2 1/2 inches. Each star shaped flower cluster is formed from five tips of petals sitting atop a tube that protrudes from a short stem. Each individual flower itself is less than two inches.

649. What type of flower is Stock?

Stock traces its origins to ancient times. This extremely fragrant, spiked flower has a hairy clustered appearance. The flowers are available in white, red, pink, salmon, lavender and yellow. It is extremely useful in mixed bridal bouquets and large arrangements because its blooms are so tightly packed. A skilled floral designer can also transform this inexpensive flower into a wisteria-looking vine to drape an arch or trellis. Stock, also called Gillyflowers, are botanically identified as Matthiola. They are available throughout most of the year, with lesser amounts of the assortment during the Thanksgiving and Christmas seasons. Matthiola will last at least one week.

650. What type of flower is the Sunflower?

Americans have fallen in love with sunflowers. Botanically, a sunflower is called Helianthus, coming from the Greek words "Helio," meaning sun, and "Anthos," meaning flowers. The flower is self-descriptive. From its dark colored center, yellow ray-like petals project out much like the sun's rays. Helianthus is one of the few major flowers that found its origin in the United States. These flowers grow wild in the southwest and are now professionally cultivated throughout the world. Giant varieties can have flower heads that are 15 inches in diameter. Because of their huge size, giant helianthus are best suited to single placement or in large arrangements. Smaller varieties measuring 3-4 inches across make excellent filler and can be worn in the hair during informal ceremonies. These fragrant-free flowers will last up to 12 days.

651. What type of flower is the Sweet Pea?

This vividly-colored, climbing flower is a native of Italy. Its scientific name is Lathyrus. Since its colors are strong oranges, lilacs and purples and its flowers are extremely fragrant, Italian royalty used this as part of the altar setting at weddings. One common variety identifies this wedding connection through the name "Royal Family." Once the flowers were cultivated professionally, breeders eliminated much of their scent. Now smaller Sweet Peas have absolutely no fragrance. Most varieties of Sweet Peas are readily available in the spring.

652. What type of flower is Tuberose?

Often confused with Snapdragon, Tuberose is a small, rose-like bud flower that grows atop 3-foot long stems. This flower has many fragrant florets that grow and open from the bottom up and look a bit like stephanotis. The maximum size of each white, star-shaped flower is 2 1/2 inches when fully opened. Tuberose originated in southern Mexico and is now grown primarily in Israel, Africa and the south of France. An extremely fragrant flower, it is frequently used for corsages and small bouquets. It can also be used to decorate small cocktail tables at the wedding reception. In fact, Tuberose flowers are so fragrant that they are greatly in demand by the perfume industry in France. Due to their limited availability and perfume industry demands, they can be quite expensive.

✿ Flowers

653. What type of flower is the Tulip?

For variety of shape and color, few flowers surpass the tulip. Hundreds of species of tulips originally grew wild in Turkey and Iran. They were first formally cultivated in The Netherlands in the 1500s. At one time this flower was so highly valued that it was used as money. At that period of time, extremely wealthy Holland traders used tulips at weddings as a sign of affluence. Botanically called "Tulipa," its name is derived from the turban shape of the flower. Today there are thousands of different species available at different times of the year. They are cupped, fringed, spiked, single-colored, multicolored, large and small. All are stately adornments in large and small floral arrangements. A popular and yet unusual tulip is the "Parakeet" tulip which has irregularly shaped, two-tone streaked petals on flowers that are so large that they have to be braced so as not to collapse their stems. Another is the "Kees Nelis Triumph" tulip that features a dramatic red cup petal that appears to change instantly into a flaming yellow border. Since tulips are available in greatest abundance in the spring, they are sought after as wedding decor to symbolize a new beginning. Since limited life span does not adversely affect wedding use, the tulip is a wedding standard. However, their hollow stems restrict them to floral designs with a water source. A special note of care: avoid mixing tulips with daffodils in the same arrangement. These flowers are allergic to each other.

654. What type of flower is the Waxflower?

The waxflower, or Chamelaucium ciliatum, is sometimes known as the Pink Tea Tree. It is a very small, light, airy flower with a diameter that is less than an inch. Each branching stem contains a lot of buds. Its foliage is needle-like. Because of the delicate nature of its flowers, the Waxflower is frequently used as filler in floral design. Its primary use is in bouquets and as decoration for a bridal table. It is available in pink, lavender and white. It is available starting in December and may be easily obtained through the end of May. Historically, the waxflower was used as a setting for tea service when the bride-to-be was first introduced formally to the groom's parents.

CHAPTER 22

Transportation

655. When should we book transportation for the wedding day?
Two to four months before the wedding.

656. How does the couple, their families, and their wedding party typically get to the ceremony?
It is customary for the bride and her father to ride to the ceremony site together on the wedding day. You may also include some or all members of your wedding party. Normally a procession to the church begins with the bride's mother and several of the bride's attendants in the first vehicle. The bride and her father will go in the last vehicle. This vehicle will also be used to transport the bride and groom to the reception site after the ceremony.

657. What kind of transportation can I use on my wedding day?
There are various options for transportation. The most popular choice is a limousine since it is big and open and can accommodate several people as well as your bridal gown. You can also choose to rent a car that symbolizes your personality as a couple. You can rent a luxury car such as a Mercedes, sports cars such as a Ferrari, or a vintage vehicle such as a 1950s Thunderbird or 1930s Cadillac. Make sure the company you choose is fully licensed and has liability insurance. Do not pay the full amount until after the event.

658. How much does transportation cost?
It can range from $35 to $100 per hour, depending on the type of transportation you choose. Many limousines are booked on a 3-hour minimum basis.

659. If I want our wedding parties to ride to the ceremony in a luxury stretch limo, can I ask them to help pay for it?
No. A special or luxurious form of transportation is not a necessity; thus, if you must have the expensive limo, you should pay for it.

660. How should the wedding party's dates or spouses get from the ceremony to the reception? Do we need to provide transportation for them?
You should recommend that several of the spouses or dates of wedding party members ride together to the reception.

661. Can I book a horse-drawn carriage to take me to my ceremony?

If your ceremony and reception sites are fairly close together, and if weather permits, you might want to consider a horse-drawn carriage. This is a very elegant and special way to arrive in style; however, you should check with the venue to make sure their location can accommodate the carriage. For instance, if you are getting married in a big city, it may be a traffic obstruction to have a carriage.

662. How can I save money on transportation on my wedding day?

Consider hiring only one large limousine. This limousine can transport you, your parents and your attendants to the ceremony, and then you and your new husband from the ceremony.

663. What kind of questions should I ask the transportation service?

- What is the name of the transportation service?
- What is the website and e-mail of the transportation service?
- What is the address of the transportation service?
- What is the name and phone number of my contact person?
- How many years have you been in business?
- How many vehicles do you have available?
- Can you provide a back-up vehicle in case of an emergency?
- What types of vehicles are available?
- What are the various sizes of vehicles available?
- How old are the vehicles?
- How many drivers are available?
- Can you show me photos of your drivers?
- How do your drivers dress for weddings?
- Do you have liability insurance?
- What is the minimum amount of time required to rent a vehicle?
- What is the cost per hour? Two hours? Three hours?
- How much gratuity is expected?
- What is your payment/cancellation policy?

664. Should I hire a valet service?

At a large home reception, you should consider hiring a professional, qualified valet service if parking could be a problem. If so, make sure the valet service is fully insured.

✳ Transportation

665. What should I do if I am having a wedding at home and there isn't enough room for our guests to park?

Find a nearby church or school where guests can park their cars. Then hire a shuttle service to take them to the house.

666. How should I let guests know where to park for my reception?

Have the officiant make an announcement at the close of the ceremony or include it in the ceremony program.

667. What is a parking fee?

Many reception sites such as hotels, restaurants, etc. charge for parking.

668. Should I pay for my guests' parking?

It is customary, although not necessary, for the host of the wedding to pay this charge. When comparing the cost of reception sites, don't forget to add the cost of parking to the total price.

669. How much are parking fees?

Parking fees can range from $3 to $10 per car.

CHAPTER 23

Gifts

670. When should we register for gifts?

Four to six months before the wedding.

671. What kinds of things should we register for?

You should register for a variety of items in a broad price range so guests can make purchases within their budgets, or perhaps combine funds for a larger gift. While online registries are very easy, you want to make sure you choose at least one store that has brick-and-mortar locations so people who are not as Internet-savvy feel comfortable.

672. How should we tell our guests about our registry?

Never include your registry information on your invitations; it is in poor taste. Instead, have your wedding party spread the word or include a link to your registry on your wedding website.

673. Can we tell our guests that we don't need or want them to bring gifts?

You can have your wedding party spread the word that you wish not to receive gifts, but expect that some guests will feel a bit caught off-guard by this and many will still bring a gift.

674. Is it tacky to ask for money instead of gifts?

Couples are getting married later in life these days, which means less need for a registry full of household appliances. If you want to ask for money, inform your wedding party members, who can spread the word to guests. However, be aware that some guests will still want to get you a gift, so it's polite to create a small registry anyhow.

675. What is a gift attendant?

It is customary for guests to send gifts to the bride before the wedding day. However, there are always some guests who bring gifts with them to the big event. The gift attendant is responsible for watching over your gifts during the reception so that no one walks away with them.

676. Is a gift attendant necessary?

This is necessary only if your reception is held in a public area such as a hotel or outside garden where strangers may be walking by.

677. How much should I pay a gift attendant?

You can pay your gift attendant anywhere from $20 to $100.

678. Who should I hire to be my gift attendant?

It is not proper to have a friend or family member take on this duty as he or she would not enjoy the reception. The gift attendant should also be responsible for transporting your gifts from the reception site to your car or bridal suite. If you want to save money, hire a young boy or girl from your neighborhood to watch over your gifts at the reception.

679. What should I give for bridesmaids' gifts?

Bridesmaids' gifts are given by the bride to her bridesmaids and Maid of Honor as a permanent keepsake of the wedding. The best gifts are those that can be used both during and after the wedding, such as jewelry or a pashmina wrap. The gift to the Maid of Honor may be similar to the bridesmaids' gifts but should be a bit more expensive.

680. When do I present my bridesmaids with their gifts?

Bridesmaids' gifts are usually presented at the bridesmaids' luncheon or at the rehearsal dinner.

681. What should I give as ushers' gifts?

Ushers' gifts are given by the groom to his ushers as a permanent keepsake of the wedding. For ushers' gifts, consider a nice watch, tie, money clip, sports tickets, or bottle of wine. The groom should deliver his gifts to the ushers at the bachelor party or at the rehearsal dinner. The gift to the Best Man may be similar to the ushers' gifts but should be a bit more expensive.

682. How much do the bridesmaids' gifts cost?

This amount depends on how much you want to spend on your bridal attendants and the Maid of Honor. It can range from $20 to $200 or more.

683. How much do the ushers' gifts cost?

This depends on how much you want to spend on your ushers and what you want to buy them. The cost can range from $20 to $200 or more.

684. Should I give out gifts to family members?

Gifts are a wonderful way to show your appreciation to

family members who have assisted you in your wedding planning process. Generally gifts are only given to the parents of the bride and groom, but anyone who has contributed monetarily for the wedding should receive a small, thoughtful gift. A nice gift is a picture frame or small album of wedding photos.

685. What is the bride's gift?

The bride's gift is traditionally given by the groom to the bride. It is typically a personal gift such as a piece of jewelry or something than bride can wear on her wedding day.

686. How much does the bride's gift cost?

The cost can vary greatly on this, as it is up to the bride and groom to decide how much they want to spend on each other.

687. What is the groom's gift?

The groom's gift is traditionally given by the bride to the groom. A nice watch is an example of a groom's gift that he can use on his wedding day.

688. How much does the groom's gift cost?

This amount must be decided between the bride and groom, depending on how much they want to spend on each other.

689. How can I save money on bridesmaids' gifts?

Ask your photographer to take, at no extra charge, professional portraits of each bridesmaid and her escort for use as bridesmaids' gifts. Select a beautiful background that will remind your bridesmaids of the occasion, such as your cake table. Put the photo in a pretty frame. This makes a very special yet inexpensive gift for your attendants.

690. How can I save money on ushers' gifts?

Negotiate with your photographer to take, at no extra charge, professional portraits of each usher and his escort for use as ushers' gifts. Put the photo in an elegant frame. This makes a very special yet inexpensive gift for your attendants.

691. How can I save money on the bride's gift?

If you and your bride decide not to exchange gifts (many couples do this to save money), consider writing her a heartfelt card telling her all the reasons you love her and are excited to be getting married. This will make a lovely, free gift.

692. **How can I save money on the groom's gift?**

Consider omitting this gift. A pretty card proclaiming your eternal love is a very special yet inexpensive gift. Consider exchanging these cards if you opt to see each other prior to the ceremony. This makes for a very emotional and happy moment.

693. **When should we send thank-you notes for the gifts we receive?**

Send thank-you notes within two weeks of receiving a gift that arrives before the wedding, and within two months after the honeymoon for gifts received on or after your wedding day. Mention the specific gift and detail how you will spend any monetary gifts you were given.

CHAPTER 24

Parties

694. What types of parties take place before the wedding?

Weddings are often much more than a day-long celebration. There can be plenty of festivities before and even after the actual wedding day. Typically, the events that take place before a wedding include the engagement party, bridal shower, bachelor party, bachelorette party, bridesmaids' luncheon, and rehearsal dinner. Some couples also like to have a brunch the day after the wedding to relax and relive the previous evening's celebration.

695. What is the engagement party?

The engagement party is generally thrown by the bride's family to celebrate the big news. Gifts are not required at this party. An engagement party is typically held in your parents' home; however, renting a space or having dinner in a nice restaurant are also acceptable.

696. What is the bridal shower and who hosts it?

Traditionally, your wedding shower is thrown by your Maid of Honor and bridesmaids, unless they are a member of your immediate family. Because a shower is a gift-giving occasion, it is not considered socially acceptable for anyone in your immediate family to host this event. If your mother or sisters wish to be involved, have them offer to help with the cost of the event or offer their home for it.

697. Who should I invite to my bridal shower?

Invite your close friends and the females in your fiancé's family. You may have several showers thrown for you, so be sure not to invite the same people to multiple showers (the exception being members of the wedding party, who may be invited to all showers without the obligation of bringing a gift). Only include people who have been invited to the wedding, with the exception being a work shower, to which all coworkers may be invited, whether or not they are attending the wedding.

698. What are some options for my bridal shower?

Tea parties, spa days, cocktail parties, and traditional at-home events are all good ideas. Generally an event is themed (lingerie, cooking, home decor) and the invitation should give guests an idea of what type of gift to bring. The agenda usually includes some games and gift opening. Be sure to have someone keep track of which gift is from whom.

699. Does the groom attend the bridal shower?
It is becoming more popular to host showers with co-ed
guest lists; however, he should skip any all-girls parties.

700. What is the bachelor party?
The bachelor party is a male-only affair typically organized
by the Best Man. He is responsible for selecting the date and
reserving the place and entertainment as well as inviting the
groom's male friends and family. Your Best Man should also
assign responsibilities to the ushers, as they should help with
the organization of this party.

701. What are my options for the bachelor party?
You have probably heard stories of wild bachelor parties,
complete with strip clubs and extreme amounts of alcohol;
however, that is usually an exaggeration. The bachelor party
is simply a night or weekend for the guys to spend time
together. Good options include dinner and drinks, golf, a
casino trip, weekend cruise, sporting event, brewery tour or
tasting, renting a boat, skydiving, or camping.

702. When should we have the bachelor party?
Your Best Man should not plan your bachelor party for the
night before the wedding, since you don't want to have a
hangover or be exhausted during your wedding. It is much
more appropriate to have the bachelor party two or three
nights or a few weeks before the wedding. Your Best Man
should also designate a driver for you and for those who will
be drinking alcohol. Remember, you and your Best Man are
responsible for the well-being of everybody invited to the
party.

703. What is the bachelorette party?
The bachelorette party is typically organized by the Maid
of Honor for the females in the wedding party. She should
choose the date, organize activities, and make any necessary
reservations. Oftentimes the bride will wear a funny
accessory, such as a feather boa or tiara, so other partygoers
see that she is the honored guest of the night.

704. What are some great bachelorette party ideas?
The bachelorette party should be a time of celebration for
close girlfriends. Some nice options include dinner and
drinks, a spa day, wine tasting, a short cruise, a weekend

yoga or Pilates retreat, a mini-vacation to the beach, or a scavenger hunt.

705. We want to have a joint bachelor-bachelorette party. What are some options?

It is becoming more popular for couples to celebrate together, and it provides a nice opportunity for the wedding parties on each side to get acquainted. You should discuss with your wedding parties what you all might be interested in — you could attend a concert, sporting event, wine tasting, or simply have a night out for dinner and drinks.

706. What is the bridesmaids' luncheon?

The bridesmaids' luncheon is given by the bride for her bridesmaids. It is not a shower; rather, it is simply a time for good friends to get together formally before the bride changes her status from single to married. You can give your bridesmaids their gifts at this gathering. Otherwise, plan to give them their gifts at the rehearsal dinner.

707. When should I hold my bridesmaids' luncheon?

The morning or afternoon of the wedding, depending on what time you are getting married.

708. What is the rehearsal dinner?

It is customary that the groom's parents host a dinner party following the rehearsal, the evening before the wedding. The dinner usually includes the bridal party, their spouses or guests, both sets of parents, close family members, the officiant, and the wedding consultant and/or coordinator.

709. Where should I have the rehearsal dinner?

The rehearsal dinner party can be held just about anywhere, from a restaurant, hotel, or private hall to the groom's parents' home. Close relatives and out-of-town guests may be included if budget permits. Restaurants specializing in Mexican food or pizza are fun yet inexpensive options.

710. How much does the rehearsal dinner cost?

It depends on the number of people invited and where you decide to hold the dinner, but it can cost from $15 to $100 or more per person.

711. When should we set the date, time and location of our rehearsal dinner?

Four to six months before the wedding.

712. Can we have an after-party following the wedding reception?

An after-wedding party can mean inviting everyone to continue the party at a local lounge or bar, or reserving another part of your reception venue for late-night celebration. Although most older guests won't attend, you should still be polite and extend the invitation to everyone at the reception.

713. What is the day-after wedding brunch?

Many times the newlyweds will want to host a brunch the day after the wedding to spend one last bit of time with their guests and to thank them for coming to the wedding. This is especially true if many guests came from out of town or if you are having a destination wedding.

714. What should we serve at the day-after brunch?

Brunch can be much less formal than the rest of the wedding. Ask your family to help create this casual get-together by cooking or picking up brunch foods. Consider keeping the brunch menu simple: have bagels, croissants, jams, fruit, coffee, and juice.

715. Where should we have the brunch?

A family member who still wants to contribute to your wedding is a perfect choice to host, or if many guests are at one hotel, consider having the brunch there. If the hotel offers a continental breakfast, ask the hotel to reserve space in the breakfast room for your group.

716. What is the best time for a day-after wedding brunch?

Choose a reasonable time for the brunch: Not too early, as many guests will be recovering from the festivities of the reception, but not too late, as out-of-town guests will have travel arrangements to attend to.

✿ Notes

....
....
....
....
....
....
....
....
....
....
....
....
....
....
....
....
....
....
....
....
....
....
....
....
....

CHAPTER 25

Traditions & Etiquette

717. What is the symbolism behind wedding rings?

The circle of the wedding ring represents eternal love and devotion. The Greeks believed that the fourth finger on the left hand has a vein which leads directly to the heart, so this is the finger onto which we place these bands.

718. What is the tradition behind the bride's bouquet?

In history, a bride carried her bouquet for protective reasons — carrying strong-smelling spices or garlic could help to drive away evil spirits which might plague the wedding. Eventually the floral bouquet became prevalent and symbolized fertility and the hope for a large family. Each flower was assigned a particular meaning when carried in a bride's bouquet.

719. What is the tradition behind the bride's veil?

The veil has historically symbolized virginity and innocence. It is believed that in ancient times, a bride was veiled to protect her from evil spirits or to shield her from her husband's eyes. Arranged marriages were common and often the couple would not officially meet until after the wedding. Now, the veil is simply a beautiful accessory to complement the wedding gown.

720. What is the tradition behind Something old, Something new, Something borrowed and Something blue?

Something old is carried to represent the history of the bride and ties her to her family. Something new represents the future and the bride's ties to her new family. Something borrowed should come from someone who is happily married and is carried in the hopes that their good fortune may rub off on you. Blue is the color of purity and is carried to represent faithfulness in the marriage. Many people don't realize that there is one more item — a sixpence in your shoe — which represents wealth.

721. Why aren't the bride and groom supposed to see each other before the wedding?

In ancient times, the bride and groom often had not even met before their wedding day, so they weren't permitted to see each other. Modernly, couples often like to build excitement and anticipation by waiting until they walk down the aisle to see each other. However, First Look photos are becoming increasingly popular — this is where the bride and groom elect to see each other just before the ceremony and have the photographer capture this moment. It is up to you whether you want to see each other or wait.

722. What is the tradition behind the white aisle runner?
Using a white aisle runner symbolizes bringing God into your union and is indicative of walking on holy ground.

723. What is the tradition behind the seating of the families?
The families are traditionally seated on opposite sides of the church, because in ancient times families would often have a wedding in order to bring peace to warring clans. In order to prevent fighting from taking place during the wedding, they were kept separated.

724. What is the tradition behind the groom entering first?
Traditionally, the groom enters first, and gives his vows first, because he is considered to be the one who has initiated the wedding.

725. What is the tradition behind the father walking the bride down the aisle?
In historic times, brides were literally given away by their fathers — women were betrothed, often at birth, to men they did not know. Now, giving the bride away is simply a way for the bride's family to publicly show their support of the union.

726. What is the tradition behind the bride standing on the left?
Because times were so violent and unpredictable, in ancient times a bride was likely to be kidnapped and held for ransom at her wedding! The bride was placed on the groom's left in order to leave his sword-hand free in case he had to defend her.

727. What are some traditional Bible readings for a wedding ceremony?
Beatitudes
Corinthians 13:1-13
Ecclesiastes 3:1-9
Ephesians 3:14-19; 5:1-2
Genesis 1:26-28
Genesis 2:4-9, 15-24
Hosea 2:19-21

Isaiah 61:10I
John 4:7-16
John 15:9-12, 17:22-24
Mark 10:6-9
Proverbs 31:10-31
Romans 12:1-2, 9-18
Ruth 1:16-17
Tobit 8:56-58

728. **What are some unique alternatives to traditional Bible readings?**

Excerpts from *The Prophet* by Kahlil Gibran, *The Alchemist* by Paulo Coelho, *The Velveteen Rabbit* by Margery Williams Bianco, poems by Pablo Neruda, Shakespeare's Sonnets, and song lyrics are all modern choices for readings.

729. **What is the tradition behind kissing the bride?**

During the Roman empire, the kiss between a couple symbolized a legal bond — hence the expression "sealed with a kiss." Continued use of the kiss to seal the marriage bond is based on the deeply rooted idea of the kiss as a vehicle for transference of power and souls.

730. **What is the tradition behind the couple being pronounced husband and wife?**

This establishes their change of names and a definite point in time for the beginning of the marriage. These words are to remove any doubt in the minds of the couple or the witnesses concerning the validity of the marriage.

731. **What is the tradition behind the signing of the guest book?**

Your wedding guests are official witnesses to the covenant. By signing the guest book, they are saying, "I have witnessed the vows, and I will testify to the reality of this marriage." Because of this significance, the guest book should be signed after the wedding ceremony rather than before it.

732. **What is the significance of the bride and groom feeding cake to each other?**

This represents the sharing of their body to become one. A New Testament illustration of this symbolism is The Lord's Supper.

733. What is the symbolism of tossing the bride's garter?

It is customary for the bride to wear a garter just above the knee on her wedding day. After the bouquet tossing ceremony, the groom takes the garter off the bride's leg. All the single men gather on the dance floor. The groom then tosses the garter to them over his back. According to age-old tradition, whoever catches the garter is the next to be married. This tradition originated because guests would actually tear at the bridal gown, thinking any part of the bride's attire gave good luck. So, instead, she threw the garter to fend off unruly guests.

734. Why do guests throw rose petals or rice as the bride and groom leave the reception?

This tradition was initiated in the Middle Ages whereby a handful of wheat was thrown over the bridal couple as a symbol of fertility. Rose petals are used to symbolize happiness, beauty, and prosperity. Rose petals, rice, or confetti is often used. Keep in mind that rose petals can stain carpets; rice can sting faces, harm birds and make stairs dangerously slippery; and confetti is messy and hard to clean. Clubs and hotels sometimes won't permit the use of any of these. Ask about their policy.

735. What are alternatives to throwing rose petals or rice?

An environmentally correct alternative is to use grass or flower seeds, which do not need to be cleaned up if tossed over a grassy area. Also, sparklers have become a popular sendoff for the newlyweds. Another popular idea is using bubbles.

736. What is behind the tradition of the groom carrying the bride over the threshold?

Ancient people believed that evil spirits would wait for the newlyweds in the threshold of their home, so the groom would carry the bride to protect her.

CHAPTER 26

Eco-Chic Wedding Ideas

Eco-Chic Wedding Ideas

737. How can I make my invitations eco-friendly?

You can use organic or soy ink on recycled paper. Or choose paper alternatives such as bamboo, hemp, banana stalks, and even cotton. Save paper by skipping the multi-envelope invitations and using a postcard for your Save the Date. Use online invitations or create a wedding website to give guests details of events such as the bachelor/bachelorette parties, rehearsal dinner, and bridal shower.

738. What are some eco-friendly options for reception venues?

Have the wedding outside, instead of in an energy-inefficient reception hall. If you have an outdoor wedding, you can utilize the natural beauty of the site to have fewer wasteful decorations. You can also locate an LEED-certified space to have an indoor wedding. LEED stands for "Leadership in Energy and Environmental Design" and means the space is sustainable and conserves water, energy, and electricity using solar power, insulation panels, and other state-of-the-art technology. Visit the U.S. Green Building Council's website to search a list of LEED-certified locations by city or state — www.usgbc.org. You can also have your wedding and reception in the same place to avoid wasting energy and natural resources on transportation.

739. What are my "green" options for flowers?

Purchase organically grown flowers, meaning they are grown without pesticides or insecticides. Consider organic roses, which are a beautiful option and have an amazing, real fragrance. (Non-organic roses are actually sprayed with perfume.) Get flowers from a local nursery to avoid using up natural resources during shipping. Just be aware that organic flowers won't last as long, however, so make sure your florist considers timing. Another option is to use potted plants instead of flowers and then have your guests take them home as favors and reuse them. Or have them donated to a local hospice or elderly care center.

740. What should I consider when having an organic menu?

Choose a menu with seasonal or locally grown products to avoid shipping costs. You may be hard-pressed to find an all-organic caterer, so simply instruct your caterer to shop at local farmer's markets and choose fresh, in-season ingredients. Be aware that with a seasonal menu, you should find a caterer you really trust, because it's not likely you'll be able to taste the menu ahead of time. Donate any extra food to a homeless shelter!

741. With so many table settings for our guests, how can we avoid wasting energy and resources?

Use recycled napkins and table linens. You can also request biodegradable utensils and plates made out of potatoes, cornstarch, or sugarcane. Then have them composted after the wedding.

742. Can we have organic alcohol at the bar?

When choosing organic wine or beer selections, make sure they are registered with the USDA National Organic Program.

743. We would like to incorporate elements from nature into our reception décor. What are some easy suggestions?

Use natural products for placecards, such as a pressed tree leaf with each guest's name on it as a placemarker, or writing guests' names on a smooth river with a paint pen. Choose beeswax or soy-based candles over those made with petroleum, a non-earth friendly product. Also consider using shells, stones, wood, or other natural elements in your centerpieces.

744. Is having an eco-friendly wedding more expensive than a traditional wedding?

Be aware that a green wedding can cost up to 20 percent more than a traditional wedding. For instance, having an organic menu can raise food costs by 10 percent.

745. How can I be eco-friendly when choosing our wedding attire?

Purchase a secondhand or vintage gown. Have it altered to look more modern and to fit your body perfectly. Consider selling or even donating your gown after the wedding. The groom can wear a hemp tux. Also, have your bridesmaids buy dresses of their choosing that they will wear again.

746. How can I find an environmentally friendly wedding ring?

Buy a conflict-free diamond. Blood Diamonds are diamonds mined in war-torn African countries that help fund rebel armies, finance arms purchases, and other illegal activities.

✳ Eco-Chic Wedding Ideas

Be sure to ask for certified "conflict-free" diamonds. Opt for a vintage piece, or have an old piece of jewelry melted down and made into a new ring.

747. We want our guests to think "green" with their wedding gifts. What are some good options?

Create a registry where guests donate to a favorite charity instead of buying you gifts. Avoid something political that guests might take issue with — stick to organizations that benefit international aid, nature, animals, disease prevention, or relief efforts. You can also register for a home-delivery service that delivers organic food products, or ask for national park passes.

748. We have heard of carbon credits to offset energy used by guests traveling to the wedding. What are carbon credits?

Carbon dioxide emissions from guest travel are the single biggest environmental impact from your wedding. The energy needed for lighting, catering, DJs, etc. always plays a role. Use an online "wedding carbon footprint" calculator to determine the amount of greenhouse gases and carbon emissions that will be generated by guests flying and driving into town. Then, the couple can purchase "carbon credits," which put money toward U.S. carbon-reducing energy projects to help offset the environmental damage from the wedding. One site designed specifically for wedding planning is www.terrapass.com. You might also ask your guests to contribute to carbon credits, instead of buying a wedding gift.

749. Can we take an eco-chic honeymoon?

Take a low-impact honeymoon by staying in a green resort or go camping. Or, instead of a lavish honeymoon, go on a volunteer trip! Build houses for Habitat for Humanity or help hurricane victims.

CHAPTER 27

Legal
Matters

750. What is wedding insurance?

Wedding insurance protects couples planning a wedding from financial loss, due to unforeseen mishaps or cancellations on their wedding day. Because you can't plan for everything, you or your parents may want to consider purchasing some type of wedding insurance. Companies generally offer two types of wedding insurance products that can be purchased individually or as a package:

- Wedding Event Cancellation / Postponement Plus Insurance — protects your financial investment in your wedding; covers cancellation / postponement, lost deposits, and more

- Wedding Liability Insurance — protects you against financial liability arising from your wedding; required by many venues

751. How much does wedding insurance cost?

Wedding insurance — specifically cancellation/postponement insurance — is affordable and can provide great peace of mind. The cost should be about 1-2% of the amount of coverage — for example, a plan that provides $25,000 in coverage should cost about $300.

752. If we are having a wedding at our home, do we need to purchase insurance to protect us in case of an accident during the wedding?

Your homeowners insurance may already provide enough coverage for your wedding, but you should contact your provider to be absolutely sure. If you need additional coverage, you can purchase a liability policy from a wedding insurance provider, which is similar to what many venues have.

753. When should we get our marriage license?

Six to eight weeks before the wedding.

754. How do I go about obtaining my marriage license?

Marriage license requirements are state-regulated and may be obtained from the County Clerk in most county courthouses. Some states (California and Nevada, for example) offer two types of marriage licenses: a public license and a confidential one. The public license is the most common one and requires a health certificate and a blood test. It can only be obtained at the County Clerk's office. The confidential license is usually less expensive and does not require a health certificate or blood test. If offered, it can usually be obtained from most Justices of the Peace. An oath must be taken in order to receive either license.

Requirements vary from state to state but generally include the following points:

- Applying for and paying the fee for the marriage license.
- There is usually a waiting period before the license is valid and a limited time before it expires.
- Meeting residency requirements for the state and/or county where the ceremony will take place.
- Meeting the legal age requirements for both bride and groom or having parental consent.
- Presenting any required identification, birth or baptismal certificates, marriage eligibility or other documents.
- Obtaining a medical examination and/or blood test for both the bride and groom to detect communicable diseases.

755. How much does the marriage license cost?
It depends upon the state where you live, but marriage licenses can cost anywhere from $20 to $100.

756. How do I get certified copies of my marriage license?
Certified copies of your marriage certificate are available at the clerk's office of the county in which you were married. When you apply for your marriage license at the county clerk's office, ask them how long it will take after the wedding before certified copies are available and the cost for each one. In some states you can get copies immediately, while in others the wait might be as long as six weeks.

757. Can I provide a photocopy of my marriage license as proof of my name change?
While some entities will accept a photocopy of the certified copy as proof of your name change, others, such as the Social Security office and many state drivers' license agencies, will require an original certified copy.

758. Who is responsible for filing my marriage license?
Often it is your officiant who is responsible for filing your

marriage license with the county clerk or records office.

759. **How do I show my proof of marriage if I leave on my honeymoon immediately following my wedding?**
If you will be traveling immediately after the wedding, be sure to ask your officiant to make a copy of the marriage license. This copy will suffice as proof of your marriage during the honeymoon and until you officially change your name. You may even want to ask for a couple of extra photocopies to keep on hand.

760. **What is a prenuptial agreement?**
A prenuptial agreement is a legal contract between the bride and groom itemizing the property each brings into the marriage and explaining how those properties will be divided in case of divorce or death. Although you can write your own agreement, it is advisable to have an attorney draw up or review the document. The two of you should be represented by different attorneys. If you are going to live in a different state after the wedding, consider having an attorney from that state draw up or review your document. Nobody likes to talk about divorce or death when planning a wedding, but it is very important to give these issues your utmost consideration. By drawing a prenuptial agreement, you encourage open communication and get a better idea of each other's needs and expectations. You should also consider drawing up or reviewing your wills at this time.

761. **Should I have a prenuptial agreement?**
Consider a prenuptial agreement if one or both of you have a significant amount of capital or assets, or if there are children involved from a previous marriage.

762. **How much does it cost to have a prenuptial agreement drawn up?**
It depends upon the attorney you go to, but it can cost from $500 to $3,000.

763. **How can I save money on a prenuptial agreement?**
Some software packages allow you to write your own will and prenuptial agreement, which can save you substantial attorney's fees. However, if you decide to draw either agreement on your own, you should still have an attorney review it.

764. When should I change my name on my legal documents (drivers' license, passport, credit cards, etc.)?

Six to eight weeks before the wedding.

765. Who do I need to notify first about my name change?

Notifying the federal government is the first thing you want to accomplish when changing your name. All other government agencies, including state and local entities, require that their records contain the same information that is on file with the Social Security office. The Social Security office will require an original, certified copy of your marriage license as well as a completed SS-5 form. If you were born outside the United States you will also need to provide proof of U.S. citizenship or lawful alien status.

Some examples of acceptable proof of citizenship or lawful alien status are:
- U.S. consular report of birth
- U.S. passport
- Certificate of citizenship
- Certificate of naturalization
- A current document issued by the U.S. Immigration and Naturalization Service (INS) such as Form I-551, I-94, I-688B, or I-766

766. What federal agencies do I need to inform of my new name and/or address?

The following are the major agencies that should be informed of your name/address change:
- Social Security Office
- Internal Revenue Service
- Passport Office
- Voter Registration

767. Do I have to inform the IRS of my name change?

It is not necessary to notify the Internal Revenue Service (IRS) of a name change, because their records will be automatically updated when you apply for a Social Security card in your new name. However, if you are moving as a result of your new marriage, you will want to notify the IRS of your new address. It is especially important to notify the IRS of a new address if you are waiting for a refund or any other form of communication from them.

768. Do I need a new passport when I change my name?

After you have notified the Social Security office of your new name, you will need to apply for a new passport. To receive a passport in your new name you will need to send an original, certified copy of your marriage license.

You will also need to send in the following information:
- A certified copy of your marriage license
- The completed DSP-82 form
- Two identical, recent photos with a light, plain background. Please make sure that the photographs you submit are 2" x 2" in size so they can be correctly attached.
- A check or money order made payable to "Passport Services" for $60 with your name and date of birth clearly printed on the front (please contact the National Passport Center to verify the current cost of a duplicate passport.)
- Your most recent passport

Passport Services will return the certified copy of your marriage license along with your new passport, which you should receive within six weeks. If you do not wish to wait for the certified copy of your marriage license to be returned to you in the mail, you may choose to go in person to any one of the 4,500 offices across the United States. To find a passport office, look in your local phone book or online.

769. Do I have to change my name on my voter registration?

In all states except North Dakota, which has no voter registration, you are required to update your voter registration anytime you move or change your name.

770. How do I change my name on my drivers' license?

Rules vary from state to state, but almost all states will require the original, certified copy of your marriage license, and you will need to go into your local office. Call ahead to ensure that you bring all the proper documentation and to verify the cost of the new license. All drivers' licensing offices should also allow you to change your voter registration at this time as well, with the exception of North Dakota, which has no voter registration.

771. How do I change my name on my vehicle's title?

The procedure for changing the name on your vehicle title varies from state to state. In most states you can change the name on your vehicle title at the same time you apply for a drivers' license in your new name. Most states will ask for the original, certified copy for the vehicle title change as well, so it may be best to make a trip into the office. Some states allow you to call ahead and make an appointment; taking advantage of this service will save you time.

772. How do I notify my State Taxation Board of my name change?

The means of notifying your state's taxation board about name and address changes varies from state to state. Some states have a form; others will accept a letter informing them of your name and/or address change. You are not required to send in a copy of your marriage certificate as proof of a name change for any of the states at this time. Be sure you have notified the Social Security office of a name change before you notify your state government agencies. Each state will want their records to contain the same information that the Social Security office has on file.

773. What other organizations, besides federal and state agencies, do I need to inform of my name change?

Once you have notified both the federal and state government agencies of your new name and change in marital status, you can move on to companies, institutions, organizations, and individuals. Below is a list of the various non-government agencies/groups that should be informed of your new name and marital status:

- Financial Records
- Insurance Records
- Legal records
- Memberships
- Household records
- School records
- Employment records
- Publications
- Medical records
- Children's records

774. How do I inform my bank of my name change?

To change the name and address of your current checking

and/or savings accounts at most banks, you will need to bring a copy of your marriage license into a branch and fill out a new signature card. This is also true for most money market accounts, IRAs, timed deposits, and certified deposits. If you are only changing your address, and not your name, many banks will allow you to mail in a change of address notification. Call your local branch to verify that they will accept a letter as notification of an address change. If you bank with an Internet bank, contact the customer service department to find out the proper procedure for changing the name on your accounts.

775. How do I change my name on my safety deposit box?

You will have to go visit the office that houses your safety deposit box to change your name, as they will require a new signature card that reflects your new name. For most institutions, a copy of your marriage certificate will be accepted as proof of your name change, but call ahead to verify.

776. What financial institutions do I need to inform of my name/address change?

You will need to notify all the individual financial institutions with which you have lines of credit, including all your existing loans and credit card companies. This is especially true of your credit cards. You will want your credit card companies to issue you a new card reflecting your new name as soon as possible, so your card will match your new identification. Begin by making a list of all the accounts that you have. Call the financial institution to check for the correct address to use for change of name and address since it is often a different address than you use when sending in payments. You will want to notify the major credit reporting bureaus of a name change as well. This will help to ensure that they have accurate information on your credit reports.

In general, the three major credit reporting bureaus are: Experian (formerly TRW), Equifax, and Trans Union. Notifying the people who help you with your finances now will make record keeping and filing your taxes easier in the long run. Tax advisors and investment counselors will then make sure all your financial records reflect your new name. It is also important to inform investment counselors, stockbrokers, and mutual fund administrators of your new address so you can be sure to receive financial statements.

777. How do I change my name on existing insurance policies?

Many couples now bring existing life insurance policies into the marriage, ones that they purchased on their own or ones that they have received through their employers. If you have an existing life insurance policy, you will want to notify your insurance issuer of your new name, and you may also want to change the beneficiary to your spouse. Most insurance companies will accept a photocopy of your marriage license as proof of your name change; however, be sure to contact your insurance agent to verify that a certified copy is not needed. Also, make a list of all outstanding insurance policies. Once you have compiled a list you may want to compare your existing coverage with your spouse's coverage, as you may have overlapping policies. In some cases, such as automobile insurance, it may be more cost effective to have both you and your spouse on the same policy. Decide which policies to keep and which to cancel. If you are keeping policies that were in your previous name, you will want to notify the insurance company of your name change. Also be sure to ask for information on adding your spouse to the policy where applicable. Most insurance companies will accept a photocopy of your marriage license as proof of your name change; however, be sure to contact your insurance agent to verify that a certified copy is not needed.

778. How do I update my legal documents with my name change?

It is a good idea to notify your lawyer about your new married status as well as any name or address changes. Your lawyer can then update any legal documents, such as wills and trusts, to reflect your new name. When notifying your lawyer, be sure to enclose a copy of your marriage license so it can be kept in your legal file as proof of your name change.

779. Do I need to change my name with the various memberships that I belong to?

You will need to update any memberships you have to reflect your new married status, as well as your name and/or address change. Some memberships, such as certain fitness clubs or warehouse clubs, will require you to go in person to change your name as you will need to have a new photo taken and a card issued in your new name.

780. How do I inform my employer of my name change?
You will need to notify your place of employment of your new married status as well as of any name or address changes. Most payroll departments will not update your records to reflect your new name until you have notified the Social Security office. Your employer will most likely have forms on hand that will allow you to change your name and/or address on all your employee-related benefits at the same time, but be sure to ask about each one individually to ensure that everyone is notified.

781. What do I have to update after my name change if I am self-employed?
Be sure to update your business licenses, accounts, and any business loans you might have. The procedure for updating business licenses varies from state to state, so call your area's licensing board for information. Most states will require an original certified copy of your marriage license to change your legal name. Don't forget to order new business cards with your new name as well!

782. How do I change my name/address with the various publications I receive?
Make a list of all the magazines, newspapers, journals, and newsletters you receive, and check to be sure you and your spouse don't have overlapping subscriptions. After canceling any publications that might be doubles (like the daily newspaper for instance), inform the others of your changes. It is especially important to notify publications of a change in address as the United States Post Office will only forward periodicals for a short period of time.

783. Why should I update my medical records with my new name/address?
To avoid confusion, and to update your emergency contact information to include your spouse, it is important that you let your doctors know of your new name. You will also want to make sure that your doctor's office has the same information as your insurance companies for billing purposes.

784. What do I need to do regarding my children or my spouse's children after I change my name/address?

If either you or your spouse have minor children, it is important to remember to update all of their records as well. You will want to be sure that either you or your spouse be added to any emergency contact records for the child. Also, be sure that when your name is listed in the child's record it is the same as the one on your new ID or drivers' license.

✿ Notes

....

....

....

....

....

....

....

....

....

....

....

....

....

....

....

....

....

....

....

....

....

....

....

....

....

CHAPTER 28

Destination Weddings

785. **What are the advantages of having a destination wedding?**

In recent years, destination weddings have enjoyed a tremendous growth in popularity. Couples are realizing that the time, effort and expense of planning a wedding and a honeymoon can be too much and decide to combine them to create the perfect destination wedding. A five-day extended wedding weekend at a lovely beach resort can also be considerably cheaper than a reception and wedding for 200 guests at a luxury hotel in your preferred city or town. It is also a wonderful opportunity for friends and family to take a vacation while celebrating your happy union. These days, more brides and grooms are paying for their own weddings and finding it a huge expense. Then they must scale back on guest lists or skimp in other areas of the wedding, perhaps not ending up with the dream wedding they envisioned. You can save a considerable amount of money by having a destination wedding. It's also about quality time spent together, as you and your fiancé are surrounded by your closest friends and family, making it a wedding — and trip — to remember.

786. **Should we provide welcome gift bags for guests when they arrive at their hotel at our destination wedding?**

It is a nice gesture to place welcome gift bags in their hotel rooms, if budget permits. Include something small and useful, such a map of the area and list of things to do, a bottle of sunscreen for a beach destination, or a CD of good music.

787. **Are we obligated to pay for our attendants' accommodations?**

You are not obligated to pay for your attendants' accommodations; however, you may consider it as a loving gesture if budget permits.

788. **Should we provide breakfast or brunch for our guests the day after our destination wedding?**

It is not required, but a nice gesture to host a day-after breakfast or brunch for guests who have traveled a long way to attend your wedding. This is a change to thank them for coming and to spend a little extra time with them.

789. What are the most popular destinations for out-of-town weddings?

- Las Vegas
- Hawaii
- U.S. Virgin Islands
- Jamaica
- Bahamas

790. Some close family members say they can't attend our destination wedding because of expense. Am I wrong to feel hurt?

Unfortunately, having a destination wedding means you must assume some people won't be able to attend because of time and money constraints. If you want your loved ones to celebrate with you, and they can't attend the wedding, host a party when you return.

791. Do we need travelers' health insurance coverage?

If your health insurance policy does not cover you abroad, consider acquiring a temporary health insurance policy. Travel agencies, health insurance companies, travelers' check companies, and your local phone book should be able to provide names of relevant companies for you. In addition to health insurance coverage, many policy packages also include protection in case of trip cancellation and baggage loss.

Keep prescription medications in their original pharmacy containers with the original labels. Bring a copy of your prescriptions and note the drug's generic name. You may consider getting a letter from your physician warranting your need for the medication.

✿ Notes

....

....

....

....

....

....

....

....

....

....

....

....

....

....

....

....

....

....

....

....

....

....

....

CHAPTER 29

Honeymoon Planning

792. How do we create a budget for our honeymoon?

You want your honeymoon to give you luxurious experiences and priceless memories. But you don't want to return from your vacation faced with debts and unnecessary feelings of guilt for not having stayed within a reasonable budget. This should be the vacation of a lifetime. You can make this trip into anything your imagination allows. Pay attention to which experiences or details you would consider a "must have" and prioritize from there. As you work with your budget, stay focused on those top priority items and allow less "elaborate" solutions for lower priority items. If you stay true to your most important vacation objectives, the minor sacrifices along the way will barely be noticed. Perhaps, at this point, you don't know how many days your honeymoon will last. Often, the number of days you'll vacation depends on the type of honeymoon you choose. If you (and your travel agent) are designing your own honeymoon, the typical cost-per-day will most likely determine your length of stay. If you opt for a cruise or another type of prearranged vacation, your length of stay will probably be dependent upon the designated length of the travel package. By determining a basic, overall budget at the start, you will know what your limits are. Yes, this is a very romantic time, but try to remain realistic! Once you have an idea of your spending limits, your choices will be much easier to make.

793. What are the most popular honeymoon destinations?

· Hawaii
· Jamaica
· Mexico
· Tahiti
· St. Lucia
· Italy
· U.S. Virgin Islands
· Aruba
· Las Vegas
· Bermuda

794. What are the most affordable honeymoon destinations?

· Mexico
· Las Vegas
· Florida
· Jamaica
· Dominican Republic

- Bahamas
- California
- Hawaii
- Canada
- Poconos

795. When should we start planning our honeymoon?
Four to six months before the wedding.

796. When should I confirm all my honeymoon reservations?
Two to six weeks before the wedding.

797. Who plans the honeymoon?
The honeymoon is traditionally the groom's responsibility. However, the planning of your honeymoon should be a joint decision as to where to go, how long to stay, and how much money to spend.

798. Who pays for the honeymoon?
Traditionally, the groom paid for the honeymoon, but as these trips get more extravagant and expensive it has become common for the couple to pay for it together. Many couples will also set up a honeymoon registry before the wedding so guests can help contribute to the cost of the honeymoon instead of giving traditional gifts.

799. When should we start planning the honeymoon?
Start planning your honeymoon about six months before the wedding. Many locations that are popular with honeymooners tend to book fairly quickly, so the earlier you plan your trip, the better values you'll usually find. There are many choices to make and many plans to be made but most of them seem to fall into place once you've made the toughest decision ... where to go.

800. Do we have to leave for our honeymoon immediately after the wedding, or can we wait?
You can take your honeymoon at any time, and many couples do elect to wait because of money, time off from work, or other issues.

801. What can we expect from a honeymoon on a cruise?
Cruises are a popular retreat for those who want the luxury of a hospitable resort with the added benefit of visiting one

or more new areas. There are hundreds of different cruise options available to you. Typically, almost everything is included in the cost of your cruise: extravagant dining, unlimited group and individual activities, relaxing days and lively nights. Certain things may not be included in the price, such as alcohol, sodas, excursions, special dinners, spa treatments, and wellness classes — so be sure to check with the cruise line. Request a helpful publication entitled Answers to Your Most Frequently Asked Questions, published by Cruise Lines International Association, (754) 224-2200, www.cruising.org.

802. What is included in the cost of a cruise?
Even though most everything is included in your cost, be sure to ask about those items that may not be included (alcoholic beverages, sundries, spa treatments and tips generally are not included).

803. How much does a cruise cost?
Costs vary greatly depending on the location the cruise will visit (if any) and your cabin accommodations. Locations range from traveling the Mississippi River to encircling the Greek Isles. Spend some time choosing your cabin. Most of them are small, but pay attention to distracting things, such as noisy areas and busy pathways, that might be located close by. Even though most everything is included in your cost, be sure to ask and clarify which items may or may not be included.

804. What can we expect if we go to an all-inclusive resort for our honeymoon?
"All-inclusive" means that, in addition to room and board, all meals, drinks, tour fees, and other excursions are included in your price. One way of considering if this is a good option for you is to list all of the activities that the vacation package offers that you are interested in. Add up the individual costs and compare. If you won't be participating in many activities, food, and drink, you may actually save money by arranging your own trip at an independent resort. However, if you are interested in activities such as boat trips, island tours, water sports, and more, an all-inclusive package is a great option. You can enjoy as many excursions as you like without paying any extra fees. Many all-inclusive resorts

will also offer nice perks with your package, such as rounds of golf, spa treatments, or a bottle of champagne. Be sure to ask about the special extras just for honeymooners.

805. What is the benefit of going to an all-inclusive resort for our honeymoon?

Many newlyweds, tired from the previous months of wedding planning and accompanying stress, opt for the convenience and worry-free guarantee of an all-inclusive resort. All-inclusive means everything is included in your package, so you won't have to worry about meals, drinks, excursion fees or even tips. Some resorts are for the entire family, some are for couples only, and some are strictly for honeymooners. Most of these resorts are nestled on a picturesque island beach catering to your relaxation needs, making them perfect honeymoon destinations.

806. What do all-inclusive resorts offer us on our honeymoon?

Most all-inclusive resorts offer numerous water activities, daily excursions in the area, nightly concerts and entertainment, casinos, golf, luxury spa treatments, fine dining, and exceptional service and attention. Many rooms also cater to honeymooners with complimentary extras, such as in-room Jacuzzis, flowers, champagne, and more. Your costs will vary depending on the location and type of room you choose. With the exception of Hawaii, most popular honeymoon destinations offer a wide variety of these types of resorts.

807. What are some various options we have for our honeymoon?

Many people have a preconceived notion of where a honeymoon should take place. And indeed, certain locations are, year after year, frequently visited by newlyweds. Think about what you and your fiancé might find appealing (and also unappealing) in a vacation. It is all up to the bride and groom, depending on where they want to go and what they want to do, but we've compiled just a few fun ideas:

- Enjoying the beaches and unique treasures of the Hawaiian islands
- Exploring Northern California's romantic wine country
- Ski and snowboard package getaways in Vermont, New Hampshire, Colorado, and Northern California
- Camping and hiking within beautiful and

    serene National Parks
- Sightseeing, touring, and exploring a variety of points in Europe via the rail system
- Island hopping on a cruise ship around the Greek Isles
- Enjoying an exciting and adventurous journey on the Orient Express

808. **What are some less traditional honeymoons we can take?**
- Bicycling in Nova Scotia while relaxing at quaint bed and breakfast inns
- Participating in a white water river rafting expedition
- Mingling with the owners and fellow guests on an Old West Dude Ranch
- Visiting landmarks and parks while enjoying the convenience of a traveling home in a rented RV
- Mustering up the courage and stamina for an aggressive hiking tour of the Canadian Rockies
- Training for and participating in a dog sled race in the brisk tundra of Alaska
- Roughing it while enjoying the splendor of a safari in East Africa

809. **How do we choose a destination for our honeymoon?**
Maybe your idea of a perfect honeymoon is ten days of adventure and discovery; but for your fiancé, it may be ten days of resting in a beach chair and romantic strolls in the evening. The choices for honeymoon vacations are as varied as the bride and groom themselves. Deciding together on a honeymoon destination is a wonderful opportunity to discover more about each other and negotiate a vacation that will leave both of you relaxed, fulfilled, and even more in love. First, determine the type of atmosphere and climate you prefer. Then consider the types of activities you would like to engage in. Do you want the weather to be hot for swimming at the beach, warm for guided tours, cooler for day-long hikes in the woods, or cold for optimum skiing conditions? Keep in mind the time of year in which your wedding falls. Will you be escaping from extreme temperatures? If you have a specific destination in mind, you (or your travel agent) will need to do some research to be sure the weather conditions will be suitable for your planned activities. Note what you feel are the pros and cons of each type of vacation. The two of you should have lots of images and possibilities

in your mind at this point! The next step is to determine the most perfect atmosphere to provide the setting for your honeymoon. Once you've made a list of all the things you desire from your honeymoon, you can choose your location!

810. **Should I hire a travel agent to help plan my honeymoon?**
Hiring the services of a good travel agent will take a lot of unnecessary pressure off of you. In the past, you may have felt you did not need the assistance of a travel agent when planning a vacation. Planning a honeymoon, however, can often be far more involved and stressful than a "regular" vacation, due to the simple fact that you are also deeply enmeshed in the planning of your wedding! Therefore, you should take advantage of the professional resources available to you when working out the small details and finding the best values. Keep in mind, though, that you will still probably want to do some research on your own, ask for second opinions, and, most of all, read the fine print. Since a travel agent can become one of your most valuable resources, you will want to consider a few important things when trying to select one. Ask family, friends, and coworkers for personal recommendations (especially from former honeymooners). If you are unable to find an agent through a personal referral, then select a few agencies that are established nearby (from newspapers, phone books, etc.) Next, you will want to make an appointment with an agent or speak to one over the phone. Pay close attention to the following and then make your decision.

811. **How do I choose a travel agent to use to plan my honeymoon?**
Find out if they are a member of the American Society of Travel Agents (ASTA). Additionally, find out if they are also a Certified Travel Counselor (CTC), or possibly a Destination Specialist (DS). Aside from just offering information and arrangements about locations and discounts, a good travel agent should also provide you with information about passports, customs, travel and health insurance, travelers' checks, and any other information important to a traveler.

ASTA: Members of this organization are required to have at least 5 years travel agent experience. They also agree to adhere to strict codes and standards of integrity in travel issues as established by the national society. In most states, there are no formal regulations requiring certain qualifications for being a travel agent. In other words, any person can decide to call him or herself a travel agent.

CTC: Certified Travel Counselors have successfully completed a 2 year program in travel management.

DS: Destination Specialists have successfully completed studies focusing on a particular region of travel.

For a list of ASTA agencies in your area, call or write:
American Society of Travel Agents
Consumer Affairs Department
1101 King Street, Suite 200
Alexandria, VA 22314
(703) 739-2782, www.ASTAnet.com

812. What kind of questions should I ask the travel agent before using him or her to plan my honeymoon?
- How long has the travel agency been in business?
- How long has the travel agent been with the agency?
- How much experience does the travel agent have? Any special studies or travels?
- Do they have a good resource library?
- Does the agent/agency have a variety of brochures to offer?
- Do they have travel DVDs to lend?
- Do they have a recommended reading list of travel aid books?
- Does the agent seem to understand your responses on your wish list and budget?
- Does he or she seem excited to help you?
- Does the agent listen carefully to your ideas? Take notes on your conversations? Ask you questions to ensure a full understanding?
- Is the agent able to offer a variety of different possibilities that suit your interests based on your wish list? Do the suggestions fall within your budget?
- Can the agent relay back to you (in his or her own words) what your wish list priorities are? What your budget priorities are?
- Is the agent prompt in getting back in touch with you?
- Is the agent reasonably quick in coming up with

suggestions and alternatives? Are the suggestions exciting and within reason?
- Does the agent take notes on your interests (degree of sports, leisure, food, etc.)?
- Does the travel agency provide a 24-hour emergency help line?
- Are you documenting your conversations and getting all of your travel plans and reservations confirmed in writing?

813. What other sources can I use to help plan my honeymoon?

National bridal magazines and general travel magazines are a great place to search for honeymoon ideas. But remember, you cannot always believe every word in paid advertising. In addition to the information your travel agent provides, you can also obtain maps, brochures, and other useful items on your own. If you have Internet access, you can acquire volumes and volumes of information and titillating pictures about your possible destinations. You can even chat with fellow soon-to-be honeymooners or recent honeymooners about their experiences. Local libraries often provide limited free time and user-assistance for their members. Your local library, the travel section of bookstores, and travel stores are also excellent sources for finding information and tips relevant to your travel needs. You will find books on traveling in general as well as books specific to the region or destination you will be visiting. There are numerous tour books, maps, language books and tapes, as well as books about a location's culture, traditions, customs, climate, and geography. These books are a great source of information since they are independent from the locations they describe and are therefore impartial, objective, and usually contain correct, unbiased information. You can also find books and other resources describing (and sometimes rating) restaurants, hotels, shows, and tours. Books on bargain hunting and finding the best deals are common as well.

814. What should we pack on our honeymoon?

The following is a list of the carry-on items you may want to consider packing when you leave on your honeymoon:
- Travelers' first aid kit
- Wallet (credit cards, traveler's checks)

- Jewelry and other sentimental and valuable items that you feel you must bring
- Identification (Passport, Drivers' License or Photo ID)
- Photocopies of the following important documents:
- Hotel/resort street address, phone number, written confirmation of arrangements and reservations
- Complete travel itinerary
- Airline tickets
- Name, address and phone number of emergency contact person(s) back home
- Medicine prescriptions (including generic names) and eyeglass prescription information (or an extra pair); list of food and drug allergies
- Phone numbers (including after-hour emergency phone numbers) for health insurance company and personal physicians
- Copy of your packing list. If a piece of your luggage gets lost, you will know the contents that are missing.
- List of your travelers checks' serial numbers and 24 hour phone number for reporting loss or theft
- Phone numbers to the local U.S. embassy or consulate
- Any "essential" toiletries and one complete casual outfit in case checked baggage is delayed or lost
- Foreign language dictionary or translator
- Camera with film loaded
- Maps
- Small bills/change (in U.S. dollars and in the appropriate foreign currency) for tipping
- Currency converter chart or pocket calculator
- Reading material
- Eyeglasses
- Contact lenses
- Contact lens cleaner
- Sunglasses
- Kleenex, gum, breath mints and any over-the-counter medicine to ease travel discomfort
- Inflatable neck pillow (for lengthy travel)
- Address book and thank you notes (in case you have lots of traveling time)
- Your budget sheet

815. What should we pack in our checked baggage for our honeymoon?

Casual Wear:
- Shorts
- Pants
- Tops
- Jackets/sweaters
- Sweatshirts/sweatsuits
- Belts
- Socks
- Underwear/panties & bras
- Walking shoes/sandals/loafers
- Athletic Wear
- Shorts
- Sweatpants
- Tops
- Sweatshirts/jackets
- Swim suits, swim suit cover-up
- Aerobic activity outfits
- Athletic equipment
- Socks
- Underwear/panties & exercise bras
- Tennis/athletic shoes

Evening Wear:
- Pants or pants/skirts/dresses
- Belts
- Dress shirts/blouses
- Sweaters
- Jackets/blazers/ties
- Socks or pantyhose/slips
- Underwear/panties & bras
- Accessories/jewelry
- Shoes

Other Clothing Items:
- Pajamas
- Lingerie
- Slippers
- Robe

Miscellaneous Items:
- An additional set of the important document photo copies as packed in your carry on bag

- Travel tour books, Tourism Bureau Information
- Journal
- Special honeymoon gift for your new spouse
- Any romantic items or favorite accessories
- Camera charger, extra camera batteries or film
- Plastic bags for dirty laundry
- Large plastic or nylon tote bag for bringing home new purchases
- Small sewing kit and safety pins
- Travel alarm clock
- Travel iron, lint brush
- Compact umbrella, Fold-up rain slickers
- Video camera

816. **What information do I need to leave with a trusted contact person when we leave on our honeymoon?**

You should leave the following with a trusted contact person while you and your spouse are on your honeymoon:

- Photocopy of all travel details (complete itineraries, names, addresses, and telephone numbers)
- Photocopy of credit cards along with 24-hour telephone number to report loss or theft. (Be sure to get the number to call when traveling abroad. It will be a different number than their U.S. 1-800 number.)
- Photocopy of travelers checks along with 24-hour telephone number to report loss or theft
- Photocopy of passport identification page, along with date and place of issuance
- Photocopy of drivers license
- Any irreplaceable items

817. **How can we make sure our honeymoon plans run smoothly?**

Use the expert knowledge of a travel agent, and research, research, research your destination. Travel agents have relationships with hotels and vendors and can help you get great deals and upgrades. They also have extensive knowledge of the area you're thinking of, so you don't end up honeymooning in the tropics during hurricane season, for instance. Use a travel agent and you'll have fewer surprises. You'll also want to do a lot of research yourself. Read reviews and blogs about resorts you're interested in, from several different sites. Also, check travel sites for weather and updates about the city you're heading to. If you're traveling abroad, be sure your passport is up to date. Lastly, make sure you get all the proper shots and medications to prevent illness. By doing all that, you're well on your way to having an incredible honeymoon.

818. **Do we tip while we are on our honeymoon?**

Tipping customs vary from country to country. It is advisable to inquire about tipping with the international tourism board representing the country you'll be traveling in. Simply ask for information about tipping customs and social expectations. You will also want to discuss gratuities with your travel agent or planner. Some travel packages include gratuities in the total cost, some leave that to the guests, and some even discourage tipping (usually because they have built it into the total package price). Be sure to discuss this with your travel planner.

819. **What do we need to know if we are honeymooning internationally?**

There are over 250 U.S. embassies and consulates around the world. After contacting the Tourism Bureau for the area you will be traveling to, it is also a wise idea to contact the U.S. Embassy or Consulate for that region. With assistance from both of these sources you will be able to determine the travel requirements and recommendations for your chosen travel destination. Call for a list of U.S. embassy and consulate locations with emergency phone numbers: (202) 647-5225 or visit http://travel.state.gov.

820. **What do we need to know about passports and visas when traveling abroad?**

Your travel agent should be able to provide you with information to adequately prepare you for your international travels. Additional information (and possibly more detailed and current information) can be obtained by contacting the appropriate sources listed in this section. As a U.S. citizen, you generally need a passport to enter and to depart most foreign countries and to reenter the United States. Some countries also require Visas. A Visa is an endorsement by officials of a foreign country as permission to visit their country. You first need a passport in order to obtain a Visa.

Inquire with the resources listed in this section for requirements of your specific destination. As mentioned, you will be required to prove your U.S. citizenship upon reentry to the United States. If the country of your destination does not require you to possess a current passport, you will still need to produce proof of citizenship for U.S. Immigration.

Items that are acceptable as proof of citizenship include a passport, a certified copy of your birth certificate, Certificate of Nationalization, a Certificate of Citizenship, or a Report of Birth Abroad of a Citizen of the United States. Proof of identification can include a drivers' license or a government or military identification card containing a photo or physical description.

821. Should the bride have her passport in her maiden name or new husband's name?

The bride should have her passport and airline tickets reflect her maiden name for ease in proof of identification while traveling. Name changes can be processed after returning from the honeymoon with your marriage certificate.

822. What do we do if our passports are lost or stolen?

Contact the local U.S. Embassy immediately if your passport becomes lost or stolen. Have a photocopy of your passport's data page, date and place of issuance, and passport number to be kept with a contact person at home. You should also travel with a set of these photocopies in addition to an extra set of loose passport photos for speed in attaining a replacement. Passports can be obtained from one of the 13 U.S. Passport Agencies or one of the thousands of authorized passport locations, such as state and federal courts as well as some U.S. post offices. Additional, and very helpful, official information for U.S. citizens regarding international travel can be found at http://travel.state.gov.

823. What health concerns do we need to be aware of before traveling abroad on our honeymoon?

Your travel agent should be fully informed about current conditions and health requirements. Your personal physician should also be able to provide you with health-related information and advice for traveling in the region you visit.

CHAPTER 30

Destination Weddings or Honeymoons in North America

824. I want to have a destination wedding or honeymoon in
California. Can you tell me about this destination?
Ten reasons to visit and fall in love with California:
1. Three drive-through redwood trees along Highway 101
between Laytonville and Klamath.
2. A herd of 400 buffalo on Catalina Island.
3. 700 wineries (and counting).
4. 90 types of mammals in Sequoia and Kings Canyon
National Parks, including 10 kinds of bats.
5. Romantic, organic architecture of the Post Ranch
Inn, with dramatic views of the famous Big Sur coastline.
6. 45 snow resorts offering downhill and cross country
skiing, snowboarding and more.
7. World's tallest living tree (367.5 feet).
8. 2,425 feet of falling water at Yosemite Falls, the longest
drop in the United States.
9. Huntington Beach, 8.5 miles of uninterrupted strands of
pristine beach.
10. 20 million acres of national forest.

825. Can I find out more local information about California as
a potential destination wedding or honeymoon location?
California is so large that it has a wide variety of climate
zones. Southern California tends to be temperate and warm
year-round, though it can be rainy on and off from October
to June. Near the coast in Northern California, it can be
chilly, even during the summer. Inland, in the mountains,
expect seasons as visitors will find in the rest of the country,
snowy in the winter and hot during the summer.

Peak Season: California is popular year-round due to its
beautiful weather, though it tends to be busiest in the
summer when other parts of the country get too hot.

Standard Time Zone: UTC (Coordinated Universal Time/
GMT (Greenwich Mean Time) — 8 hours: PST — Pacific
Standard Time.

For more information, contact: California Tourism;
Telephone: 916-444-4429; Website: www.visitcalifornia.com

826. I want to have a destination wedding or honeymoon in
Florida. Can you tell me about this destination?
No matter what a visitor's interests, they will find an

attraction in Florida to enjoy. Mouse ears and the major theme parks of the Orlando area are what first come to mind as Florida attractions, but they are only the beginning. Wildlife and botanical attractions are among the most popular and include both large parks and zoos and small private gardens. Florida's rich history is reflected in museums, monuments, forts and homes throughout the state. For a cultural excursion, fine art museums have works from Dali to Rubens, sculpture and architecture by names such as Frank Lloyd Wright.

Secluded hideaways and lively, bustling cities are perfect for a honeymoon or destination wedding. Florida has beautiful white-sand beaches, historic mansions, old-fashioned paddleboats and many other beautiful places to set the stage for romance.

827. Can I find out more local information about Florida as a potential destination wedding or honeymoon location?

Florida's temperature varies depending on whether visitors are in the southern or northern areas of the state. In northern and central Florida, from November through March, they can expect temperatures to be in the low forties to the high-60s and low-70s. The rest of the year, temperatures will generally fall from the mid-60s to the low-90s. In southern Florida, from December through March, expect mid- to high-50s to mid-70s and the remainder of the year, mid-70s to low-90s. It tends to be very humid year-round but especially in summer months.

Peak Season: Florida is popular year-round, though it peaks during the winter, as it remains temperate while the rest of the east coast grows very cold.

Standard Time Zone: UTC (Coordinated Universal Time/ GMT (Greenwich Mean Time) — 5 hours: EST (Eastern Standard Time)

For more information, contact: Visit Florida; Telephone: 850-488-5607; Website: www.flausa.com

828. I want to have a destination wedding or honeymoon in Las Vegas. Can you tell me about this destination?

The Entertainment Capital of the World, Las Vegas'

entertainment scene offers a lineup of award-winning magicians, Broadway-caliber productions, world-renowned concert headliners and unique-to-Vegas production shows. Nevada law permits a wide variety of gaming, including traditional card and dice games, race and sports books, slot machines, cashless slot machines, high-tech electronic gambling devices, and international games of chance originating in Europe and Asia.

On average, 150 couples tie the knot each day in Las Vegas. From formal black tie affairs to renewing vows in front of a rhinestone-studded Elvis impersonator to cruising through a 24-hour drive-through chapel, with more than 100,000 couples obtaining licenses each year, Las Vegas is the marriage capital of the world.

829. What is the shopping like in Las Vegas if we go there for our destination wedding or honeymoon?

The Forum Shops at Caesar's Palace has 110 shops and restaurants including Versace, Gucci, Escada, Valentino, Juicy Couture, Armani, Burberry, Fendi, Christian Dior, FAO Schwartz, and many more.

830. Can I find out more local information about Las Vegas as a potential destination wedding or honeymoon location?

Las Vegas weather tends to be hottest in June, July and August with temperatures soaring above 100 degrees. It may not feel as hot due to very low humidity however, it is important to remember to drink plenty of water and wear sun protection outdoors. At night, them temperature will drop considerably, most notably in winter. Rain is not common although July and August hold threats of severe thunderstorms and flash floods. Winters are mild with snow fall virtually non-existent.

Peak Season: Las Vegas is located in the desert where the summers are hot and the winters are cool, making spring and fall the best times to visit.

Standard Time Zone: UTC (Coordinated Universal Time/ GMT (Greenwich Mean Time) — 8 hours: PST — Pacific Standard Time

For more information, contact: Las Vegas Visitor

Information Center, 3150 Paradise Road, Las Vegas, NV 89109-9096; Telephone: (702) 892-7575; Website: www. vegasfreedom.com

831. I want to have a destination wedding or honeymoon in Mexico. Can you tell me about this destination?

The country's enormous cultural and natural diversity means that it has something to offer newlyweds from anywhere in the world, from those seeking privacy and beautiful surroundings to those who would like to explore some of the country's cultural and natural attractions.

· The climate varies from tropical to desert
· Approximate population: 106,202,900
· Capital: Mexico City
· Currency: Mexican Peso (MXN)

832. What are our destination wedding options in Mexico?

Getting married in Mexico is becoming more and more popular, as it has a multitude of locations and options to offer. Be sure to note that only civil marriages are legal in Mexico; you can have a religious ceremony, but it will have no affect on the legality of the marriage.

Beach Weddings: There are tons of beaches on which you can marry in Mexico, from Los Cabos to Cancun, Playa del Carmen to Acapulco. The choices are limitless. You can go through a wedding coordinator who specializes in or offers packages for beach weddings or through a resort on whose beach you can marry, provided you are staying at that resort. The beaches of Mexico are stunning and provide the perfect setting for a romantic and unique wedding.

Resort Weddings: Resorts are everywhere in Mexico and usually offer spectacular and luxurious accommodations, as well as wedding packages and coordinators that help plan the wedding from start to finish. Below are a handful of resorts and hotels that are popular locations to stay:

· Club Cascadas de Baja
· Fiesta Americana Grand Aqua
· Acapulco Princess
· One&Only Palmilla
· Iberostar Playa Paraiso, Cozumel and Playa del Carmen
· Club Med Cancun and Ixtapa
· Secrets Riviera Cancun

- Dreams Cancun, Los Cabos and Puerto Vallarta
- Riu Cabo San Lucas, Riviera Maya, Cancun and Puerto Vallarta
- SolMelia Cancun, San Lucas, Cabo Real, Cozumel, Turquesa and Puerto Vallarta
- Sunscape Riviera Maya and Puerto Aventuras
- Palace Resorts Cancun

Church Weddings: Many faiths and religions are represented in Mexico, so you should have no trouble locating a chapel, synagogue or mosque in which to marry. To be married in a church, your local parish priest needs to sign a statement of Freedom to Marry, as well as a statement that asserts that you and your fiancé have undergone and completed premarital counseling. As stated before, however, religious weddings have no affect on the legality of the marriage, so you must still be married by a Justice of the Peace if you want a ceremony in a church.

833. What is the nightlife like in Mexico?
Acapulco's nightlife has something for everyone, and its illuminated glass porches are now legendary. The discotheque, dance halls, and bars are designed for all sorts of people wishing to have a good time. Many of these establishments have a panoramic view of the bay.

Nightlife in Cancún is intense and goes on until dawn in its many discotheque and nightclubs. Visitors will find all kinds of music there as well as the finest Mexican and imported drinks. The bars are very entertaining and the waiters make sure there's always a lively atmosphere. Boats offering dinner with music and an open bar cruise around the bay and Laguna Nichupté.

Los Cabos boasts a variety of nightlife, particularly in La Concepción, north of the Marina. Popular venues include Squid Roe, a dance club, and Kokomo's, a contemporary music bar on the Boulevard Marina.

834. What is the dining like in Mexico?
Whether visitors are at a lively beachfront eatery along the boardwalk, a romantic hilltop restaurant, or one of the leading hotels, dining in Mexico is a memorable experience. Even the most modest restaurant can offer fresh-from-the-

sea fish and shellfish grilled to perfection, accompanied by ice-cold chelada — beer and lemon juice on ice, served in a salt-rimmed glass. Mexican specialties include ceviche — fish or shellfish marinated in lime juice and mixed with onion, tomato and cilantro.

835. What is the shopping like in Mexico?

Mexico has modern shopping centers with all types of shops and boutiques. Visitors can find costume jewelry, silver, leather goods, perfumes and souvenirs made from seashells. You can always find a great deal if you barter with sellers.

836. What are our accommodation options in Mexico if we go there for our destination wedding or honeymoon?

- Boca Chica
- Camino Real Acapulco Diamante
- Camino Real Cancun
- Casa del Mar Golf Resort & Spa
- Casa Natalia
- Casa Terra Cotta
- Esperanza
- Fairmont Acapulco Princess
- Fiesta Americana Condesa Acapulco
- Hilton Cancun Beach & Golf Resort
- Hotel Cabo San Lucas
- Hotel El Rey del Caribe
- Hotel Los Flamigos
- JW Marriott Cancun Resort & Spa
- Las Brisas
- Las Ventanas al Paraiso
- Le Meridien Cancun Resort & Spa
- Ritz-Carlton Cancun
- Sun Palace
- Twin Dolphin
- Villa Vera Hotel & Raquet Club

837. Can I find out more local information about Mexico as a potential destination wedding or honeymoon location?

Climate: From May through October, Mexico has a rainy period, with hurricane season lasting through the summer. Peak Season: Mid-December through April.

Language: Spanish, though English is sometimes spoken in touristy areas. Don't fear attempting to speak Spanish.

Currency: Mexican Pesos — MXN.

Standard Time Zone: UTC (Coordinated Universal Time/
GMT (Greenwich Mean Time) —6 hours: CST Central
Standard Time

For more information, contact: Mexico Tourism Board,
Telephone (From US): 800-446-3942 or 305-347-4338;
Website: www.visitmexico.com

838. What are the marriage requirements for Mexico?
All Mexican civil marriages are automatically valid in
the United States, but you may want to call ahead to your
specific destination to be sure you are following the rules
for that particular city and state. A religious ceremony can
be had, but it isn't considered official. Your hotel can often
arrange for a professional wedding planner to assist you with
your preparations. It typically requires two to four days in
Mexico to complete the arrangements, though having the
assistance of a coordinator may shorten this. Foreigners
wishing to get married in Mexico must submit the following
documents to the appropriate Mexican Registry Office, at
least two days before the intended date of the ceremony.

All foreign documents listed must be "apostilled," or
legalized in their country of origin and translated into
Spanish by a registered translator in Mexico:
  · Current passports
  · Certified copies of birth certificates
  · Tourist cards or visas
  · Names, addresses, nationalities, occupations and ages of
    both parties' parents
  · Health certificates and blood tests performed in Mexico
  · Four witnesses (each must have a photo id)

If either you or your fiancé has previously been married, you
will also need verification that at least a year has passed from
the date of your divorce or the death of your spouse in the
form of a certified copy of the divorce decree or a certified
copy of the spouse's death certificate.

839. What are our destination wedding options in Canada?

You can get married in a variety of locations in Canada, from the beautiful shores of Vancouver Island to the edge of Niagara Falls. Canada is a stunning country and you will not be disappointed no matter where you choose to marry.

Beach Weddings: Weddings on the beach are more rare in Canada than the Caribbean or South Pacific, but no less memorable or lovely. The shores of Vancouver Island or Prince Edward Island beckon for weddings, where you can be surrounded by dense forests with a splendid mountain in the backdrop. You can also be married lakeside, on a sandy beach before a sparkling mountain lake.

Resort/Villa Weddings: Resorts and villas are abundant in Canada and there's no lack of options for you in terms of marrying at one of these luxurious and elegant locations. It is relatively easy for you and your fiancé to marry in Canada, so you have a wide variety of options to choose from, including resorts in the mountains to resorts on the beach or on a small, forested island. Below we've listed a few popular resorts and places to stay:

- Fairmont Chateau Lake Louise
- The Keltic Lodge
- The Aerie
- Langdon Hall Country House Hotel
- Delta Chelsea
- The Wickaninnish Inn
- Le Chateau Frontenac

Niagara Falls Weddings: What could be better than getting married by one of the nation's most spectacular natural creations? Niagara and Horseshoe Falls are stunning sights and many wedding coordinators will help you in planning your dream wedding at either of these sites. You can marry in a beautiful garden beside the falls, in front of the falls, aboard the Maid of the Mist or atop the Minolta Tower. Some non-denominational ministers will also offer their services for these weddings.

Church Weddings: Roman Catholicism and Protestantism are the two most dominant religions in Canada, but many, many others are equally represented. You can find chapels, churches or other houses of worship.

840. What are the marriage requirements for Canada?

It is indeed possible for foreign visitors to get married in Québec. First, you must complete and file the Marriage Civil form along with your two original birth certificates. The future married couple will be summoned to an interview at which time the date of the marriage will be determined. Additional information is available at the courthouses or by visiting the Ministry of Justice's website, www.justice.gouv.qc.ca/english/accueil.asp.

CHAPTER 31

Destination Weddings or Honeymoons in Europe

841. **I want to have a destination wedding or honeymoon in Italy. Can you tell me about this destination?**

Italy is geographically divided into 20 regions. Of these regions, three of the most popular destinations with romantic travelers are Veneto (home to Venice) and Latium (home to Rome), and Tuscany (home to Florence).

Fast Facts:
- A democratic republic replaced the monarchy in 1946
- The climate is mainly Mediterranean
- Approximate population: 58,103,000
- The official language is Italian
- Capital: Rome
- Currency: Euro (EUR)

842. **What is the nightlife like in Italy?**

Night spots will generally fall into three categories. The "osterie musicali" offer full meals, cicheti (little savory snacks), beer, inexpensive wine, and live music. Many of them also serve as galleries for local artists. Then there are the English and Irish style pubs, with beer on tap and occasional live music. These pubs tend to be especially popular with the younger crowd. Finally, there are the late-night cafes and piano bars that offer more late-night enjoyment.

843. **What is the dining like in Italy?**

The cuisine of Venice is based on fish and seafood. A classic first course here and elsewhere in the Veneto region is pasta e fagioli (thick bean soup with pasta). Roman cooking is predominantly simple; dishes rarely have more than a few ingredients, and meat and fish are most often baked or grilled. The typical Roman fresh pasta is fettuccine, golden egg noodles at their best with ragù, a rich tomato and meat sauce. One of the great joys of a meal in Italy is that most restaurants will not rush diners out. Service is relaxed and the bill will not be brought until a visitor asks for it. A rustic-looking spot that calls itself an osteria may turn out to be chic and anything but cheap. Generally speaking, however, a trattoria is a family-run place, simpler in decor, cuisine, and service — and slightly less expensive — than a ristorante.

844. **What is the shopping like in Italy?**

There are jewelers, antiques dealers, and high-fashion

boutiques. The best buys here are still leather goods of all kinds and silk goods and knitwear. Boutique fashions may be slightly less expensive in Italy than in the United States. Some worthy old prints and minor antiques can be found in the city's interesting little shops, and full-fledged collectors can rely on the prestigious reputations of some of Italy's top antiques dealers. Shops still stock pottery and handwoven textiles made in Italy.

845. What are our accommodation options in Italy?

Moderately priced hotels and accommodations in Rome and Venice can bring a variety of amenities with them. As a general rule, you will have to be willing to pay more for a bathroom en suite or other such comforts or luxuries. The prospect of opening a window and seeing the Grand Canal in Venice or the dome of St. Peter of Rome is everywhere, so you will have a multitude of options.

- Abbazia
- Alimandi
- American
- Casa Verardo
- Cavalieri Hilton
- Colombina
- Danieli
- Giuliana
- Grand Hotel de la Minerve
- Hotel Art
- Hotel des Bains
- Hotel Eden
- Hotel Raphael
- Hotel Scalinata di Spagna
- Istituto San Giuseppe
- Luna Hotel Baglioni
- Pensione Guerrato
- St. Regis Grand

846. Can I find out more local information about Italy as a potential destination wedding or honeymoon location?

Climate: Thanks to the moderating influence of the sea as well as the protection from the cold north winds given by the Alpine barrier from the cold north join together to bless Italy with a temperate climate. Nevertheless, the weather in any given area can vary considerably based on how far one is from the sea or the mountains. Typically, it is warm all over

Italy in summer. The high temperatures begin in Rome in May, often lasting until sometime in October. Winters in the northern part of Italy are cold, with rain and snow, but in the south the weather is warm all year, even in winter.

Peak Season: In general, April/May/June and September/ October are the best times to travel to Italy. Temperatures are comfortable and the tourist crowds are not too bad. July and August mark the busiest tourist time, even though temperatures are hotter and the air is muggier. In August, many Italians are on holiday resulting in many hotels, restaurants and shops being closed.

Language: Italian is the language of the majority of the population but there are minorities speaking German, French, Slovene and Ladino.

Currency: The Euro - EUR is the official form of currency.

Standard Time Zone: UTC (Coordinated Universal Time/ GMT (Greenwich Mean Time) +1 hours: CET (Central European Time)

For more information, contact: Italian Government Tourism Board, 630 Fifth Avenue, Suite 1565, New York, NY 10111; Telephone (From US): 212-245-5618; Website: www. italiantourism.com

847. What are the marriage requirements for Italy?

U.S. citizens to be married in Italy must present the following documents:

· Passports
· Certified copies of each Birth certificate. A translation (certified by a Consular Officer) of each document into Italian is required as well as its Apostille. An Apostille is a seal affixed to a public record by the Secretary of State Notary Public of the State where the document was originated.
· If applicable, Final Divorce Decree, Annulment Decree or Death Certificate of previous spouse. A translation of each document into Italian is required as well as its Apostille.
· If under 18, sworn statement by parents or legal guardian consenting to the marriage. A translation of each

document into Italian is required as well as its Apostille.

- To be legal in Italy, the translated documents must be given the Apostille Stamp by the Secretary of State in the state where each document was originally issued.
- Obtain an Atto Notorio from an Italian Consul in the United States. This is a declaration that according to U.S. laws there is no obstacle to the marriage, and it must be sworn to by two witnesses.

Upon arrival in Italy, you will need to schedule appointments for:

- Another Declaration (Nulla Osta), sworn to by the U.S. citizen at the U.S. Consulate in Italy stating that there is no legal impediment to his or her marriage under Italian Law and U.S. Law.
- Legalization of the Nulla Osta must be done by the office of the Prefecture. There is one in every provincial capital.
- A waiver for a woman who has been divorced within the last 300 days must be obtained from the Procura della Republica (District Attorney), issued upon presentation of a medical certificate that she is not pregnant.

Some Registrars require that couples sign a Declaration of Intent to Marry 2 to 4 days before the marriage ceremony, so you should check with the Registrar to be certain. Civil ceremonies can take place in the office of the Registrar, in which case they are conducted in Italian and last about thirty minutes. If you choose to have a Roman Catholic ceremony, it will automatically be registered with the Italian Authorities and thus a civil ceremony is not required. Ceremonies of other religions are not recognized by Italian Authorities, in which case you must have a civil ceremony prior to the religious one.

848. I want to have a destination wedding or honeymoon in Greece. Can you tell me about this destination?

Greece is a series of beautiful islands, where the landscape contains many historic sites and relics; elegant pieces of architecture; world-class museums; ancient ruins, fortresses, castles and monasteries; and so much more. Culturally, visitors will find an area filled with fellow travelers enjoying wondrous sights, sounds and flavors.

Fast Facts:
- In 1974, democratic elections abolished the monarchy and created a parliamentary republic
- The climate is mostly temperate
- Approximate population: 10,668,350
- Greek is the official language
- Capital: Athens
- Currency: Euro (EUR)

849. What is the nightlife like in Greece?

Greece is famous for its lively lifestyle. Visitors will find lots of theatres, cafes, shops, music performances, cinemas, bars, casinos and night clubs. Typically, night clubs open around midnight and don't shut down until dawn. With their nights covered, it is also quite easy to find places for entertainment during the day. Whether with fellow vacationers or seasoned locals, visitors will find something to suit their individual desire for entertainment.

850. What is the dining like in Greece?

Greek cuisine is healthy and delicious, a true reflection of the culture and locally grown produce and seafood. Greek food incorporates many spices and herbs, such as oregano, mint, clove, garlic, onion, and cinnamon. Other common ingredients include lemon, grape leaves, ground lamb, olive oil, figs, honey, feta and other cheeses, and fresh fish.

851. What is the shopping like in Greece?

Greece's rich tradition in hand-woven fabrics, embroideries, wood-carvings and jewelry is readily seen in shops throughout the islands. Visitors should take advantage of all the markets around the island, as well as late-night shopping. During the summer months, most shops stay open until midnight, making for an exciting and different shopping experience.

852. What are our accommodation options in Greece?

We advise you to travel in the early summer or early autumn (U.S. seasons), so there will be fewer tourists.
- Asteras Villas
- Atlantis Hotel
- Atrina Houses
- Casa Delfino
- Doma

- Elounda Beach
- Hotel Fortezza
- Istron Bay
- Lato Hotel
- Louis Creta Princess
- Mare Monte Beach Hotel
- Minos Beach
- Pegasus Suites

853. Can I find out more local information about Greece?

Climate: Greece enjoys mild winters and very hot, dry summers cooled by seasonal breezes, the meltemi, which moderate even the hottest months of July and August. Rainfall is rare during the summer months. Autumn is the mildest season, when temperatures are often higher than in spring. The mountains that run across the island act as a barrier to the weather, often creating different conditions in northern and southern Crete. Santorini is relatively dry and sunny throughout the year, the brightest months from April to October. The summer months can be hot, so advise travelers to visit in the fall or spring.

Language: The primary language spoken in Greece is Greek. English is spoken in hotels, most restaurants, department stores and by the "Tourist Police," who wear a badge on their lapel depicting the English or American flags.

Currency: The official currency of Greece is the Euro - EUR.

Time Zone: UTC (Coordinated Universal Time/GMT (Greenwich Mean Time) +2 hours: EET (Eastern European Time)

For more information, contact: Greek National Tourist Organization, Olympic Tower, 645 Fifth Avenue, 9th Floor, New York, New York 10022; Telephone: (212) 421-5777; Website: http://www.greekembassy.org

854. What are the marriage requirements for Greece?
Foreign nationals in Greece may be married either in a civil ceremony or a religious ceremony; both are recognized as legal under the laws of Greece. Marriage licenses can be obtained from your current place of residence, prior to coming to Greece, and are generally accepted by the Greek

authorities. This only applies, however, if neither you nor your fiancé is a resident of Greece. Valid American Marriage Licenses are accepted in Greece provided that they do not contain restrictive statements (for example: "This license is valid for county X" or "Marriage will take place in the state of California," etc.). If these statements cannot be removed, the license should be amended by the issuing authority to include Greece as one of the places in which the marriage can take place. It is also recommended that the marriage license be endorsed with the Apostle stamp, a special authentication for documents to be used outside the United States and can be obtained from your local State Secretary.

The following documents are required for marriage in Greece:
· A passport or other travel document.
· A certified copy of both parties' birth certificates, along with an official translation. Official translations can be obtained at the Translation Department of the Greek Ministry of Foreign Affairs, 3 Voukour-estious Street, 3rd floor in Athens. The translation may take up to a week to prepare.
· If applicable, documentary evidence (death certificate or final divorce decree) of the termination of a previous marriage (the most recent, if more than one), along with an official translation.
· Confirmation by an American Consular Officer that there is no impediment to the marriage (i.e. neither party is under 18 years of age, there is no existing undissolved marriage, etc.). This confirmation is issued in the form of an Affidavit of Marriage signed under oath by the American citizen bride or groom before a Consular Officer in Athens or Thessaloniki. (For minors under 18 years of age, a court decision approving the marriage is required.) The affidavit must be completed in English and Greek. The Embassy's Notorial Unit and the Consulate General perform Notorial services. The fee for the affidavit is approximately US$10.00.
· A copy of the newspaper in which the wedding notice was published. Wedding notices should be published in one of the local newspapers in the Greek language (the names should be phonetically written in Greek and not in Latin characters) before the application for a marriage license is submitted. In small towns where newspapers are not published, notices are posted by the

mayor or president of the community at the City Hall or Community Office.

· Following the ceremony, the marriage must be registered at the Vital statistics Office (Lixiarcheio). This applies to all marriages, whether civil or religious, and must be done within 40 days following the ceremony. After 40 days, the marriage can only be registered with the payment of revenue stamps. After 90 days, the marriage can only be registered with the District Attorneys' authorization (addressed to the Registrar of the Office of Vital Statistics) and the payment of revenue stamps. Marriages can be registered by either spouse, or by a third party who is in possession of a power-of-attorney signed before a Greek Notary Public giving him/her authority to take all steps necessary to effect registration of the marriage. Marriages that are not registered have no legal validity.

855. I want to have a destination wedding or honeymoon in France. Can you tell me about this destination?

France offers enough diversity in landscape and culture to fill a lifetime of vacations. The landscapes range from the coasts of Brittany to the hills of Provence, the canyons of the Pyrenees to the bays of Corsica, and from the valleys of the Dordogne to the peaks of the Alps. Each region, with its own local culture and style, has its own style of architecture, food, fashion and even its own dialect. Like all the world's greatest capitals, Paris lives at a fast pace, by day and night, and especially at rush hours. It is divided into 20 arrondissements that spiral out like a snail shell from the first, centered around the Louvre, of which certain quarters like the Montmartre, Montparnasse, and the Marais are real villages within the city. Paris is the world capital of art and culture because it has some of the most famous museums and monuments in the world like the Eiffel Tower, the Notre-Dame cathedral, and many more. With its history and architectural patrimony, Paris is living, moving, and evolving every day.

Fast Facts:
· Has been a presidential democracy since 1958
· Is the largest Western European nation
· Approximate population: 60,656,170
· French is the official language

- Capital: Paris
- Currency: Euro (EUR)

856. What is the nightlife like in France?

Nightclubs are everywhere, in the remotest corners of France. Their style and music vary a lot from one place to another, but closing time is fixed at 5 o'clock in the morning.

857. What is the dining like in France?

Throughout France, visitors will find all sorts of restaurants, from simple, small, cozy ones to famous, gourmet restaurants, along with brasseries, inns, and tearooms.

The majority of restaurants serve food from noon to 3 p.m. and from 7 to 11 p.m. Some will welcome visitors even later — larger brasseries and those near to railway stations. In large towns, small grocery shops stay open until midnight. During the day, visitors can eat at any time in sandwich shops, fast-food restaurants, or again in some brasseries.

858. What is the shopping like in France?

Paris is one of the fashion capitals of the world. Go window-shopping at the great couturiers, along the Avenue Montaigne. Paris has many and various markets: the flower market on the Ile de la Cité, bird markets, organic markets, and food markets in every quarter. A real walkabout in a good natured and typical Parisian atmosphere! In the Regions, the town centre often has a number of clothes shops which are just as good as those in Paris. Every town or village in the different regions also has their weekly market; here visitors will find lots of regional products.

859. What are our accommodation options in France?

Paris has many eclectic and beautiful neighborhoods where you can choose to stay. Make sure you know something about the areas of Paris, including the differences between the Left Bank and Right Bank, so you'll be able to know what you're looking for.
- Ermitage Hotel
- Four Seasons Hotel George V
- Grand Hotel Jeanne d'Arc
- Hotel Balzac
- Hotel Bellevue et du Chariot d'Or
- Hotel Costes

- Hotel de l'Academie
- Hotel de Nesle
- Hotel La Manufacture
- Hotel Lancaster
- Hotel Langlois
- L'Hotel
- Relais Christine
- Residence des Arts
- Terrass Hotel

860. Can I find out more local information about France?

Climate: Usually, the temperature in Paris will range between 50 to 75 degrees from May to October. July and August are the warmest months. Brittany in the far west is the wettest French locale, especially between October and November. May is the driest month for the Bretons. In the South, the Mediterranean coast has the driest climate with any noticeable rain coming in spring and autumn.

Peak Season: Varies by region.

Language: The national language of France is French.

Currency: The national currency in France is the Euro - EUR. U.S. dollars are not accepted in most establishments; however, some hotels, shops and restaurants may accept U.S. dollars at an agreed upon exchange rate.

Standard Time Zone: UTC (Coordinated Universal Time/ GMT (Greenwich Mean Time) + 1 hour

For more information, contact: France Tourism Development Agency, 825 Third Avenue, 29th floor, New York, NY 10022; Telephone: 514-288-1904; Website: www. franceguide.com

861. What are the marriage requirements for France?

Because of France's strict requirements, it is not possible to marry there during a short stay. Either you or your fiancé must have lived in France for at least 40 consecutive days prior to the wedding. Banns must be posted at least 10 days before the wedding, at least 30 days into the stay in France. The banns and civil ceremony must take place at the city hall in the area in which the party lives. Before having a religious ceremony, you must have a civil ceremony. The religious officiant will require proof that the marriage has already been performed civilly. The 40-day period cannot be waived, no matter what. You will receive a booklet that is an official document and in which all births, deaths, divorces and name changes are then recorded for your new family. You may also receive a marriage certificate by writing to the city hall in which your civil ceremony is performed, including a self-addressed envelope with the correct postage, the date of the marriage and the full names of both parties, including the wife's maiden name.

In order to be married, you must each present the following:
- A valid U.S. passport or French residence permit.
- A certified copy of their your certificates less than 3 months old along with a sworn translation. You can find a list of sworn translators at the city hall where you will be married.
- An affidavit of marital status (certificate of celibacy) less than 3 months old. It can be done in the form of a notarized affidavit executed before an American Consular office in France.
- An affidavit of law and customs. It is a statement about U.S. marriage laws, certifying that the American citizen is free to contract marriage in France and that the marriage will be recognized in the United States.
- A medical certificate less than 2 months old. The marriage banns cannot be posted until each party has obtained a pre-nuptial medical certificate attesting that the individual was examined by a doctor *en vue de mariage*.
- Two proofs of domicile (i.e., electricity or telephone bills, lease, etc.).
- If you wish to have a prenuptial contract, the French notary preparing the contract will give you a certificate that must be presented.

Each city hall has its own requirements and may not require all of the above documents. You should check well in advance with the city hall in which you plan to be married to be sure you have the correct documents.

CHAPTER 32

Destination Weddings or Honeymoons in Asia

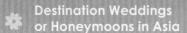

862. I want to have a destination wedding or honeymoon in Bali. Can you tell me about this destination?

The Indonesian island of Bali has been widely known as an exotic heaven filled with unique arts and ceremonies. The people of Bali, a friendly and remarkably artistic people, living amid breathtaking panoramas, have created a dynamic society with unique arts and ceremonies, making Bali an island almost unreal in today's hectic and changing world. Terrace rice fields dominate the landscape, with rivers and small irrigation streams dissecting a luscious green landscape, filling the air with enchanting sounds of running water. The island of Bali is one of over 17,000 islands that make up Indonesia's archipelago with a total population of more than 200 million, scattered over a land area of some 2.02 million square kilometers. Lying across a region of immense volcanic activity, Indonesia has some 400 volcanoes, with at least 70 still active. Bali is an island divided by a string of impressive volcanoes running almost through the center of the island. Shrouded in mystery and magic, they stretch skyward in majestic splendor. Bali's main volcano is the still active and sometimes explosive Gunung Agung, which is considered sacred among local people as it is believed to be the center of the universe.

Fast Facts:
- Approximate population: 3,000,000
- Tropical climate
- Official language is Bahasa Indonesia, but English is also spoken
- Currency: Indonesian Rupiah (IDR)
- Capital: Gorontalo

863. What is the nightlife like in Bali?

Bali's best nightspots are in the south, a popular gathering place for young travelers looking to party. Legian has become the club town, with discos and after-hours bars that keep jumping until dawn. Kuta and Tuban, just south of Legian, offer 24 hours of dancing and music supplied by the local bars. Ubud is the dance center of Bali. Hotels often provide shows, sometimes abbreviated in length and adapted for Western visitors. Performances held elsewhere around Ubud are more likely to reflect local culture. Night life as commonly known in the West also exists in Bali, especially in Kuta. The cafés, pubs, and discotheques lining the streets of Kuta and Legian are definitely the place to be and to be seen. Pub crawls can require many nights, and the varieties beat even the wildest western college towns. So, if a visitor's idea of fun consists of nightly pub crawls and daily sun bathing to cure the hangover, simply stay in Kuta, day and night. They won't be disappointed. Up North near Singaraja, Lovina Beach also has its own collection of pubs, restaurants, and discotheques. The environment is nice, friendly, and relaxed, certainly not as hectic as Kuta.

864. **What is the dining like in Bali?**

A traveler's visit to Bali is not complete unless they also partake in a delightful gastronomical tour of the food and fruit of Bali. Typical Balinese cuisine includes suckling pig, tender duck, meat kebabs, vegetables, and fresh fruits, all with rice as a centerpiece. For an exotic experience, visitors can step forward to the hustle of Kuta for an exclusive range of selected international and Indonesian cuisines, wine and cocktails.

865. **What is the shopping like in Bali?**

Shopping in Bali is not simply walking into a shop, picking something from a shelf and paying for it. Shopping is an art. In every traditional market and art shop around Bali, bargaining is a must. This traditional way makes shopping in Bali a fun time, where visitors can feel the warmth of human value in every transaction. Before they begin their shopping tour on this island, please obtain cash because most places do not accept credit cards. Even if visitors are not seasoned negotiators, they can be prepared to enjoy the bargaining process. It is a fun activity — they should be patient and they will get the best (and maybe even local) price. The biggest traditional market stands near Badung's river, Kumbasari market. It can give visitors an insight into the traditional Indonesia market where local people do their daily shopping. Fruit, vegetables and meat can be found in the basement; on the second level is the place for spices and dried goods; while household wares, clothing, art and craft is on the third level. Here visitors can get a very good price if they're good at bargaining.

866. **What are our accommodation options in Bali?**

Bali offers a pleasing assortment of places to stay, ranging from traditional hotels to bungalows nestled in the island's beautiful scenery. Be sure to keep in mind that prices for traditional hotels are often cheaper here, so you should take that into considering when deciding where to go or stay.

- Aditya Beach Bungalows
- Alam KulKul
- Amandari
- Amankila
- Ananda Cottages
- Balina Beach Bungalows
- Bounty Hotel
- Hotel Inter-Continental Bali
- Hotel Mas Lovina
- Poppies Cottages
- Puri Bagus
- Rambutan Beach Cottages
- The Oberoi
- The Sanctuary
- Villa Tugu

867. Can I find out more local information about Bali?

Climate: The climate in Bali is tropical — hot and humid all the time! There are two seasons, dry (April to September), and rainy (October to March). The timing of these seasons has varied considerably in the past few years, however, due to El Niño and other climatic interference. Temperatures range from 21 to 33°C in the low lands, but it can get quite chilly at night in the highlands of Central Java. Visitors should bring a jacket if they intend to do any volcano climbing.

Language: Bahasa Indonesia is the official language. English is frequently used in commerce.

Currency: Indonesian Rupiah - IDR. Exchange facilities for the main foreign currencies are available in banks or at authorized money changers in major cities of Indonesia. Rupiah comes in denominations of 100,000, 50,000, 20,000, 10,000, 5000, 500 and 100 in bank notes, and 1000, 500, 100, 50, 25, 10 and 5 coins.

Time Zone: UTC (Coordinated Universal Time)/GMT (Greenwich Mean Time) +8 hours

For more information, contact: Republic of Indonesia, 3457

Wilshire Blvd., Los Angeles, CA 90010; Telephone: 213-383-5126; Website: http://kjri-la.net

868. What are the marriage requirements for Bali?

To qualify as a legal marriage in Indonesia, the service has to be performed according to the laws of the respective religious beliefs of the parties concerned. All couples who marry in Indonesia must declare a religion. The Civil Registry Office can record marriages of persons of Islam, Hindu, Buddhist, Christian-Protestant and Christian-Catholic faiths. Agnosticism and Atheism are not recognized. Marriage partners must have the same religion; otherwise one partner must make a written declaration of change of religion. The U.S. has a Consular Representative in Bali that can offer assistance to couples.

A Christian, Hindu or Buddhist marriage is usually performed first in a church or temple ceremony. After the religious ceremony, every non-Islamic marriage must be recorded with the Civil Registry (Kantor Catatan Sipil). Without the registration by the Civil Registry, these marriages are not legal. Recording by Civil Registry officials can be performed directly at the religious ceremony for an additional fee.

All persons of non-Islamic faith are required to file a Notice of Intention to Marry with the Civil Registry Office in the Regency where you are staying as well as a "CNI" (Certificate of No Impediment to Marriage) obtained from you consular representatives. A CNI is simply a letter from your Consular Representative or Embassy Representative in Indonesia stating that there is no objection for you to get married in Indonesia. You can contact the Consular Representative of your country for details well before your intended date of marriage.

The U.S. Consular Representative in Bali can be reached at 62-361-233-605. The Civil Registry office has a Mandatory Waiting Period of ten (10) working days from the date of filing. This waiting period may be waived for tourists presenting a guest registration form (Form A).

All Marriage Certificates (except Islamic Marriage Certificates) will be issued by the Civil Registry usually on the same or next day. A sworn English translation of the marriage certificate should be obtained for use abroad. It is not necessary for the marriage certificate or translation to be registered by your Consular Agency. However, it might prove beneficial to have the sworn translation of the marriage certificate verified or a special translation made by the Consular Agency of your home country.

Most hotels and resorts can offer assistance with your arrangements for getting married in Bali. Many resort wedding packages include necessary arrangements for religious and legal ceremonies, rental of bridal dresses, hair styling, makeup, photography, cake, etc.

869. I want to have a destination wedding or honeymoon in the Maldives. Can you tell me about this destination?
The Republic of Maldives consists of 1,190 total coral islands — 202 are inhabited and 87 are exclusive resort islands. Visitors can imagine having their own little island as a vacation home. A short barefoot walk from their bungalow takes them to every little corner of the island, whether it is the restaurant, bar or the dive school. While the rooms are individual or semi-detached bungalows built around the island facing the beach, or built over water in the shallow lagoon that surround the island, the restaurants and the bars, game rooms, gymnasium, spas and swimming pool may be built in a centralized area or scattered around the island to give each an individual and unique feel. What surprises many is that in all of these resort islands the only inhabitants other than the guests are the resort staff. Accommodations range from detached individual cottages to over water bungalows. All resorts have deserted white sandy beaches and translucent clear lagoons enclosed by rich house reefs. Every island has its individual charm, character and ambience.

Fast Facts:
· Became a republic in 1968, 3 years after independence from British protection
· Tropical, humid and dry climates
· Approximate population: 349,100
· Official language is Maldevian Dhivehi
· Capital: Male'
· Currency: Rufiyaa (MVR) and Laaree

870. What is the nightlife like in the Maldives?

Every resort offers a variety of excursions and a selection of evening entertainment. The excursion could be a day long trip or a half-day trip out to fishing villages, resorts and uninhabited desert islands. In the evenings there is usually a weekly disco, the popularity of which often depends on the composition of guests on the island at the time. Fishing enthusiasts can enjoy fishing expeditions' big game fishing, trolling or night fishing, which is a relatively relaxing option.

871. What is the shopping like in the Maldives?

The Local Market, just a block away from the Male' Fish Market on the northern waterfront, is divided into small stalls. Here the pace is slower and the atmosphere peaceful, compared to the hectic activity in the rest of this neighborhood. Each stall is filled with a variety of local produce mainly from the atolls. Here visitors will find different kinds of local vegetables, fruits and yams, packets of sweetmeat, nuts and breadfruit chips, bottles of homemade sweets and pickles, and bunches of bananas hanging from ceiling beams. Another building just next door sells smoked and dried fish. It is not difficult for visitors to find their way around Male', especially if they carry a map with them. After all it is only two square kilometers. The main street, Majeedhee Magu, runs right across the island from east to west. Chaandhanee Magu on the other hand runs from north to south. Most souvenir shops line the northern end of Chaandhanee Magu, earlier known as the Singapore Bazaar for its many imports from Singapore. Guides and vendors speaking in English and other foreign languages patiently wait to serve the visitors. These shops are stocked with an ample supply of gifts and souvenir items. Best buys include the "thudu kuna," the Maldivian mat woven with local natural fibers. Attractive too are the wooden miniature "dhonis." When shopping for souvenirs, do keep in mind that export of products made of turtle shell, black coral, pearl oyster shell and red coral is prohibited.

872. What are our accommodation options in the Maldives?

Resorts and hotels in the Maldives are located on independent islands through the Pacific and offer a wide variety of rooms for you to choose from, depending upon your tastes and desires. Make sure you know the details of the facility where you choose to stay, such as if it is air-

conditioned or not.
- Angsana Resort & Spa
- Bathala Island Resort
- Biyadhoo Island Resort
- Dhiggiri Tourist Resort
- Equator Village
- Filitheyo Island Resort
- Komandoo Island Resort
- Medhufushi Island Resort
- Nika Island Resort
- Royal Island Resort
- Velavaru Resort

873. Can I find out more local information about the Maldives?
Climate: The Maldives has a tropical climate with warm temperatures year round and a great deal of sunshine. The warm tropical climate results in relatively minor variations in daily temperature throughout the year. The hottest month on average is April and the coolest, December. Average temperature is around 84 to 89 degrees. The weather is determined largely by the monsoons. There is a significant variation in the monthly rainfall levels. February is the driest with January to April being relatively dry; while May and October record the highest average monthly rainfall. The southwest monsoon or hulhangu from May to September is the wet season. Rough seas and strong winds are common during this period. The northeast monsoon iruvai falls between December to April. This is a period of clear skies, lower humidity and very little rain. The Maldives is in the equatorial belt and therefore severe storms and cyclones are extremely rare events.

Peak Season: January through April

Language: Dhivehi is the language spoken in all parts of the Maldives. English is widely spoken by Maldivians, and visitors can easily make themselves understood around the capital island. In the resorts, a variety of languages are spoken by the staff, including English, German, French, Italian and Japanese.

Currency: Rufiyaa (MVR) and Laaree (1 Rufiyaa = 100 Laarees) (Coins: MRf. 2, 1, 50 larees, 20, 10, 5, 2, and 1 laaree; Bills: 5, 10, 20, 50, 100 and 500 Rufiyaa.) US dollars are commonly used, though not everyone will accept them.

Standard Time Zone: The Maldives are 10 hours ahead of Eastern Standard Time.

For more information, contact: Maldives Tourism Promotion Board, 4th Fl, Bank of Maldives Building, Male 20-05, Republic of Maldives; Telephone: 960-332-3228; Website: www.visitmaldives.com

✿ Notes

CHAPTER 33

Destination Weddings or Honeymoons in Oceania and the South Pacific

874. What are our destination wedding options in Hawaii?

There are countless options regarding getting married in Hawaii. You can do almost anything you can dream up.

Beach Weddings: Hawaii's beaches are numerous and all stunning in their own way. Beach weddings are common in Hawaii and can be arranged through a wedding coordinator or on one's own. Some companies will offer beach wedding packages that you can take advantage of. All of Hawaii's beaches are free and public, so there are no fees or special permits required to get married on them. The only problem may be an overcrowding of people, so try to locate a more secluded beach.

Resort/Hotel Weddings: Hawaii does not have any all-inclusive hotels, but it does have a number of gorgeous resorts and hotels that offer wedding packages.

Church Weddings: There are many seaside chapels where you can get married on Hawaii's islands. Some companies and wedding coordinators offer packages for church weddings in specific locations, such as Waikiki Beach or the North Shore. Hawaii is incredibly diverse when it comes to religions and faiths, so you should not have a problem finding the type of officiant or house of worship you are seeking.

875. I want to have a destination wedding or honeymoon on the Big Island of Hawaii. Can you tell me about this destination?

· Hawaii is the most isolated population center in the world
· It is the only state that grows coffee
· Hawaii was the 50th state
· There are no racial majorities on Hawaii — everyone is a minority

The ocean is never out of view on Hawaii's Big Island. And here, there are all kinds of ways to have fun in, on, or under the warm, crystal-clear water. There are 266 miles of coastline and 47 beaches here with diverse sand colors from pristine white to green to rich volcanic black. From mid-November through May, the great humpback whales make their annual visit to Hawaii's Big Island. Visitors should keep their cameras handy if they're on a whale watching tour; these gentle giants can take to the air at any moment.

876. **What is the dining like on the Big Island of Hawaii if we go there for our destination wedding or honeymoon?**
In the last hundred years, cuisine from around the world migrated to Hawaii's Big Island. Starting with the Polynesians then flavored by an endless march of immigrants from Japan, China, the Philippines, Korea, U.S. mainland, and Europe; Hawaii's favorite foods are a carnival of compound tastes that are exciting and delicious. The result is called "Hawaii regional cuisine" and reflects the best of those places — combined with the freshest locally grown, and often exotic, ingredients of Hawaii. Of course, this includes exceptional fresh-caught ocean fish like ahi, mahi-mahi, onaga, ono, opakapaka and opah.

877. **What is the shopping like on the Big Island of Hawaii?**
Browse treasures carved from local woods like Koa and Milo, such as bowls so thin that they're translucent. Find tropical wear for everyone in the family — at every level of fashion sophistication. Discover books and works of art reflecting Hawaii and the Pacific, along with Hawaiian quilts and pillows. And, don't forget to take home "made only in Hawaii" products such as fruit jams, Kona coffee, Hawaii Vintage Chocolate, macadamia nuts, and recipe books containing the secret ingredients and preparations of the Island's many exotic cuisines. They make wonderful gifts for friends, family, and co-workers who weren't lucky enough to come along.

878. **What are our accommodation options in Hawaii if we go there for our destination wedding or honeymoon?**
Hawaii's islands offer some of the most beautiful resorts and hotels around. You will have any number of choices of places to stay, but keep in mind that Hawaii does not have any all-inclusive resorts on any of its islands.
- Aloha Beach House
- Dunbar Beachfront Cottages
- Four Seasons Resort Hualalali
- Four Seasons Resort Maui
- Grand Wailea Resort
- Halekulani Hotel
- Hideaway Cove Villas
- Hilton Waikoloa Village
- Hotel Lanai
- Moloa's Beach House

· Princeville Resort
· The Lodge at Koele
· Turtle Bay Resort
· Waikiki Beach Marriott

879. Can I find out more local information about Hawaii as a potential destination wedding or honeymoon location?

Climate: Year round in the Hawaiian Islands, the weather is wonderful. Because they're located at the edge of the tropical zone they really have only two seasons. In "summer," the average daytime high temperature is 85 degrees; in "winter," it's 78 degrees. Ocean temperatures are always warm; trade winds keep the islands cool and the humidity comfortable. Beach-goers will be happy to learn that the temperature of Hawaii's near-shore waters stay comfortable throughout the year. The average year round water temperature is 74 degrees, with a summer high of 80 degrees. If visitors favor a dry and sunny destination, they can check out the leeward side of each island. (That's the region sheltered from the prevailing winds — generally the west and south.) If they want lush, tropical and wet, check out an island's windward side (the regions facing the prevailing winds - generally the east and north). But even to windward the showers usually last just long enough to create the legendary, blazing rainbows. And what would Hawaii be without them?

Peak Season: Unlike other destinations, Hawaii's "high" and "low" seasons aren't dictated by the weather here (it's always great), but rather the weather everywhere else. Expect premium rates during the winter months, mid-December through March. Family travel is most popular during the summer. Spring and Fall, while considered "low" season, offer great travel values and fewer visitors.

Language: While Hawaii is an exotic destination, it's still the 50th state in the United States and English is their official language. But their rich, multi-ethnic heritage means visitors will hear echoes of Asia, Europe and South America in their delightful local "pidgin."

Currency: US Dollars, USD

Standard Time Zone: UTC (Coordinated Universal Time/ GMT (Greenwich Mean Time) — 10 hours

For more information, contact: Hawaii Visitors and Convention Bureau, Waikiki Shopping Plaza, 2250 Kalakaua Avenue, Room 502, Honolulu, HI 96815; Telephone: 1-800-GO-HAWAII (464-2924); Website: www.gohawaii.com

880. I want to have a destination wedding or honeymoon in Kauai. Can you tell me about this destination?

Kauai has a lush, rural feel and a laid-back lifestyle all its own. After all, Kauai is Hawaii's oldest island and, as first-born, has a legacy of paradise to uphold. And what a paradise! A trip around Kauai is a feast of green, tropical forest, cascading waterfalls, golden sand beaches. Visitors' circumnavigation will be interrupted by one of the world's greatest natural wonders, the Napali Coast.

On Kauai, visitors don't have to go far to find the kind of beach they're craving. There's more beach per mile of coastline here than on any other Hawaiian Island. Forty-three beaches in total, varying from quiet white-sand lagoons, to perfectly carved calm water bays, to expansive pounding ocean shores. Kauai is also Hawaii's water world. With rivers, waterfalls, and the deep blue Pacific, if it involves water, they'll find it here.

881. What is the dining like in Kauai?

On Kauai, like its people, visitors will find a delightful cultural mix of foods — Chinese, Japanese, Italian, American, Filipino, Thai, Korean, Mexican and more. Pacific Rim cuisine is a favorite indulgence here, marrying the exotic flavors of Polynesia and Asia. Fresh fish, meats, and produce grown in the Islands are an inspiration for imaginative dishes that are so beautifully presented, they double as works of art.

882. What is the shopping like in Kauai?

Shopping on Kauai is good, laid-back fun. Most of the retail stores shoppers will find here are the small, boutique-sized variety, so their experience is anything but hectic. Visitors will find treasure after treasure browsing through the tiny shops and casual shopping centers in Kapaa, Wailua, Poipu, Koloa, Hanapepe and Hanalei. The most common finds include hand-carved koa bowls and boxes, Hawaiian quilts, and fine art from paintings and sculptures to jewelry, ceramics and photography.

883. **I want to have a destination wedding or honeymoon in Maui. Can you tell me about this destination?**

Maui No Ka ʻOi (Maui is the best) is what the locals say, and visitors couldn't agree more. The island weaves a spell over the more than 2 million people who visit its shores each year, and many visitors decide to return for good. The island was formed by two volcanoes that erupted long ago — the extinct 5,788-foot Puʻu Kukui and the dormant 10,023-foot Haleakala (now the centerpiece of a national park). The resulting depression between the two is what gives Maui its nickname, the Valley Isle. Maui's volcanic history gives it much of its beauty. The roads around the island are lined with rich red soil, Central Maui is still carpeted with grassy green, and the deep blue of ocean and sky mingles with the red and green of Maui's topography. And the three planned resort communities along Maui's lee shore — Kapalua, Kaʻanapali, and Wailea — offer self-contained environments of such luxury and beauty that the effect is almost surreal.

Kaanapali Beach is four miles long and one of Maui's finest beaches. There is a paved beach walk that stretches the length and meanders past condominiums, hotels, restaurants and the Whaler's Village Shopping complex. One of Maui's best spots for snorkelers is a Kaanapali's doorstep fronting the Sheraton Maui. Visitors can't miss "Black Rock." Below it, schools of tropical fish are in session all year long.

884. **What is the dining like in Maui?**

Here, visitors' dining options are as varied as Maui's multi-cultural population. From small cafés featuring Filipino, Thai, Chinese, and Portuguese specialties to lavish, five-star restaurants featuring the finest in European-inspired haute cuisine, Maui offers something to satisfy every appetite. No matter what type of food visitors prefer, they should be sure to enjoy a special meal of Hawaii Regional Cuisine — a style unique to the islands that features fresh island seafood, locally grown herbs and spices, and flawless presentation.

885. **What is the shopping like in Maui?**

No trip to Maui is complete without a little souvenir of a stay on this sensational island oasis. From charming boutiques of locally crafted creations to some of the world's most celebrated name brand stores, the sheer variety of shopping outlets is enough to satisfy the demands of shopping fans.

886. **I want to have a destination wedding or honeymoon in Oahu. Can you tell me about this destination?**

Oahu, the third largest Hawaiian Island, has an area of 608 square miles and a coastline of 112 miles. It reaches from sea level to 4,003-foot Mt. Ka'ala. This is the most populated island, where Honolulu is the Capital City, the principal port, the major airport, business and financial center, and the educational heart of the state. Oahu is the military command center of the Pacific, and Waikiki is the visitor center.

On Oahu, visitors will experience the diversity of an island paradise where cosmopolitan conveniences are surrounded by breathtaking scenery. Visitors can envelop themselves in the Aloha Spirit — a way of life in the islands that will leave visitors longing to return to Oahu, the heart of Hawaii. Visitors can "Hang loose" at the world-famous Waikiki Beach or find their own secluded stretch of sand. A short drive out of town in any direction will bring visitors face to face with uncrowded beaches, natural wonders and beautiful scenery.

887. **What is the nightlife like in Oahu?**

Discover the magic of Oahu at night. With a bustling city and resorts, Oahu offers a myriad of nightlife. From luau and Polynesian shows to cool clubbing and martini bar hopping to theater performances and comedy acts to romantic dining and the sounds of the ocean breeze and ukuleles, Oahu is a night owl's paradise.

888. **What is the dining like in Oahu?**

Oahu is known for its eclectic and innovative fare, each with an exotic cultural background. The cuisine is as interesting and diverse as the people who live here. To "eat" one's way through Oahu would literally take months, maybe longer. Its variety of ethnic foods and preparations are some of the most extensive in the world. So extensive in fact, visitors may never sample the same flavors twice. The assortment of Asian restaurants is truly astonishing, as is the seemingly endless venues for fresh seafood.

889. **What is the shopping like in Oahu?**

Explore Oahu's malls with their unique blend of local stores and national chains. In one stop, pick up clothes for the kids, local macadamia nuts, and pikake-scented lotion — only on Oahu. Find bargains at the swap meet and at the International Marketplace. Pick up t-shirts, lauhala placemats and dried tropical fruit. Discover Asian and Hawaiian surprises in Chinatown. Taste mango or li hing mui seed; buy fresh fruit; and don't forget to get those special leis to take back home. Pick up a one-of-a-kind piece at the many craft fairs and at local shops around the island, such as up at the North Shore. Visitors can select a koa bowl, a Niihau shell necklace, a blown glass dolphin, plumeria-shaped bowls, feather lei or poha berry jam that will remind them of the islands and wanting to come back. Oahu is a shopper's dream.

890. I want to have a destination wedding or honeymoon in Australia. Can you tell me about this destination?

Australia is an exciting country full of spirit, color and contrast: green, pristine wilderness; lush rainforest; blue skies; sparkling water; silver beaches; and the red earth of the Outback. Contrast is a way of life in Australia. Australia itself is an ancient land as illustrated in its landscape. A good amount of the central and western portion of Australia is an arid, flat span of dry land. Yet, in contrast, its coastal cities boast a youthful buzz and energy — justified since most of which were founded as recently as the mid-19th century. It is this harshness of the interior landscape that has forced modern Australia to become a coastal country. Most of the population lives within 12 or 13 miles of the ocean. This metropolitan sector embraces the modern, values of materialism and self-indulgence while the beach climate is a playground for entertainment and socializing. Buzzing cities, long sandy beaches, turquoise blue of the ocean, luxurious hotels, majestic landscapes and natural wonders, Australia has it all.

Fast Facts:
- Captain James Cook made the first territorial claim on the island in 1770
- Arid to semiarid and tropical climates
- The world's smallest continent, but the sixth-largest country
- Approximate population: 20,090,400
- English is the official language, but many others are also spoken, including Chinese and Italian

· Capital: Canberra
· Currency: Australian Dollar (AUD)

891. What are our destination wedding options in Australia?

Beach Weddings: Beach weddings in Australia can take place almost anywhere — Perth, Cairns, Sydney, the Gold Coast or Port Douglas, to name a few.

Resort/Villa Weddings: With its vast surface area, Australia has many resorts and villas that can accommodate the couple wishing to marry there.

Church Weddings: Chapels and churches can be located on the beach or downtown in metropolitan Sydney, in the Outback or on a private island off Queensland. Christianity is the predominant religion, but there are many, many other faiths that can accommodate a couple wishing to get married.

Sydney Opera House Weddings: Set against the city skyline and on Sydney's beautiful harbor, Sydney Opera House is a spectacular backdrop for your wedding. Some planners will offer an Opera House package, so be sure to search around.

Tall Ship Weddings: There's nothing more majestic than the image of a tall ship sailing across the ocean. Svanen is Australia's oldest tall ship and wedding coordinators in Sydney can help you plan your wedding aboard this timber beauty, sometimes offering special packages.

Rainforest/Wildlife Weddings: Couples can marry amid Australia's rainforests or wildlife. Wedding coordinators will sometimes offer packages that allow you to marry beneath a spectacular waterfall or in one of Australia's wildlife parks while the animals look on.

892. What is the nightlife like in Australia?

Each of Australia's major cities has a nightlife attraction, whether it's an international-style casino with all the glitter of Las Vegas, a waterfront area where the barstools come with a view of yachts and dancing waves, or an entire district that sparkles by night.

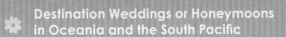
893. **What is the dining like in Australia?**

Fine wine and dining are now as characteristically Australian as warm sun and booming surf. Australian cuisine is marked by its fresh, eclectic take on dishes gleaned from all the cultures of the world. There's a huge variety available in every state — some examples are chevre from Queensland, prosciutto from Western Australia, brie and cold-pressed olive oil from South Australia, balsamic vinegars and snails from Victoria, milk-fed lamb from New South Wales, smoked salmon from Tasmania, and mud crabs from the Northern Territory. There are many reasons for Australia's culinary success, including a diversity of micro-climates that allow it to produce mangoes as well as strawberries, custard apples, citrus fruits and coffee beans. Its lush coastal pastures are well suited to farmhouse cheeses, its native forests produce honeys of exceptional fragrance and flavor, and its vast coastline yields succulent oysters, crayfish and tuna. Australian chefs have been quick to make the most of this natural bounty, experimenting with ingredients and drawing inspiration from the cultural cross-currents of modern Australia. Over the past 30 years, Australia has become one of the most ethnically diverse nations on earth. In addition to world-class cuisine, Australia is ranked as the world's seventh-largest wine producer, and the finest Australian wines are among the best in the world.

894. **What is the shopping like in Australia?**

New Age meets suburban chic at Sydney's favorite, fashion-conscious churchyard bazaar, Paddington Markets, where the range of goods includes crystals, tribal silver, plants or just slinky socks at knockdown prices. The north Queensland village of Kuranda has a flourishing market, Rainforest Market — the place to go for arts and crafts, fashions, and a range of exotic rainforest products. Part country fair, part rock festival and part country show, the monthly Byron Bay Market combines music, spectacle, exotic fruit salads, ethnic finger-food and people skilled in basket weaving. Salamanca Markets brings a dash of excitement to the historic stone warehouses on the Hobart waterfront every Saturday with a dazzling array of crafts by some of Australia's finest artisans.

895. **What are our accommodation options in Australia?**

Sydney, Melbourne and Southern Queensland are the most

popular destinations for travelers, but some prefer to rough it and brave the Outback or travel to the western coast to visit Perth or north to see Darwin. There are far too many places where you could stay to even begin to list them all, but we'll cover a few of the more popular hotels and resorts located in Sydney and Melbourne.

- Adelphi
- Bedarra Island
- Crown Towers
- Hotel Lindrum
- Hotel Sofitel
- Lizard Island
- Observatory Hotel
- Ravesi's on Bondi Beach
- Robinson's by the Sea
- Silky Oaks
- Sir Stamford at Circular Quay
- Swiss-Grand Hotel
- The Hotel Como
- The Sebel Pier One Sydney
- The Windsor
- Toad Hall
- Victoria Court Sydney

896. Can I find out more local information about Australia?
Australia's seasons are the reverse of those in the northern hemisphere. From Christmas on the beach to mid-winter in July, Australia's climate is typically mild in comparison with the extremes that exist in both Europe and North America. Australia's seasons: Spring is September to November, summer is December to February, autumn is March to May, and winter is June to August. Australia also features a diverse range of climatic zones from the tropical regions of the north, the arid expanses of the interior and the temperate regions of the south. It's worth noting that the temperate regions have all four seasons, while those in the tropical zone have only two (summer "wet" and winter "dry").

Language: While it's common knowledge that Australians speak English, Australia also has a unique colloquial language that can confuse visitors when they first hear it. From "fair dinkum" to "cobber," colloquial language is common throughout the land.

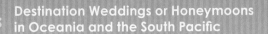

Currency: Australian dollars — AUD.

Standard Time Zone: There are three time zones in Australia: Eastern Standard Time (EST), which includes New South Wales, Victoria, Queensland, Tasmania and the Australian Capital Territory; Central Standard Time (CST), which includes South Australia and the Northern Territory; and Western Standard Time (WST) - Western Australia. CST is Coordinated Universal Time/GMT (Greenwich Mean Time) +9:30 hours.

For more information, contact: Australian Tourist Commission, 6100 Center Drive, Suite 1150, Los Angeles CA 90045; Telephone: 310-695-3200; Website: www.australia.com

897. What are the marriage requirements for Australia?
If you and your fiancé wish to be married in Australia, you will be required to submit a Notice of the Intended Marriage with your chosen celebrant. Civil and religious marriage celebrants are listed on the Attorney General's Commonwealth website, at http://www.law.gov.au/celebrants. The form must be submitted at least one month and one day before the marriage is to take place (and not more than 18 calendar month's notice of an intended date of marriage.) This form must be signed and witnessed either by an Australian Consular Official or Diplomatic Officer. Personal identification (such as a passport, birth certificate, etc.) is also required. You should check with your celebrant to ensure that you have the correct legal identification.

898. I want to have a destination wedding or honeymoon in Fiji. Can you tell me about this destination?
The Fiji Islands are 1,000 miles of pristine white sand beaches, fabulous coral gardens and azure lagoons. More then anything else, Fiji is an exotic destination. It's the exhilaration of a dolphin arching high into the air beside a visitor's boat, the long gliding swoop of an orange dove through the rainforest, or the smiles of excited children performing in unison to the beat of a hollow log drum. Fiji's 333 islands can sizzle with excitement or murmur with the quiet calm of pristine nature. Where else can visitors swim with huge, harmless manta rays congregating by the shore, snorkel over giant rainbow gardens of soft coral, or scuba

dive the White Wall and famous Astrolabe Reef? Fiji is also where the Cloud Breaker, the incredible 6-metre wave found offshore at Tavarua, draws surfers from around the world.

Fast Facts:
- Became independent from the British in 1970
- Tropical marine climate
- Approximate population: 893,350
- English is the official language, but Fijian and Hindustani are also spoken
- Capital: Suva
- Currency: Fijian Dollar (FJD)

899. What is the dining like in Fiji?

Dining in Fiji offers a multiethnic culinary experience. Whether visitors are dining at their hotel, island resort or "in town," they'll find a palette painted by flavors from India, China, Korea, Japan, Italy and the best of Europe as well as Australia, New Zealand and the South Pacific waters. Restaurants run the gamut from five-star international to 24-hour air-conditioned coffee shops. Steaks and local seafood can be found in most restaurants as can the specialties of our own Fijian cooking heritage. Most hotels and resorts also offer specific culinary themed nights, magiti (Fijian feasts), beach or poolside barbecues, as well as Fiji's best-known outdoor cooking experience — the lovo. A lovo is an underground oven of heated rocks, cooking a variety of foods wrapped in banana leaves, covered with earth and coming out after several hours of cooking with a faintly smoky flavor. Lovos produces succulent, tender meats, chicken, seafood, and given the proper occasion, a whole suckling pig! Visitors shouldn't leave Fiji without having experienced other traditional Fijian dishes. Kokoda, Fiji's most popular specialty, is portions of fresh fish marinated in lime juice and served in a half coconut.

900. What is the shopping like in Fiji?

Some popular items to bring home for friends, family and business associates to enjoy include Fijian-inspired designer T-shirts; carved tanoa bowls, from which the national drink yaqona (kava) is mixed and served; Fijian replica war clubs; cannibal forks; and Fijian combs. Handicraft like woven baskets and mats, masi (tapa cloth), animal wood carvings and pottery items are best sellers. And, for international

fashion buffs, the ubiquitous sulu for men and women is Fiji's all-purpose, one-size-fits-all garment. Women wear them 100 different ways from a beachside wrap to an evening dress while men in business and government wear them as a day skirt.

901. What are our accommodation options in Fiji?

Fiji's resorts and hotels are many, and one option you have is to stay in a bungalow several miles offshore. These can be romantic and intimate, but limit the amount of Fiji scenery you actually see.
· Beachcomber Island Resort
· Coconut Grove Beachfront Cottages
· Homestay Suva
· Moody's Namena
· Qamea Resort & Spa
· Rakiraki Hotel
· Shangri-La's Fijian Resort
· The Wakaya Club
· Tokoriki Island Resort
· Turtled Island Resort
· Vatulele Island Resort

902. Can I find out more local information about Fiji?

Climate: Fiji enjoys an ideal South Sea tropical climate and can get hot in the summer but seldom reaches above 96 degrees. Trade winds from the southeast bring year long cooling breezes late afternoon and early evening. Fiji sits far enough from the equator to have relatively mild summer heat but close enough to have warm balmy winters too! The "dry" season in Fiji is May to October, and the "wet" season is November to April. But Fiji's weather varies greatly geographically. The leeward (west) sides of the major high islands including Viti Levu and Vanua Levu are protected from the prevailing southeast trade winds and receive less rainfall than the windward sides of the islands.

Peak Season: June to October.

Language: Fiji is an English-speaking country.

Currency: The Fijian dollar - FJD.
Standard Time Zone: UTC (Coordinated Universal Time/ GMT (Greenwich Mean Time) +12 hours

For more information, contact: Tourism Fiji, 5777 W. Century Blvd., Suite 220, Los Angeles, CA 90045; Telephone: 310-568-1616 or 800-YEA-FIJI; Website: www. bulafijinow.com

903. What are the marriage requirements for Fiji?

There is neither a residence requirement nor a minimum period of stay required for marriage in Fiji. The required documents are listed below:

- Birth certificates of you and your fiancé. Birth certificates must either be originals or copies certified by and bearing the seal of the issuing authorities.
- If either you or your fiancé was previously married, legal proof of termination of the prior marriage(s). Death and/or divorce certificates must either be originals or copies certified by and bearing the seal of the issuing authorities.
- U.S. passport if either you or your fiancé is a U.S. citizen.
- Two witnesses over the age of 21 years.
- If either of you is under the age of 21 years, a written notarized consent is required from the father; the consent may be signed by the mother only if the father is deceased or cannot be located. If the parent(s) unreasonably refuses to consent, a written consent from a Court Magistrate will suffice.
- Fees are approximately US$10. For a special license, it costs approximately US$8 and applicants must marry within 28 days from the date the license is issued.

District Officers and Registrars may perform marriages without a marriage license. After the ceremony, it may take 15 working days to obtain the marriage certificate: 10 days for the Minister or District Officer's document to reach the Registrar General and 5 or 6 days for the Registrar to search its records and issue the certificate. A special license is required if the marriage ceremony is to be performed by a Minister of Religion or performed at a venue other than the Registrar-General or District Offices. If you decide to have a civil ceremony, it is advisable to make an appointment either a day or two in advance.

A marriage performed in accordance with the legal requirements of the country in which it takes place is recognized as valid in the United States. For specific information, you can consult an attorney in the jurisdiction where you reside. The two main offices of the Registrar General in Fiji are located in Suva and Lautoka: Suva: (679) 315-280, Lautoka: (679) 655-132.

904. I want to have a destination wedding or honeymoon in Tahiti. Can you tell me about this destination?

Tahiti and its islands comprise an area officially known as French Polynesia. The islands are scattered over 4 million square kilometers of ocean in the eastern South Pacific. French Polynesia offers many exciting recreational activities. Visitors can find a new activity to suit their sense of adventure each day of their vacation.

Unless you are a French National, getting married in Tahiti is very complicated, and requires a minimum of one month's residency. All legal weddings are basic civil ceremonies, which are carried out at the Town Hall in front of the mayor.

Get a sense for the local color by registering for a circle island tour. These bus tours, which are available on selected islands in French Polynesia, visit the small villages, fields, hills and plantations of the region, giving tourists a feel for every day Tahitian life.

For thrill-seekers looking for a pulse-quickening experience, helicopter tours offer a bird's-eye view of Tahiti and her islands. Soar above velvety green volcanic peaks, past sprawling crystalline waters and sparkling sands.

Rent a bicycle or scooter and see French Polynesia up close and personal. Rentals are an excellent way for curious visitors to mix with the natives, take in the sights, and customize their vacation experience.

The International Golf Course of Atimaono, located on Tahiti's west coast some 25 miles from Papeete, is one of the most contemporary and beautiful courses in the South Pacific, and is open to visiting golfers.

The campgrounds of French Polynesia are popular with backpackers, students, and other visitors who enjoy "roughing it." Campgrounds are always private and there are no facilities in parks or other public areas. Trails are numerous on the islands, and it's a good idea to seek out a guide to ensure against getting lost. Examining the mountains, hills, valleys and volcanic peaks on horseback is also a marvelous way for visitors to commune with nature.

Fast Facts:
- The French annexed multiple Polynesian groups in the 19th century
- Tropical, moderate climate
- Approximate population: 270,480
- French is the official language, but English and Polynesian languages are also widely spoken
- Capital: Papeete
- Currency: Comptoirs Francais du Pacifique franc (XPF or CFP)

905. **What is the nightlife like in Tahiti?**
Get lucky at one of three hotel casinos in Tahiti. Or visitors should toss off their inhibitions — and their shoes — and dance the night away at one of Tahiti's many clubs. They provide an excellent opportunity for visitors to mingle with the locals. Some of Tahiti's clubs boast a ballroom ambiance, while others jump to the driving rhythms of disco beat or rock and roll. Tahiti's local bars possess are classic, smoky, music-filled nightspots that present a great opportunity for visitors to mix with the locals.

906. **What is the dining like in Tahiti?**
The Tahitian diet consists mostly of fish, shellfish, breadfruit, taro, cassava, pork, yams, chicken, rice and coconut. Polynesian eateries on the island prepare tempting and exotic seafood dishes. Visitors will also find American, Chinese, French and Italian cuisine here, as well as Polynesian variations on the aforementioned themes. In addition, Les Roulottes are colorful food-vans that provide good, fast food at reasonable prices, and every evening hundreds of Tahitians and visitors gather to eat, laugh and enjoy the end of the day. Meals range from barbecue steaks, chicken and shish-kabob to pizza cooked in a wood-burning stove or freshly cooked delicacies.

907. **What is the shopping like in Tahiti?**
Visitors can select from an array of goods, including black pearl jewelry, paintings, pottery, sculpture, wood

carvings and woven artifacts. Moorea's laid-back lifestyle is chronicled in the work of many of the island's local artists. Tahiti's premier marketplace, Le Marche, is a great place to pick up handicrafts and souvenirs. Shoppers will find an assortment of jewelry, hats, skirts, carvings, mats and weaving here, as well as small cafes and vendors offering tempting fruits, vegetables and fish.

908. **What are our accommodation options in Tahiti?**
French Polynesia offers you a myriad of places to stay, but be sure you are aware that quality is often reflective of cost, meaning if you choose to stay at a cheaper location, you will probably get what you pay for.

- Bora Bora Beach Resort
- Hotel Bora Bora
- Hotel Kaveka
- Hotel Les Tipaniers
- Hotel Maitai Polynesia
- Hotel Tiare Tahiti
- Inter-Continental Tahiti Beachcomber Resort
- Le Meridien Tahiti
- Le Royal Tahitian Hotel
- Moorea Pearl Resort & Spa
- Sheraton Hotel Tahiti
- Sofita Ia Ora
- Sofitel Maeva Beach
- St. Regis Bora Bora Nui Resort & Spa

909. **Can I find out more local information about Tahiti?**
Climate: The temperature averages about 79 degrees year round, both air and water. It is a tropical destination blessed with lots of sun and enough rain to keep the waterfalls flowing and the flowers growing. The summer is from November through April, when the climate is slightly warmer and more humid. Winter is from May through October, the climate is slightly cooler and dryer.

Peak Season: July and August

Language: Official languages are Tahitian and French, but Paumotu (language of the Tuamotu Islands) and Mangarevan (spoken in the Gambiers) are also native tongues. English is also widely spoken.

Currency: Comptoirs Francais du Pacifique franc — XPF or
CFP, though US dollars and credit cards are common.
Notes: 500, 1000, 5000, and 10000; Coins: 1, 2, 5, 10, 20,
50, 100.

Standard Time Zone: UTC (Coordinated Universal Time/
GMT (Greenwich Mean Time) — 10 hours.

For more information, contact: Tahiti Tourism Board,
1300 Continental Blvd., Suite 160, El Segundo, CA 90245;
Telephone: 310-414-8484; Website: www.tahiti-tourism.com

✼ Notes

CHAPTER 34

Destination Weddings or Honeymoons in the Caribbean

910. **I want to have a destination wedding or honeymoon in Barbados. Can you tell me about this destination?**
In Barbados, cliffs of sandstone overlook calm bays and rugged coastlines, and cozy soft sand beaches nestle between heads of coral sculpted by the sea. Graced by gently rolling hills, sugar cane fields and spectacular beaches, Barbados is one of the most densely populated islands in the Caribbean. The people are outgoing and friendly; in fact, one of the reasons so many people enjoy going to Barbados is the friendly people and the feeling that the resort or hotel they are staying in is part of the community. Barbados is also a surfer's paradise — Barbados is guaranteed to have surf somewhere along its shores on almost any given day of the year.

Fast Facts:
· First settled by the British in 1627
· Official currency is the Barbados dollar (BD$)
· The official language is English
· Barbados is on Atlantic Standard Time, 1 hour ahead of New York, except during Daylight Savings
· Approximate population: 279,200
· Capital is Bridgetown

911. **What are our destination wedding options in Barbados?**
Beach Weddings: For a beach wedding, you may have to consider hiring a wedding planner in Barbados to aid in planning. Make note that all beaches in Barbados are public.

Resort Weddings: Resorts often offer wedding planners or coordinators to help plan your wedding, provided that you are staying at that resort. Sometimes resorts will marry you for free if you stay a certain number of nights at that location. Be sure to know which resorts offer what so you can make your decision accordingly. Some popular resorts with free weddings or that offer a wedding coordinator in Barbados are:
· Almond Beach Village Resort
· Grand Barbados Beach Resort
· Turtle Beach Resort
· Bougainvillea Beach Resort
· The Crane Resort
· Bon Vivant

On-Shore Weddings: If you want to marry in Barbados and arrive by cruise ship, the wisest thing may be to hire a wedding planner who can greet you upon docking and take you through the steps they've arranged for the wedding. The wedding planner can arrange for decoration of the location where you want to get married, as well as transportation to the Ministry of Home Affairs to obtain the marriage license, witnesses and any other services you need or desire. If you have chartered a private yacht or catamaran, you can get married aboard that surrounded by the Caribbean's azure waters.

Important Note: Many cruise ships cannot legally marry you while at sea. One of the cruise lines that does allow this is Princess Cruise Lines. For all other cruise lines, you must wait until the ship has docked and be married onboard then or at one of the ports of call.

Church Weddings: An assortment of churches is available on Barbados where you can marry, including Anglican, Methodist and Roman Catholic. Make sure you know that some reverends will require written confirmation from your minister at home that you are practicing Christians and have gone through pre-martial counseling. For Roman Catholic weddings you must complete a premarital questionnaire, have a signed declaration of freedom to marry by your priest from home, statements from the bishop of the your diocese from home and a certificate stating that you have gone through premarital counseling. For Jewish weddings on Barbados, you must bring your own Rabbi, as there are none on the island.

Plantation/Villa Weddings: Plantation or villa weddings are common in Barbados, thanks to the abundance of such houses and estates located all over the island. When staying at any one of these locations, you are guaranteed an intimate, private wedding and accommodations. There are many to choose from, so be sure to do your own research on weddings in Barbados on plantations or at villas:
· Sunbury Plantation House
· Cove Spring House

912. What is the nightlife like in Barbados?
As the sun sets, the action shifts from the beaches and clear

waters to a wide selection of nighttime dining, dancing and entertainment fun! Visitors can take in an exciting murder mystery show, a romantic cruise, a historic dinner play, or jump to the beat in nightclubs throughout the St. Lawrence Gap. Visitors should check with their hotel for the latest information on all the current happenings on the island.

913. What is the dining like in Barbados?

There is an abundance of fine restaurants on the island that offer local cuisine, seafood and continental cuisine. Besides the fresh bounty drawn from the sea, the island keeps thousands of acres under cultivation so that restaurants can receive fresh vegetables and fruits, as well as island grown pork, chicken and beef. The wide range of dining options available in Barbados ensures that there is something to suit every taste and budget. By day, informal attire is acceptable in most Barbados restaurants, but at night a more formal dress code is enforced. It is also recommended that dinner reservations be made in advance, especially during the winter.

914. What is the shopping like in Barbados?

Barbados is an island filled with artistic talent, from skilled local potters at work fashioning their wares as has been done for centuries, to modern fashion designers, abstract artists and poets. Pelican Village, on the outskirts of Bridgetown, is the place to get local handicrafts, including straw bags, wall hangings, batik, paintings, rum cakes, and much more. The heart and soul of shopping in Barbados is Broad Street. There, visitors will find several large department stores and duty-free shops.

915. What are our accommodation options in Barbados?

There are many options available to you for accommodations in Barbados. You can choose to stay at a resort, a hotel, a vacation apartment, villa, cottage and more.

- Accra Beach Hotel & Resort
- Almond Beach Village Resort
- Cobblers Cove Hotel
- Coral Reef Club
- Divi Southwinds Beach Resort
- Little Arches Hotel
- Mango Bay Hotel & Beach Club
- Sandpiper

- Sandy Beach Island Resort
- Sandy Lane Hotel & Golf Club
- Tamarind Cove
- The Crane
- The Fairmont Glitter Bay
- The House
- The Savannah
- Turtle Beach Resort
- Villa Nova

916. Can I find out more local information about Barbados?

Climate: It is mostly sunny and fair in Barbados, featuring warm days with cool winds and cozy nights. It rains most in summer and a good rainfall is refreshing and much needed. Rain is usually followed quickly by sunny skies and within minutes everything is dry. Tropical rainstorms sometimes occur in the hurricane season, which runs from June to October (as is said in Barbados, "June too soon, October all over!"). Tropical rains are spectacular but the island is very porous and the heaviest rains quickly drain off into the underground lakes or the sea.

Language: The official language of Barbados is English with a broad dialect.

Currency: The official currency is the Barbados Dollar — BD$. Most establishments will also accept U.S. currency.

Time Zone: GMT (Greenwich Mean Time) — 4 hours. There is no Daylight Savings Time in Barbados.

For more information, contact: Barbados Tourism Authority, 800 Second Avenue, New York, NY 10017; Telephone: 1-800-221-9831; Website: www.barbados.org

917. What are the marriage requirements for Barbados?

It is very easy to get married in Barbados. There is no required waiting period or minimum length of stay. Application for a marriage license must be made by both parties in person at the office of the Ministry of Home Affairs. Both you and your fiancé will need valid passports or the original, or certified, copies of your birth certificates. If either of you have been divorced, an original Decree Absolute or a certified copy of the Final Judgment must be presented. If either of you were previously married and widowed, a certified copy of the Marriage Certificate and Death Certificate in respect of the deceased spouse must be presented. Where necessary, all documents not in English must be accompanied by a certified translation. The applicable fees, if neither of you are a citizen or resident of Barbados, are approximately US$75 and a US$25 stamp.

918. I want to have a destination wedding or honeymoon in Aruba. Can you tell me about this destination?

Aruba is one of the Caribbean's most beautiful treasures. With almost perpetually sunny days, dry climate, safe distance from passing hurricanes, pristine beaches and sparkling blue water, it's a paradise where visitors can travel and feel safe to explore its wonders. Travelers are likely to come back to Aruba after experiencing its splendor.

Fast Facts:
- Population: approximately 100,000
- Over 40 different nationalities are represented on the island
- Earliest Indian settlements date back to 1000 A.D.
- Capital: Oranjestad
- Currency: Aruban guilder/florin (AWG)

919. What are our destination wedding options in Aruba?

With its perfect weather, gorgeous beaches, rich history and lush tropical landscape, Aruba is the ideal location for couples who want to get married on a beautiful Caribbean island. Civil ceremonies have to take place at the City Hall, but church weddings and other ceremonies can then take place almost anywhere on the island!

Beach Weddings: You would be foolish not to take advantage of Aruba's spectacular beaches. If you are staying at a resort or hotel, you can arrange to get married through them on their beaches. With its fantastic year-round weather, Aruba's beaches promise a perfect day for couples who get married there. You can also contact a local wedding planner or coordinator who often offers packages for those looking to marry on a beach. Again, you must marry at City Hall first before you can have a ceremony on the beach.

Church Weddings: Once the Civil ceremony has taken place, you can get married in a number of Aruba's beautiful, and sometimes colorful, churches. For Catholic couples, you must provide proof that you have gone through premarital counseling at the church in your hometown, permission from your parish priest that you can marry in Aruba, a copy of your marriage certificate from the U.S., your Confirmation and Baptism certificates and valid passports. All these documents must be submitted 4 months before the ceremony is to take place. For a Jewish ceremony, you must submit a formal petition of marriage to the Aruban Jewish Community and some form of verification of Judaism from your Rabbi back home. Both you and your fiancé must be Jewish.

At Sea/On-Shore: Weddings are not allowed to be performed at sea by a ship's captain off the coast of Aruba, according to Dutch laws, but if the ship has been given authority by the country under whose flag it is registered, a wedding may take place. This may be difficult to achieve, however, as few cruise lines allow weddings to take place at sea. You may be able to contact a wedding coordinator who can plan a wedding on a catamaran, however.

Resort Weddings: With its quality hotels and resorts, getting married at a resort on Aruba is always a good idea. Many provide wedding coordinators who can help plan the wedding from start to finish, making it easy and affordable for couples looking for that perfect destination wedding. Resorts may also offer a number of locations on their property where you can marry, from the beach to a beautifully decorated gazebo overlooking the ocean. Once you have chosen your preferred resort or hotel, contact the wedding coordinator there for more information on prices and packages available. We've listed just a few popular resorts where you can marry on Aruba:
- Bucuti Beach Resort Aruba
- Tierra del Sol Resort & Country Club
- Amsterdam Manor Beach Resort
- La Cabana All-Suite Beach Resort & Casino

920. What is the nightlife like in Aruba?
Theme nights are an extremely popular kind of nightlife in Aruba. On any given night, visitors can find a themed party in any club, from carnival themes to pirates. Casinos are also

popular at night — for high rollers or the average visitor who wants to try his or her hand at slots. They can also catch Vegas-style shows at these casinos. For those with a lot of energy and stamina to burn, frequent any one of Aruba's dance clubs or discos, but be sure to show up at midnight or 1 a.m. — any earlier and the party won't have started yet. If travelers are seeking a more low-key, calm night, they can check out any of the bars or clubs in the hotels. Bars and clubs in Oranjestad can be busy and crowded, but a cozier scene can often be found in a hotel bar or on a dinner cruise.

921. **What is the dining like in Aruba?**
Dining on Aruba is an exciting experience, as there are many international cuisines from which to choose. In Aruba's capital, Oranjestad, the Bon Bini Festival — a celebration of local arts and crafts and food — takes place on every Tuesday, the whole year round. Visitors should be sure to try pan bati, a thick and sweet pancak; pastechi, deep-fried turnovers filled with spicy meat, fish or cheese; or anything containing a Madam Janette chile pepper, hotter than the jalapeño and Aruba's special way of spicing up their dishes. Meals are eclectic and delicious — diners can't go wrong when they pick a restaurant on Aruba.

922. **What is the shopping like in Aruba?**
Because aloe is one of Aruba's only exports, exceptional skincare products are available on the island, as well as a large assortment of imported products sold, including jewelry, designer fashions, crystal, chocolate, porcelain and much more. At boutiques or markets, local crafts are often sold at reasonable prices. Most shops can be found in the capital of Oranjestad and the best part — no sales tax!

923. **What are our accommodation options in Aruba?**
Visitors to Aruba can choose from anything from a high-end hotel to a motel along the beach, but almost all are quality choices:
· Tierra del Sol Aruba Resort & Country Club
· Bucuti Beach Resort Aruba
· La Cabana All-Suite Beach Resort & Casino
· Talk of the Town Beach Club
· Caribbean Palm Village Resort
· Playa Linda Beach Resort
· Amsterdam Manor Beach Resort

924. Can I find out more local information about Aruba?

Climate: Tropical marine, with little seasonal variation. Aruba's known for its almost perpetually sunny days and dry climate all year-round.

Language: Dutch is the official language of Aruba, but English, Papiamento and Spanish are also widely spoken.

Currency: The Arubian guilder/florin (AWG)

Standard Time Zone: Atlantic Standard Time — one hour ahead of New York, except during Daylight Savings, when the time is the same.

For more information: Aruba Tourism Authority, L.G. Smith Blvd. 172, Eagle, Aruba, Dutch Caribbean; Telephone: 297-582-3777; Website: www.aruba.com

925. What are the marriage requirements for Aruba?

If you are looking to get married on Aruba, you will have to provide the following documentation:

- · An "apostile" from your country of citizenship stating that both you and your fiancé are single and eligible to marry
- · An original birth certificate for each of you
- · A divorce decree if either of you have been divorced
- · A death certificate if either of you have been widowed
- · Valid passports
- · Copies of the passports of your witnesses

The proper application and documentation must be faxed to the Civil Registry (fax: 297-583-9160) and also submitted by courier (FedEx, etc.) one month before to the wedding date. Civil ceremonies must take place in the U.S. or Aruba before the church wedding, and in Aruba are performed from Wednesday through Friday, 9:30 a.m. to noon. Requirements vary for Catholic and Jewish ceremonies.

926. I want to have a destination wedding or honeymoon in the Bahamas. Can you tell me about this destination?

With hundreds of activities on land and sea to choose from, visitors to The Islands of the Bahamas will find there's not enough time in a day to do everything that the islands have to offer. Vacationers looking for an active holiday will find a myriad of choices for sports — from sailing, windsurfing, fishing and scuba diving to golf, biking and hiking on land. Those in search of edification will not be disappointed as The Islands of the Bahamas is rich in history and culture as displayed in museums, communities, and in live performances.

Fast Facts:
- British settlement began in 1647
- The islands' area is slightly smaller than Connecticut
- Currency: Bahamian Dollar (B$1)
- Approximate population: 301,790
- English is the official language, but Creole is spoken among Haitian immigrants
- The government is a Constitutional Parliamentary Democracy
- Capital: Nassau
- Gained independence from the British in July 1973

927. What are our destination wedding options in the Bahamas?

Beach Weddings: There are many businesses or wedding planners that will offer you wedding packages for beach weddings, which may be the easiest route to go.

Resort/Villa Wedding: There are a number of resorts and villas in the Bahamas that offer wedding packages for couples who stay at their location. Such packages often include a wedding coordinator, marriage license, clergyman, decorations and music, and transportation. Research various different types of packages offered by various resorts so you can know which ones are best for you. Some popular resorts in the Bahamas are:
- Bluff House Beach Hotel & Yacht Club
- Atlantis
- Sandals Royal Bahamian Resort & Spa
- Riu's Hotel Paradise Island
- Breezes Bahamas

On-Shore Weddings: For those couples wishing to marry in the Bahamas, but arriving by cruise ship, there is the option to have an on-shore wedding and then return to the ship as husband and wife. Witnesses are often supplied by the cruise lines, unless you have invited friends and family along on the cruise beforehand. Depending on the location where you choose to marry, the reception after the marriage can take place back on the ship.

Church Weddings: Church weddings are available as many religious faiths are represented in the Bahamas. Roman Catholics must receive instructions over a six-week period from your local parish priest, who will in turn communicate with the chancery in Nassau. If you want to get married in a church or other house of worship, it may be wise to hire a wedding coordinator who knows the process, or you can go about contacting the church or house of worship on your own.

928. What is the nightlife like in the Bahamas?

One of the real pleasures of The Islands of the Bahamas is that each island has its own personality. No matter what kind of nightlife entertainment visitors want, they'll find it on one of the islands. Peaceful nighttime serenity abounds on The Out Islands. A world of glamour and gaming thrive on Grand Bahama and Nassau/Paradise Island. Casinos, Las Vegas-style shows and nightclubs will keep visitors entertained well into the evening hours. And they shouldn't forget their dancing shoes! Live music fills the night air on Grand Bahama Island — Goombay, disco and jazz be found at any of the lively dancing clubs. Check out Port Lucaya's open-air Count Basie Square for live bands, fire-eaters and other local entertainers. Casinos and nightclubs here keep visitors entertained well after the sun goes down. Many local clubs offer a variety of music, dancing and a taste of live Junkanoo music — the Bahamian music of choice.

929. What is the dining like in the Bahamas?

Most dishes center on seafood like conch or rock lobster, but visitors will find a tremendous variety of fare throughout the islands. Crawfish is another island delicacy that visitors find delicious. Finally, the renowned sweet Eleutheran pineapple wine is available everywhere. To sample authentic Bahamian cuisine, visitors should look for a restaurant participating in the "Real Taste of the Bahamas" program sponsored by the Ministry of Tourism. They should be marked with the "Real Taste of the Bahamas" logo in their window.

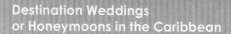
930. **What is the shopping like in the Bahamas?**

The Islands of the Bahamas is a shopper's paradise! With shelves piled high with products from around the world and the discounted duty-free prices around every corner, travelers should be armed with strong willpower or an extra stash of cash for a shopping spree. Some of the best buys include deals on perfume, crystal, leather goods, jewelry, fine linen, watches, photographic equipment, china, binoculars, and telescopes, where prices can be between 25 to 50 percent below U.S. prices.

931. **What are our accommodation options in the Bahamas?**

The Bahamas are a very popular location for couples on their honeymoon or who are planning a destination wedding. Below are some of the more romantic accommodations if you are considering the Bahamas.

- Atlantis
- Bluff House Club Beach Hotel
- Compass Point
- Green Turtle Club
- Kamalame Cay
- Ocean Club
- Old Bahama Bay
- Pink Sands
- Sandals Royal Bahamian Hotel
- Stella Maris Resort Club
- Wyndham Nassau Resort & Crystal Palace Casino

932. **Can I find out more local information about the Bahamas?**

Climate: The trade winds that blow almost continually throughout The Islands of the Bahamas give the islands a warm, agreeable climate which varies little year-round. The most refreshing time is from September through May, when the temperature averages 70 to 75 degrees. The rest of the year is a bit warmer with temperatures between 80 and 85 degrees. Rainfall is scarce from November through April each year; however, showers can occur during the months of May through October. The temperature typically never drops below 72 degrees with averages of 82 degrees in summer and 76 degrees in winter.

Language: The official language of The Islands of the Bahamas is English, more British than American, and generally intertwined with a special Bahamian dialect. Some Indian words like "cassava" and "guava" have been retained in the language.

Currency: Both US and Bahamian dollars are accepted interchangeably throughout the islands.

Time Zone: GMT (Greenwich Mean Time) — 5 hours. Daylight Savings is observed.

For more information, contact: The Bahamas Ministry of Tourism, 640 Fifth Avenue, New York, NY 10019; Telephone (From US): 1-800-BAHAMAS; Website: www. bahamas.com

933. What are the marriage requirements for the Bahamas?

Both you and your fiancé must reside in the Bahamas for one day prior to the wedding. The license costs $100 and both of you must apply in person. You will also need to obtain an affidavit from the US embassy in Nassau stating that both of you are American citizens who are free to marry (both are single, divorced, widowed, etc.). The cost is $55 per person. If one of you is divorced or widowed, they will need to provide proof at the time of application. If you have questions about current fees and requirements, the embassy can be contacted at 242-302-2034.

934. I want to have a destination wedding or honeymoon in Antigua. Can you tell me about this destination?

Antigua, the largest of the English-speaking Leeward Islands, is about 14 miles long and 11 miles wide. Antigua has many trails and tracks that are well suited to hiking. Most of the popular hikes lead to one or another of the island's many historic forts. One of Antigua's most popular and thrilling activities is swimming with the dolphins. This once-in-a-lifetime adventure gives participants the opportunity to experience playtime with dolphins. Not only is this a fun time, but it also gives participants a much greater understanding of these fascinating mammals and a greater appreciation for marine life.

Fast Facts:
· Settled early by the French and Spanish, but the English formed a colony in 1667

- Approximate population (of Antigua & Barbuda): 68,000
- Official language is English
- Capital: St. John's on Antigua
- Independence from the UK in November 1981
- Currency: East Caribbean Dollar (XCD)

935. What are our destination wedding options in Antigua?

Beach Weddings: With 365 beaches, you have any number of locations where you can get married. The setting is naturally romantic and the wedding can be as elaborate or simple as you choose. One way to plan this is to go through a wedding planner on Antigua or a business that specializes in coordinating beach weddings that offers packages to you. If you want to get married on a resort's beach, the wedding can be planned through them. It is relatively easy for you to get married in Antigua — all that may be required is a visit to the Ministry of Justice, confirmation of date and time with a Marriage Office, and payment of fees.

Resort/Villa Weddings: With its rich history and historic buildings, you can choose to marry at one of Antigua's beautiful resorts, plantations, or even among the ruins of an old fort. Listed are just a handful of popular resorts in Antigua:

- Galley Bay
- St. James's Club
- Jolly Beach Resort
- Sandals Antigua Caribbean Village & Spa

Church Weddings: Church weddings on Antigua are possible, but require permission from the church authorities where you wish to get married. You should have your pastor or clergyman from home contact the church beforehand to obtain the requirements. Some churches require couples to go through premarital counseling before allowing them to be married under their roofs. Make sure you know that you will need a little extra time to plan a church wedding.

936. What is the nightlife like in Antigua?

Although Antigua is no Las Vegas in terms of nightlife, it is one of the more happening spots in the region. The island boasts 3 casinos, many clubs and nightly entertainment at most hotels. Much of the nightlife in Antigua revolves around the resorts and hotels. Often, the hotel entertainment features some of the best steel bands and calypso singers in the Caribbean. Outside of the hotels, Antigua offers plenty of hotspots featuring good drink and great entertainment. Live entertainment can be found at many of the popular bars.

937. What is the dining like in Antigua?

Antigua has a wonderful mixture of local delicacies, West Indian, International, and exotic cuisines. There is an excellent choice of bars, restaurants, cafes and pizzerias. Visitors can sample fish and fresh seafood that are caught and served daily. If looking for a local dish, visitors should ask a native Antiguan where to get fungi and saltfish or Ducana.

938. What is the shopping like in Antigua?

Antigua offers a variety of shopping experiences for travelers, from saving money while shopping at a duty free store to window shopping for the perfect vacation memento. Antiguan folk pottery dates back at least to the early 18th century, when slaves fashioned cooking vessels from local clay. Today, folk pottery is fashioned in a number of places around Antigua, but the center of this industry is Sea View Farm Village. The clay is collected from pits located nearby and the wares are fired in an open fire under layers of green grass in the yards of the potters' houses. Buyers should be aware that Antiguan folk pottery breaks rather easily in cold environments.

939. What are our accommodation options in Antigua?

Antigua can be hard to navigate, so we advise you choose carefully when selecting a hotel or resort. They can also be very pricey, so we suggest you book a package to save on costs.

· Coco Bay Resort
· Curtain Bluff
· Galley Bay
· Harmony Hall
· Hawksbill Beach Resort
· Jolly Beach Resort
· Jumby Bay Resort
· Ocean Inn
· Sandals Antigua Resort & Spa
· Siboney Beach Club

- St. James Club
- The Admiral's Inn
- The Catamaran Hotel & Marina
- The Cooper & Lumber Store Hotel
- The Inn at English Harbour

940. Can I find out more local information about Antigua?

Climate: Temperatures generally range from 75 degrees in the winter to 85 degrees in the summer. Annual rainfall averages only 45 inches, making it the sunniest of the Eastern Caribbean Islands, and the northeast trade winds are nearly constant, flagging only in September.

Language: English is the primary language on Antigua.

Currency: The official currency is the Eastern Caribbean dollar (XCD), which is fixed to the US dollar. US dollars are widely accepted, as are traveler's checks and credit cards.

Time Zone: GMT (Greenwich Mean Time) — 4 hours. Daylight Savings is observed.

Entry Requirements: Proof of US citizenship is required in the form of a passport. Visitors will also need an onward or return ticket. No Visa is required for trips under six months in duration.

For more information, contact: Antigua and Barbuda Tourist Office, 305 E. 47th Street, 6A, New York, NY 10017; Telephone (From US): 212-541-4117; Website: www.antigua-barbuda.org

941. What are the marriage requirements for Antigua?

More and more people are getting married while on vacation, and it's now easy to do in Antigua and Barbuda. There are three simple steps you must take:
- Visit the Ministry of Justice located on lower Nevis Street in downtown with your valid passports, complete the application and pay applicable fees.
- Confirm a date and time for the ceremony with a Marriage Officer.
- Get married! There is a registration fee of US$40 that must be paid at the courthouse in the new government buildings on Queen Elizabeth Highway. The application

fee for the special marriage license is US$150, and the
Marriage Officer's fee is US$50.

Both you and your fiancé will need valid passports as proof
of citizenship. If either of you have been previously married,
you will need to bring along the original divorce decree or,
in the case of a widow or widower, the original marriage
and death certificates. Both of you must be over 15 years of
age. If you are under 18, written authorization from parents
or a guardian is required. It is important that all documents
presented are original or certified original by the issuing
departments or offices. You should ensure that all documents
are in your legal names and provide affidavits in cases where
you are known by another name. Your marriage must also
be solemnized or celebrated in the presence of two or more
witnesses, apart from the Marriage Officer (they can ask a
guest or two to do this for them).

Your Antigua/Barbuda marriage ceremony is both legal and
binding. Additionally, consent must be expressed by both
you and your fiancé to accept each other as husband and
wife. To be married in a church requires the permission from
the church authorities where you wish to be married. You
need to have your pastor contact the church to establish the
requirements. Some churches ask that you attend pre-nuptial
consultations. Therefore, allow some extra time if planning
a church ceremony. To get a list of churches in Antigua,
contact the Antigua and Barbuda Department of Tourism for
a list of churches on the island.

942. I want to have a destination wedding or honeymoon
in the U.S. Virgin Islands. Can you tell me about this
destination?
The United States Virgin Islands (St. Thomas, St. Croix,
and St. John) are among some of the most popular tourist
destinations in the Caribbean. Nowhere else offers such a
vacation value as the U.S. Virgin Islands: secluded beaches,
national parks, duty-free shopping, campgrounds, kayaking,
hiking, ecological tours, world-class diving, superb sailing.
tropical forests, local craftsmen, island art, sunbathing, fine
dining, and nightlife. Vacationers frequently visit all three
islands during their stay. St. John is only 20 minutes away
from St. Thomas by ferry, and frequent small-plane service,
sea-planes, hydrofoil, charter boats, catamaran service and

commercial airlines link St. Thomas and St. Croix.

Fast Facts:
- Subtropical climate
- Approximate population: 108,700
- English is the major language spoken, along with Spanish/Spanish Creole and French/French Creole
- Capital: Charlotte Amalie
- Island residents are US citizens, but do not vote in the US presidential elections

943. What are our destination wedding options in the U.S. Virgin Islands?

Beach Weddings: Couples wishing to get married on a beach in the U.S. Virgin Islands can seek to do so through a wedding coordinator the island offers or one a particular resort may offer. You can work with the planners to sort out all the logistics of the beach wedding, from airline tickets to who is going to officiate. These coordinators and planners know the islands and its services best, so it is highly recommended you work with them to plan your wedding.

Resort/Villa Weddings: There are numerous resorts and villas throughout the U.S. Virgin Islands — it all comes down to you picking the perfect one for you and your fiancé. Here are just a few of the popular resorts in the USVI:
- Caneel Bay
- Sapphire Beach Resort & Marina
- The Buccaneer

At Sea Weddings: Weddings on a private yacht are possible in the U.S. Virgin Islands, which are the home to many yacht brokers. The price often includes a chef, food, beverages, watersports equipment and a variety of other amenities. Your friends and family can watch as you get married amid the crystal clear waters of the Caribbean. These weddings at sea can also be arranged through a wedding planner or coordinator.

Church Weddings: If you opt for a traditional wedding, you will have no trouble finding a house of worship that will marry you according to your faith. The U.S. Virgin Islands are culturally and religiously diverse, so there are plenty of options available. The islands offer a number of synagogues, churches and mosques.

Underwater Weddings: Underwater weddings are also possible on the U.S. Virgin Islands. It is something that many couples — often adventure seekers — opt to do. One stipulation of such a wedding is that the couple — and whichever guests may be attending — must be certified to dive. The officiant must also be certified. In this case, it is best to find a company that specializes in underwater weddings.

944. I want to have a destination wedding or honeymoon on St. Croix. Can you tell me about this destination?

The largest of the U.S. Virgin Islands, St. Croix is rich in diverse history that remains alive in the architecture, national parks, historic landmarks, botanical attractions, and traditions that are an integral part of island life.

Golf is extremely popular on St. Croix. Adventure seekers can explore St. Croix's beautiful west end on horseback or by bike. Guided tours are available for all experience levels. Hikers will find several indigenous and migratory species in the forest and in the Sandy Point Wildlife Refuge. St. Croix offers some of the best snorkeling in the world. Buck Island, famous for its striking natural beauty and underwater snorkeling trails, is one of only two underwater National Monuments in the United States. Cane Bay Reef, Davis Bay and Salt River Bay are popular scuba diving spots known for the 13,000-foot deep sub-sea canyon and steep diving walls. Divers off the coasts of St. Croix may also experience close encounters with rare species of sea turtles that nest seasonally on the island's beaches. Kayakers can see snowy egrets, great barracudas, spotted eagle rays, and hundreds of other species in Salt River Bay National Park and Ecological Preserve.

945. I want to have a destination wedding or honeymoon on St. John. Can you tell me about this destination?

The smallest of the U.S. Virgin Islands, St. John retains a tranquil, unspoiled beauty uncommon in the Caribbean or anywhere else in the world. Two-thirds of St. John is part of the Virgin Islands National Park, featuring fascinating trails, secluded coves, and dazzling white beaches. The Reef Bay Trail takes hikers through dense forests, plantation ruins, and rock outcroppings marked by well-preserved petroglyphs. Cruz Bay, the center of activity on St. John, contains colorful shops, lively bars, and fabulous restaurants. Trunk Bay is one of the world's most photographed beaches and the most popular on St. John. Trunk Bay also offers an exciting underwater snorkeling trail.

946. I want to have a destination wedding or honeymoon on St. Thomas. Can you tell me about this destination?

With duty-free shopping exemptions unrivaled by any other Caribbean destination and fine dining and accommodations at an exceptional value, St. Thomas is indeed a treasured discovery for travelers. Both *National Geographic* and *Condé Nast Traveler* have named heart-shaped Magens Bay one of the most beautiful beaches in the world. Snorkeling, kayaking, and other water gear is available for rental. Coral World Marine Park & Observatory contains an underwater observatory tower, a tropical nature trail, a marine gardens aquarium, and an 80,000-gallon coral reef tank. St. Thomas is a mountainous island, so visitors will find that climbs to the peaks offer dramatic views. Visitors will also note the abundance of the yellow cedar, one of the world's most beautiful flowers.

947. What is the nightlife like in the U.S. Virgin Islands?

There are several clubs throughout the U.S. Virgin Islands, most of which feature live music. For a taste of the Caribbean's musical style, visitors should seek out one of the many local Calypso bands. There is also a casino on St. Croix. For a taste of the local beat, travelers should check out Mocko jumbies (dancers in colorful costumes wearing stilts), reggae and calypso, steel pan bands, and pulsating salsa. The Crucian Christmas Festival, one of St. Croix's most popular events, includes a month-long celebration that culminates in the Three Kings Day parade. Island traditions come alive during celebrations throughout the year. The Three Kings' Day festival on St. Croix, St. John's Fourth of July celebration, and St. Thomas' annual Carnival are just three examples of the dozens of special events that take place each year. However, on any given day, visitors can catch a glimpse of the unique culture of the islands.

948. What is the dining like in the U.S. Virgin Islands?

Caribbean lobster, wahoo, grouper, mahi-mahi, tuna and

other daily catches from the sea are staple menu items. Local specialties include "Fungi," a cornmeal based side dish; "kallaloo," a soup made from okra, spinach and fish; sweet-potato pudding; fried "johnnycake" bread; plantains; peas and rice; curried chicken; "old wife" fish; and conch fritters, a batter-fried delicacy. Since many island recipes originate from times when imports were scarce, today's typical island fare includes locally grown and raised spices, tropical fruits, root vegetables, and meats. One favorite local beverage is maubi, a slightly fermented drink concocted from ginger root, yeast, herbs, and the bark of the maubi tree. Non-alcoholic ginger beer, bush tea, soursop juice, and the creamy sea-moss cooler are also popular.

949. **What is the shopping like in the U.S. Virgin Islands?**
The U.S. Virgin Islands are a duty-free port, with no sales or luxury taxes on items such as watches, cameras, fine jewelry, china, and leather goods. Christiansted's King's Alley on St. Croix offers handmade goods and designer fashions. Mongoose Junction on St. John is a shopper's paradise, featuring jewelry, clothing, crafts, and artwork. Charlotte Amalie on St. Thomas has been hailed as the best shopping port in the world. In short, visitors are sure to find unique, inexpensive shopping no matter what island they're on. Shops in the downtown areas are usually closed on Sundays, unless a cruise ship is in port.

950. **What are our accommodation options in the U.S. Virgin Islands?**
Be sure to look into the package deals offered by many of these and other hotels and resorts in the U.S. Virgin Islands. The price of accommodations in the islands can be quite expensive if you are not considering staying at an all-inclusive resort.

· Caneel Bay
· Carambola Beach Resort
· Chenay Beach Resort
· Cormorant Beach Club & Hotel
· Cottages By the Sea
· Divi Carina Bay Resort & Casino
· Elysian Beach Resort
· Estate Zootenvaal
· Harmony Studios
· Hotel 1829

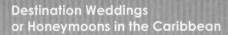

- Hotel Caravelle
- Lavender Hill Suites
- Maho Bay Campground
- Marriott Morning Star Beach Resort
- Renaissance Grand Beach Resort
- The Buccaneer
- The Ritz-Carlton St. Thomas
- The Waves at Cane Bay
- Villa Blanca
- Villa Santana
- Westin Resort St. John

951. Can I find out more local information about the U.S. Virgin Islands as a potential destination wedding or honeymoon location?

Climate: The U.S. Virgin Islands have year-round warm temperatures. The average temperature ranges from 77 degrees in the winter to 82 degrees in the summer.

Peak Season: Winter

Language: English, though approximately 45 percent of the population of St. Croix speaks Spanish. French and French Creole are also spoken on the islands.

Currency: U.S. Dollars — USD

Standard Time Zone: GMT (Greenwich Mean Time) — 4 hours

For more information, contact: United States Virgin Islands Department of Tourism, PO Box 6400, St. Thomas, USVI 00804; Website: www.usvitourism.vi; Telephone (From US): 800-372-USVI or 213-739-0138.

952. What are the marriage requirements for the U.S. Virgin Islands?

Because the U.S. Virgin Islands operate under the laws of the United States government, legal marriage requirements are simple and hassle-free. You need only request an application for a marriage license from the U.S. Virgin Islands Territorial Courts or go online to www.usvitourism.vi. There is a required eight-day waiting period after the notarized and completed application is received in the islands. (Additional documentation is required if either of you has married previously.) You should specify whether a territorial court judge or a clergy member will perform the marriage ceremony, as an appointment is necessary to be married in the court. The marriage application fee is only $25, and the marriage license is $25. Weddings performed in the court by a judge will incur another $200 fee for the ceremony.

953. I want to have a destination wedding or honeymoon in St. Lucia. Can you tell me about this destination?

St. Lucia is rich in natural beauty — and there is so much to see and do. Historical, cultural and heritage sites can be found throughout the island. There are plenty of challenges for sporting visitors. Go windsurfing, sailing, parasailing, deep-sea fishing, or water-skiing. The St. Lucia National Trust and the Department of Forestry offers a number of nature trails. Hikers will have the opportunity to see spectacular rain forest waterfalls, flora and local birds like the Saint Lucia Parrot, the Saint Lucia Oriole and the Saint Lucia Black Finch. Travelers can follow a hiking trail through an estuarine tropical forest to a wide white sand beach that is frequented by nesting Leatherback Turtles. Comfortable shoes are a must.

Fast Facts:

- Gained independence from the UK in 1979
- Tropical climate
- Approximate population: 166,300
- Official language is English, but French patois is also spoken
- Capital: Castries
- Currency: East Caribbean Dollar (XCD)

954. What are our destination wedding options in St. Lucia?

Beach Weddings: There is no better wedding scenery than the pristine sandy beaches St. Lucia. These can be arranged through island wedding planners or the resort where you are staying. The most popular time for a beach wedding is sunset, which provides for lovely pictures of the event. Sometimes companies will offer packages that include not just beach weddings, but weddings atop cliffs or underneath waterfalls, at a historic location (such as a fort) or in a tropical garden.

Resort/Villa Weddings: Resort or villa weddings are very popular in St. Lucia. Make sure you know which resorts offer wedding packages so you can make an informed decision as to where to stay. Below are some popular resorts on St. Lucia:

- Ladera Resort
- Anse Chastanet Resort
- Rendezvous
- Stonefield Estate Villa Resort
- Sandals Grande St. Lucian, Halcyon Beach and Regency St. Lucia

Church Weddings: Roman Catholics are the main religious community in St. Lucia, but other religions are represented on the island. Your local parish priest has to communicate with a priest on the island to ensure that you have completed pre-marital counseling before the marriage takes place, and that you have met all the conditions needed so you can be married in a Catholic church on St. Lucia. Such weddings take at least 3 months of planning, so be prepared.

955. What is the nightlife like in St. Lucia?

Most hotels and resorts offer some form of entertainment throughout the week, including local live bands and cultural performances. There are also a number of bars, nightclubs, and restaurants all over the island that are fun spots at night.

956. What is the dining like in St. Lucia?

St. Lucians enjoy food and this is evident by the large number of restaurants, cafes, and fast food outlets on the island. The cuisine is largely a combination of international and Creole utilizing fresh local produce. There are also specialty restaurants such as French, Italian, Indian and steakhouses. And of course, as one would expect, almost every restaurant offers fish and seafood dishes.

957. What is the shopping like in St. Lucia?

St. Lucia has a variety of shopping experiences to suit all types of travelers. The 100-year-old Castries market is a must-see for visitors to the island, where local vendors offer thousands varieties of island memorabilia, spices and foods, and local fishermen offer the daily catch. The Castries Market is particularly vibrant on Saturdays, especially during St. Lucia Jazz and Carnival.

958. What are our accommodation options in St. Lucia?

Hotels and resorts in St. Lucia can be expensive, so, you should look into a package deal or try out an all-inclusive resort. Wherever you stay, you will feel a deep sense of intimacy and isolation, which is perfect for the honeymooners or newlyweds who want to get away from it all.

- Anse Chastanet
- Bay Gardens Hotel
- Hummingbird Beach Resort
- Jalousie Hilton Resort & Spa
- Ladera Resort
- LeSPORT
- Mago Estate Hotel
- Rendezvous
- Royal St. Lucian
- Sandals Grande St. Lucian Spa & Beach Resort
- Sandals Halcyon Beach St. Lucia
- Sandals Regency Golf & Spa Resort
- Stonefield Estate Villa Resort
- Windjammer Landing Villa Beach Resort

959. Can I find out more local information about St. Lucia as a potential destination wedding or honeymoon location?

Climate: St. Lucia has tropical year-round temperatures of 70 degrees to 90 degrees with trade winds coming from the northeast. The rainy season is from June to November and the drier period is between December and May.

Peak Season: Mid-November through mid-March

Language: The main language in Saint Lucia is English, although many St. Lucians also speak French and Spanish. Kwéyòl, St Lucia's second language, is widely spoken by the St. Lucian people including doctors, bankers, government ministers and the man on the street! Kwéyòl is not just a patois or broken French, but a language in its own right, with its own rules of grammar and syntax. The language is being preserved by its everyday use in day-to-day affairs and by special radio programs and news read entirely in Kwéyòl.

Currency: Eastern Caribbean Dollar, XCD
Standard Time Zone: GMT (Greenwich Mean Time), 4 hours

For more information, contact: St. Lucia Tourist Board, 800 Second Ave Ste 400, New York, NY 10017; Telephone (From US): 888-4STLUCIA; Website: www.stlucia.org.

960. What are the marriage requirements for St. Lucia?

It's easy to get married in St Lucia. There is a 48-hour residency requirement when you are looking to marry. After you've stayed on the island for two days, a local Solicitor can apply for a license on your behalf. This license needs to be received two working days before the wedding date. You must have the following documentation:

· Passport
· Birth Certificate
· Decree Absolute (if one of you is divorced) or a Death Certificate (in the case of a widow/widower of first spouse)
· If a name has been changed, a Deed Poll is required
· If one of you is under the age of 18, evidence of a consent of parents is required in the form of a sworn affidavit stamped by a Notary Public
· If any required documents are not in English, an authenticated translation must be available.

Notorial Fees & Marriage License are approximately US$150. Registrar Fees are approximately US$37. A marriage certificate costs US$3. Typically, all of these details can be taken care of by a couple's hotel.

961. I want to have a destination wedding or honeymoon in Puerto Rico. Can you tell me about this destination?

Puerto Rico offers the excitement of overseas travel with the convenience and comfort of a domestic trip. It is a vibrant, modern, bilingual and multi-cultural society, one that has been molded by Spanish, African, Indian and U.S. influences. Whether dreaming of spectacular surfing waves, a challenging golf course, or the perfect sunbathing beach, Puerto Rico offers the active traveler a tremendous array of opportunities. Surfing and golf compete with tennis, fishing, kayaking, scuba diving, and horseback riding, not to mention windsurfing and parasailing, for visitors' active time. Puerto Rico's perpetual summer weather begs travelers to enjoy the sport of their choice! Nature lovers will not want to miss the phenomenal experience of visiting a tropical phosphorescent bay. The phosphorescence is actually bioluminescence generated by microscopic organisms in the water, and at two different protected bays, La Parguera and Vieques, visitors can see this for themselves. Truly magical! Finally, Puerto Rico is home to some of the most beautiful beaches in the world, and its hundreds of miles of coastline harbor an almost endless selection for the beach connoisseur.

Fast Facts:
· Ceded to the U.S. as part of the Spanish-American War
· Tropical marine climate
· Approximate population: 3,916,600
· Spanish and English are the official languages spoken
· Capital: San Juan

962. What are our destination wedding options in Puerto Rico?

Beach Weddings: Beach weddings can be arranged through a local wedding planner who knows the island and its requirements best. They will know which beaches offer the best views and have the softest sand, and will know how to arrange for an officiant and any other services you desire.

Resort/Villa Weddings: The numerous resorts and villas on Puerto Rico often offer wedding packages, including a wedding coordinator who can help in arranging all the necessities for the wedding. We've listed just a few of the more popular resorts at this location:
· Horned Dorset Primavera Hotel
· The Water Club
· Villa Montana
· Villa Vista Linda
· Hyatt Dorado Beach Resort & Country Club

Church Weddings: There are many religions represented in Puerto Rico, but the major ones are Catholicism and Protestantism. Locate an officiant who can perform the ceremony you desire to your specifications and wishes. Some priests are willing to perform a "non-Christian" ceremony, so be sure to ask around. Jewish, Baptist, inter-denominational and other religious ceremonies are also possible. Each religion has its own set of requirements, so be sure you learn about these before making final arrangements.

963. What is the nightlife like in Puerto Rico?

The Caribbean has a well-deserved reputation as a quiet, laid-back place, where hammocks are more common than discos. But Puerto Ricans truly know how to party, and the nightlife in the island's bigger cities and resort hotels rivals that of the world's most cosmopolitan cities! San Juan is the Caribbean capital of nightlife and entertainment, where visitors can indulge in bar hopping, fine dining, Vegas-style gaming or anything in between. Throughout the San Juan area, bars, discos and popular restaurants are found on nearly every corner of the city. Visitors can also leave the big island entirely and head to Vieques, where they can take in some live jazz before they head for a midnight swim in phosphorescent waters.

964. What is the dining like in Puerto Rico?

Dining in Puerto Rico can be an adventure. From boutique restaurants serving the latest fusion cuisine to traditional Puerto Rican Mesones, from snack shacks on the beach to classic steak houses, Puerto Rico offers as many choices of dining atmosphere and cuisine as any major city on the mainland. Visitors should be sure to eat at one of the thirty traditional eateries participating in the Mesones Gastronomicos Program sponsored by the Puerto Rico Tourism Company. These restaurants, located throughout the island, serve up Criolla cooking at its best. Criolla cuisine is a blend of Taíno, Spanish and African influences incorporating all kinds of delicious fruits and vegetables, unforgettably savory rice dishes, meat and poultry, as well as abundant seafood from local waters. One island favorite, tostones, or fried green plantains, are enjoyed alone or as a side dish with nearly every meal. Mofongo is another star preparation of mashed plantains and meat or seafood in a delicious garlic and tomato-based sauce.

965. What are our accommodation options in Puerto Rico?

You should be prepared to take things easy in Puerto Rico. When staying at a resort, you should be aware that not everything is included in the price, such as any activities you may pursue.

· Caribe Hilton
· Casa Grande Mountain Retreat
· Ceiba Country Inn
· Copamarina Beach Resort

- Doral Palmas del Mar Resort
- Embassy Suites Dorado del Mar Beach & Golf Resort
- Horned Dorset Primavera Hotel
- Hotel and Parador Joyuda Beach
- J.B. Hidden Village Hotel
- Lemontree Waterfront Cottages
- Mayaguez Resort & Casino
- Parador Hacienda Gripinas
- Parador Hacienda Juanita
- Ponce Hilton and Casino
- Tamarindo Estates
- The Fajardo Inn
- The Villas at Palmas

966. Can I find out more local information about Puerto Rico?

Climate: Puerto Rico is a tropical destination blessed with lots of sun and enough rain to keep the waterfalls flowing and the flowers growing. The climate is as close to perfect as it can get, averaging 83 degrees in the winter and 85 degrees in the summer. In other words, it's always summer! The trade winds cool the coastal towns and the temperature decreases as visitors go up into the higher mountains.

Peak Season: December 15 to April 15.

Language: Spanish & English are the official languages. Although Spanish is the norm, English is widely spoken in all major tourist areas throughout the island.

Currency: U.S. Dollars - USD.

Standard Time Zone: GMT (Greenwich Mean Time) — 4 hours.

For more information, contact: Puerto Rico Main Office, 135 W. 50th Street, 22nd Floor, New York, NY, 10020; Telephone: 212-586-6262; Website: www.gotopuertorico. com.

967. What are the marriage requirements for Puerto Rico?

With Puerto Rico's exotic ambiance and spectacular sunsets, there's no better place to be swept up in the romance of a wedding! Here's what you need to know before you can tie the knot in Puerto Rico:

- Each of you will need to bring a photo ID or passport; if either you or your fiancé has been divorced or widowed, a divorce decree or death certificate is also required.
- Both of you will need to take a blood test from a federally certified laboratory (in the U.S. or Puerto Rico) within 10 days of the wedding date.
- A marriage certificate can be acquired in advance from the Puerto Rico Department of Health; call 787-767-9120 for more information.
- A doctor will need to sign and certify your marriage certificate and blood test in Puerto Rico.
- You will then visit the Demographic Registry to obtain the marriage license, and purchase two license stamps (total stamp cost is US$30).
- You can expect to receive their marriage license within ten days of your wedding date.

968. I want to have a destination wedding or honeymoon in Jamaica. Can you tell me about this destination?

Jamaica features rich culture, vibrant art, picturesque beaches, and world famous all-inclusive resorts. The island of Jamaica is the Caribbean's largest English-speaking island. With endless coastlines, the beaches range from reef-protected white sand in the north to black sand beaches in the south. Jamaica's rich ancestry, with ties to Africa, Asia, Europe, the Middle East, Great Britain, India, China, Germany, Portugal, and South America, has woven a nation that is truly uniquely Jamaican. Visitors can catch a show at one of the many theaters and stage shows, revel at Carnival and Augus' Mawnin, or just dance in the street to the infectious reggae beat pouring from nearly every street corner and rum bar across the island. No matter where you are, music is likely to entertain you. The Jamaican people love to dance; in fact, it is an integral part of everyday life. Touring Jamaica on one's own is possible, but may be intimidating to some, as Jamaica's dramatic inequality of wealth and social tensions influence the local people. With an all-inclusive resort, visitors step off the plane and are immediately swept away to their own private paradise.

Fast Facts:
- Gained independence from the British Commonwealth in 1962

- Slightly smaller than Connecticut
- Approximate population: 2,730,000
- Official language is English and patois English
- Capital: Kingston
- Currency: Jamaican Dollar (JMD)

969. What are our destination wedding options in Jamaica?

Beach Weddings: Jamaica calls out to couples for a beach wedding. The island holds some of the most beautiful beaches in the world. There is also the option of staying at a resort and getting married on the resort's beach, with a wedding coordinator provided by the resort itself.

Resort/Villa Weddings: There are plenty of resorts and villas in Jamaica where you can have the wedding of your dreams. Be sure to do your own research and compile an extensive list of possible resorts or villas or plantations where you can marry, and whether or not the locations offer wedding packages. We've listed just a handful of the popular resorts in Jamaica:

- Half Moon Resort
- Blue Lagoon Villas
- Sans Souci Resort & Spa
- Endless Summer Villa
- Good Hope Plantation
- Couples Negril, Ocho Rios and Swept Away
- Sandals Negril, Montego Bay, Ocho Rios and Whitehouse
- Superclubs Runaway Bay, Super Sunrise and Montego Bay
- Riu Negril and Ocho Rios
- Beaches Negril and Boscobel

Church Weddings: Protestantism is the main religion of Jamaica, and Christianity in general is vastly represented throughout the island, but many other religions are also represented, so you should have no trouble getting married under the religion you choose. Once you have found a church or house of worship where you would like to wed, you should contact the priest or head to plan and organize the wedding. There may be additional fees for Catholic and Jewish ceremonies.

On-Shore Weddings: Couples who arrive at Jamaica and

dock in Montego Bay or Ocho Rios can get married on-shore. Sometimes the cruise line will provide a wedding coordinator and witnesses for you to help with the arrangements of the marriage process, and other times you will have to find a wedding coordinator on the island who can help you through the planning process. The coordinator will be able to arrange for licenses, wedding officials, witnesses and transportation.

970. What is the nightlife like in Jamaica?

Jamaica is the home of reggae, and every Jamaican town has some degree of nightlife, whether it is a cluster of small bars with a jukebox, cabaret-type entertainment, high tech dance clubs, beach parties, or karaoke ensembles. Fashionable street dances featuring sound systems have become the rage for younger, dancehall audiences. Visitors should check with local newspapers for nightlife happenings when they get there.

971. What is the dining like in Jamaica?

Jamaica's "jerk meat" is the island's most distinctive style of cooking. Meat, usually chicken or pork, and sometimes fish, is seasoned in a special blend of island-grown spices, including pimento, hot peppers, cinnamon and nutmeg, and then grilled slowly for hours over a fire of pimento wood and under a cover of wooden slats or corrugated zinc sheets in a specially designed drum. Seafood is plentiful, as is the selection of fresh fruit and vegetables. Foods of all types can be found while dining in the resorts. Further outside the resorts and outside of Kingstown, international eating options are limited.

972. What is the shopping like in Jamaica?

The Ocho Rios area has a wide variety of shopping possibilities. Main Street, in the center of town, is a shopping hub that includes the local craft market and some duty-free delights.

973. What are our accommodation options in Jamaica?

Jamaica has hundreds of options for your honeymoon or destination wedding. We've listed just a few of the more intimate and beautiful ones as a starting point.
· Blue Lagoon Villas
· Breezes Runaway Bay
· Half Moon Golf, Tennis & Beach Club

- Jake's
- Jamaica Inn
- Sandals Dunns River Resort
- Sandals Montego Bay
- Sandals Negril
- Sandals Grande Ocho Rios
- Sandals Whitehouse
- Sans Souci Resort & Spa

974. Can I find out more local information about Jamaica?

Climate: Jamaica has a tropical climate at sea level and a temperate climate towards the highlands of the interior. The island sees two rainy seasons: from May to June, and from September to November. Of note, also, is the hurricane season from June to September, during which time large storms may, but rarely do, pass over the island. The average temperature is between 66 and 99 degrees year-round.

Peak Season: Mid-December through mid-April

Language: The official language is English, but most Jamaicans speak a local patois influenced by a combination of several different languages.

Currency: Jamaican Dollars — JMD

Time Zone: GMT (Greenwich Mean Time) — 4 hours. Jamaica does not observe Daylight Savings Time.

For more information, contact: Visit Jamaica, 1320 S. Dixie Highway, Coral Gables, FL 33146; Telephone (From US): 212-856-9727; Website: www.visitjamaica.com.

975. What are the marriage requirements for Jamaica?

Unlike many countries, Jamaica does not expect you to take a blood test before getting married. However, the following documentation is required:

- Proof of citizenship — certified copy of birth certificate, which includes father's name.
- Parents' written consent if under 18 years of age.
- Proof of divorce if applicable (original certificate of divorce).
- Certified copy of death certificate for widow or widower.
- Italian nationals celebrating their wedding in Jamaica

must notify their embassy and a certified copy of their marriage certificate forwarded to their embassy to be legalized and translated.
· French Canadians need a notarized translated copy of all documents and a photocopy of the original French documents.

There are non-denominational Marriage Officers who can officiate either at their offices, in their homes or at a place chosen by you and your fiancé, and are able to provide witnesses. Marriage Officers charge anywhere from US$50 to US$250.

976. I want to have a destination wedding or honeymoon in the British Virgin Islands. Can you tell me about this destination?

Located where the Caribbean meets the Atlantic, the British Virgin Islands contains sixty islands. With hundreds of secret bays and hidden coves, they have long been a seafarers' haven. There is plenty of unsurpassed natural beauty and limitless fun on land and water all adding up to more of nature's little secrets than visitors ever imagined.

Fast Facts:
· Annexed by the English from the Dutch in 1672
· Subtropical climate
· Approximate population: 22,640
· Official language is English
· Capital: Road Town
· Currency: US Dollar (USD)

977. What are our destination wedding options in the British Virgin Islands?

Beach Weddings: There is an ample amount of beach in the British Virgin Islands where you can marry, so depending upon the island and the setting you are striving for, hiring a wedding planner is your best bet. Beach weddings in the British Virgin Islands are popular because of the spectacular sunsets and incredible vistas.

Resort/Villa Weddings: Resort and villa weddings are also widely popular and there are many options available. They will often provide their own wedding coordinators to help you plan the wedding, but in the case that they don't you can contact the resort or villa and see if special arrangements can be made. We've listed below some popular resorts in these locations:

· The Bitter End Yacht Club
· Biras Creek Estate
· Villa Renaissance
· The Sugar Mill
· CuisinArt Resort & Spa
· Long Bay Beach Resort & Villa

Church Weddings: Roman Catholicism is the predominant faith on the Spanish- and French-speaking islands of the British West Indies, while Protestantism is predominant in the Dutch territories and elsewhere. Protestantism is also predominant in the British Virgin Islands. In the British Virgin Islands, for church weddings, the banns must be published by the church of choice at least three weeks in advance. Some ministers may require proof of membership.

At Sea Weddings: Weddings on a private yacht are very popular in the British Virgin Islands. You should contact a yacht broker or go through a wedding planner on the islands to obtain more details about the specifics of planning a wedding on a yacht.

978. What is the nightlife like in the British Virgin Islands?
The nightlife in the BVI is quite different from the nightlife found on neighboring islands. Here, visitors will not find a fast-paced nightlife scene; rather, the pace of the unhurried day flows into the night. Indulge in fine food and drink at one of the many resorts or local restaurants. Absorb the local flavor and hospitality at one of the islands' many outdoor beach bars. They might find themselves sitting next to a local business owner who has just closed up shop for the night, or chatting with a financier who came ashore from a yacht. The experience will stay with visitors for a lifetime!

979. What is the dining like in the British Virgin Islands?
The local cuisine represents a variety of tropical tastes extracted from the multiple cultures that have made the BVI what they are today. The Caribbean, of course, is well known for its wealth of spices. Combine these with indigenous fruits, vegetables and seafood, and the results are a colorful and palatable taste extravaganza. From West

Indian to Cordon Bleu cuisine, the BVI has restaurants to satisfy every palate, mood and budget. Some restaurants are on the beach, others can be found along the islands' dramatic ridges offering breathtaking views of the sea. Some are located in historic sugar mills, surfside shacks and fragrant tropical gardens. Visitors can try sampling some of the local dishes — it's a fantastic way to experience the BVI culture, savor some "home food," and get a chance to mingle with the locals.

980. **What is the shopping like in the British Virgin Islands?**
The British Virgin Islands offer a variety of shopping experiences ranging from local handcraft markets to farmers' markets to traditional boutiques. Since there is no duty-free shopping, consumer goods tend to be expensive because of duty and shipping costs associated with bringing these items to the islands. Visitors should try to pack enough toiletries, film, sunblock, etc. for the duration of their vacation as familiar brand name items are limited and usually quite costly.

981. **What are our accommodation options in the British Virgin Islands?**
Here are a few options to look into if you are thinking about going to the British Virgin Islands for your destination wedding or honeymoon:
   · Anegada Beach Campground
   · Anegada Reef Hotel
   · Guana Island Club
   · Peter Island Resorts
   · Sandcastle Hotel
   · Sandy Ground Estates

982. **Can I find out more local information about the British Virgin Islands?**
Climate: The British Virgin Islands enjoy a balmy, subtropical climate. Temperatures rarely drop below 77 degrees in the winter or rise above 90 degrees in the summer. The average temperature is around 83 degrees with slight variations between seasons.

Peak Season: The peak tourist season is December to May, but this has more to do with the weather in North America and Europe than it does with the reliably balmy weather of the BVI. It can be beneficial to visit outside this period, when visitors can expect room rates to be about two-thirds of the rates charged during the busier months. And as an additional bonus, between April and August, the calmer weather tends to keep the waters clearer for diving.

Language: English

Currency: US Dollar — USD.

Time Zone: GMT (Greenwich Mean Time) — 4 hours.

For more information, contact: British Virgin Islands Tourism Board, 1 West 34th Street, Suite 302, New York, NY 10001; Telephone: 800-835-8530; Website: www. bvitourism.com

983. What are the marriage requirements for the British Virgin Islands?

You can apply immediately upon arrival in BVI for a license at the Attorney General's Office, situated on the second floor of the Central Administration Complex, Road Town, Tortol The Attorney General's office is open Monday through Friday, 8:30 a.m. through 4:30 p.m., except for holidays. The license will take three working days to process, so you should plan accordingly. Once the license is granted, it is good for three months.

At the Attorney General's office, you will be required to purchase a $110 postage stamp for a special license if you have been a resident of BVI for one day or a $50 postage stamp for an ordinary license if you have been a resident of BVI for fifteen days or more. You will have to show proof of your residency status (proof of the day on which they arrived) in the BVI, via your passports. In addition, you must show proof of marital status (including certified copies of Absolute Decree of Divorce or death certificates, if applicable), and have two witnesses to witness and sign your application form for the license. Please note that these witnesses need not be the same two witnesses who are present at your marriage ceremony. You and your fiancé can ask anyone to be the witnesses at the Attorney General's office and the ceremony.

Having applied for your license, you will need to go to the Registrar's Office in the heart of Roadtown. At the office, you will be required to fill out a form showing your names as shown on your travel documents, your ages, occupations, marital status, and the names of the two witnesses, who must then be present at the ceremony.

If you wish to be married at the Registrar's Office, you will be required to pay a fee of $35. If you wish the Registrar to perform the ceremony outside the office, there is a fee of $100. If the Registrar needs to leave Tortola to perform the ceremony, you will also be required to pay for the transportation to and from that island. If you wish to be married in the church of your choice, Wedding Banns must be published on three consecutive Saturdays or Sundays in that church. You must make advance arrangements with the minister of that church.

984. I want to have a destination wedding or honeymoon in Anguilla. Can you tell me about this destination?
Anguilla is often the destination of choice for luxurious, five-star resorts. Resorts and spas offer the latest in spa and wellness facilities, services and treatments. Unhurried, uncomplicated, easy-to-explore Anguilla invites bike tours and hiking excursions as well as a myriad of activity choices. Art galleries featuring original oils, pastels and watercolors, fine wood and metal sculptures, driftwood tables, and mantle pieces are scattered throughout the islands. With 33 beaches, beachgoers are assured of peace and serenity. It is this very nurturing, relaxed and gracious spirit that has set Anguilla apart from many other vacation destinations, in the Caribbean and around the world.

Fast Facts:
· Became a separate British dependency in 1980
· Tropical climate
· Approximate population: 13,250
· Official language is English
· Capital: The Valley
· Currency: East Caribbean Dollar (XCD)
· Has 3 airports

985. What is the nightlife like in Anguilla?
For a small island, Anguilla has a number of nightlife

options and musical entertainment to offer its visitors.
Classical pianists and guitarists, a quiet saxophone, reggae,
steel drum and calypso bands are just a few options. *What
We Do in Anguilla* and *Anguilla Life* list the what, where
and when for night owls. These publications are available
from the Anguilla Tourist Board and most properties.
Local hot spots offer an opportunity to dance barefoot to
Caribbean tunes. Generally, Sandy Ground is the hotspot on
Fridays and Saturdays, while Sundays and Wednesdays the
crowds move to Shoal Bay East.

986. **What is the dining like in Anguilla?**
Dining in Anguilla is unmatched in the Caribbean with
more gourmet choices per acre than in New York City. From
award-winning chefs and elegant restaurants to beachside
bistros and sand cay barbecues, Anguilla offers a dining
experience for every mood, taste and budget. French, Italian,
Creole, West Indian, American, and other culinary styles
are masterfully influenced by the flavors of the Caribbean to
create an eclectic mix of mouthwatering delights.

987. **What is the shopping like in Anguilla?**
Anguilla is home to a veritable colony of artists who have
come from many parts of the world. The diverse art forms
include pottery, sculpture, handcrafts, paintings and
woodcraft. There is also a growing collection of tribal
artifacts, textiles, antiques, carvings and furniture from
many exotic destinations, which can be found in art galleries
and studios around the island.

988. **What are our accommodation options in Anguilla?**
Here are a few options to look into if you are thinking
about going to Anguilla for your destination wedding or
honeymoon:
- Anguilla Great House Beach Resort
- Cap Juluca
- Cove Castles
- CuisinArt Resort & Spa
- Easy Corner Villas
- Frangipani Beach Club
- La Sirena
- Malliouhana

989. Can I find out more local information about Anguilla as a potential destination wedding or honeymoon location?

Climate: Anguilla is a dry island with an average annual rainfall of 35 inches and average monthly temperature of 80 degrees. The island is continually cooled by prevailing trade winds, with little change of temperature in the summer. Water temperatures are in the high-70s to low-80s. Optimum diving conditions are in the summer months when visibility is at its highest. Hurricane season can vary but usually runs from June to October.

Language: English.

Currency: Eastern Caribbean Dollar (XCD). US currency is also widely accepted.

Time Zone: GMT (Greenwich Mean Time) — 4 hours. Anguilla does not operate Daylight-Saving Time.

For more information, contact: Anguilla Tourist Board, 246 Central Avenue, White Plains, NY 10606; Telephone.: 914-287-2400; Website: www.anguilla-vacation.com

990. I want to have a destination wedding or honeymoon in the Cayman Islands. Can you tell me about this destination?

Nestled in the calm, turquoise waters of the western Caribbean lies the peaceful British Crown Colony known as the Cayman Islands. Consisting of three islands just 480 miles south of Miami, Grand Cayman, Cayman Brac, and Little Cayman remain a little piece of paradise. Visitors will never be short of things to do in the Cayman Islands. World-class scuba diving, snorkeling and sailing are just the beginning of their Islands' adventure. Whether it's a trip under the sea to feed the stingrays, an excursion to the Turtle Farm for a hands-on experience of one of nature's most inspiring miracles, or a journey into the past to revisit the first landing by Christopher Columbus, visitors will have an amazing time in the Cayman Islands.

Fast Facts:
· Remained a British dependency in 1962 when Jamaica became independents
· Tropical marine climate

- Approximate population: 44,270
- Official language is English
- Capital: George Town
- Currency: Caymanian Dollar (KYD)

991. What is the nightlife like in the Cayman Islands?

The Cayman Islands offers an enjoyable variety of nightlife and entertainment. The nightclubs attract a younger crowd of locals and tourists alike along Seven Mile Beach. DJs spin to the sounds of hip hop, disco, calypso, reggae, salsa and meringue. Occasionally there are live performances by bands. For a great laugh, visit a live comedy club.

992. What is the shopping like in the Cayman Islands?

An amazing variety of local items for sale include shell jewelry, thatch work, wood carvings, Caymanian-style birdhouses, crocheted items, pepper sauces, tropical fruit jams, honey, Caymanite (Cayman's semi-precious stone) jewelry and sculpture, and a unique selection of antique and treasure coin jewelry. On Grand Cayman, farmer's markets sell delicious unusual local jams, hot sauces, fruits, fresh juices and baked goods. A growing interest in developing local art and crafts has led to the opening of art and craft galleries featuring local and Caribbean art. Underwater photography services and an excellent selection of photos and framed prints are available as well.

993. What are our accommodation options in the Cayman Islands?

Here are a few options to look into if you are thinking about going to the Cayman Islands for your destination wedding or honeymoon:

- Colonial Club
- Divi Tiara Beach Resort
- Indies Suites
- Little Cayman Beach Resort
- Pirates Point Resort, Ltd.
- Treasure Island Resort
- Walton's Mango Manor

994. Can I find out more local information about the Cayman Islands as a potential destination wedding or honeymoon location?

- Language: English.

- Currency: The Cayman Islands Dollar (KYD) is the official currency; US currency is also widely accepted.
- Time Zone: GMT (Greenwich Mean Time) — 4 hours. Cayman Islands does not operate Daylight saving Time.
- For more information: Cayman Island Department of Tourism, 350 Fifth Avenue, Suite 1801, New York, NY 10118; Telephone: 877-4-CAYMAN; Website: www.caymanislands.ky

995. What are the marriage requirements for the Cayman Islands?

Getting married in the Cayman Islands is a relatively simple process. You can get married at any point from the day of your arrival on the islands. You will need an embarkation/disembarkation card to prove when you arrived and that you have an expected departure date and time. You and your fiancé can get married during a cruise ship stopover if the proper arrangements are made in advance.

A marriage license must be obtained from the Chief Secretary's Office. Before applying for the license, you must arrange for a Cayman Islands Marriage Officer to wed you. Upon your arrival in the islands, a list of marriage officers can be acquired from the Chief Secretary's Office. The following documents are needed for you to marry:

- Original birth certificates and valid 10-year passports
- A Decree Absolute if either of you has been divorced
- Death certificates if either of you is a widow or widower, and the original marriage certificates from that union
- Parental consent is either you or your fiancé is under 18 years of age — if the father of either party is deceased, consent can be given by a male guardian. If there is no male guardian, the mother may give consent

The cost of the marriage license is CI$150, plus the charge for a stamp at CI$10. These stamps can be purchased at the Chief Secretary's Office, or at any local post office.

996. I want to have a destination wedding or honeymoon in Turks and Caicos. Can you tell me about this destination?

The Turks and Caicos Islands are famous for the 1,000 square miles of reef that surrounds them. The islands have been ranked in *Rodales' Scuba Diving Magazine* as "Best Fish Life," "Best Overall Destination," "Top Fifteen Most

Popular Dive Destinations Worldwide," "Best Wall Diving" and "Best Beginner Diving." South Caicos is the center for fishing, with lobster and conch exported from the islands. Parrot Cay and Pine Cay are privately owned islands that are home to several exclusive resorts. These small yet friendly islands offer many secluded beaches with awe-inspiring views.

Fast Facts:
- Gained independence in 1982, but the policy was reversed and they remain a British dependency
- Tropical climate
- Approximate population: 22,550
- English is the official language
- Capital: Grand Turk
- Currency: US Dollar (USD)

997. What is the dining like in Turks and Caicos?

There are about 70 restaurants throughout the Turks and Caicos Islands offering local cuisine, seafood, conch, lobster and other specialties and Caribbean dishes as well as a selection of restaurants offering more Mediterranean, Italian, British and American dishes.

998. What is the shopping like in the Turks and Caicos Islands?

In Providenciales there are three main shopping centers: Ports of Call, Market Place, and Central Square. All of these centers include a place to buy souvenirs as well as clothing, beach and sportswear. For arts and crafts, there are a number of places to visit in Providenciales and in the family of islands. Visitors should notice smaller art and craft outlets as they travel around the islands. Innovative work can be found by artists who use the natural environment to create designer mirrors, lamps and other household as well as fashion items.

999. What are our accommodation options in the Turks and Caicos Islands if we go there for our destination wedding or honeymoon?

Here are a few options to look into if you are thinking about going to the Turks and Caicos Islands:
- Beaches Turks & Caicos Resort & Spa
- Club Med Turkoise
- Grace Bay Club

- Ocean Club
- Osprey Beach Hotel
- Parrot Cay Resort
- Point Grace
- Royal West Indies Resort
- The Arches of Grand Turk Island
- Turks Head Inn
- Turtle Cove Inn

1000. **Can I find out more local information about the Turks and Caicos Islands as a potential destination wedding or honeymoon location?**

Climate: The average temperature of the Turks and Caicos ranges between 85 and 90 degrees from June to October, sometimes reaching the mid-90s, especially in the late summer months. From November to May the average temperature is 80 to 84 degrees. Water temperature in the summer is 82 to 84 degrees and in winter about 74 to 78 degrees. A constant trade wind keeps the climate at a very comfortable level.

Language: English

Currency: The United States Dollar (USD) is the official currency.

Time Zone: GMT (Greenwich Mean Time) — 5 hours. Daylight Savings Time is observed from April to October. For more information: Turks and Caicos Tourist Board, 60 E. 42nd Street, New York, NY 10165; Telephone: 649-375-8830; Website: www.turksandcaicostourism.com

1001. **What are the marriage requirements for Turks and Caicos?**

You and your fiancé must reside on Turks & Caicos for 24 hours before an application for a marriage license can be made. After you have applied, you must wait 2 or 3 days to receive the license, after which the ceremony can take place. You can apply for your license through the Registrar's Office on Grand Turk Island. For more information call 649-946-2800 or fax 649-946-2821.

The following documents are necessary if you are getting married on Turks and Caicos:

- Birth certificates and valid 10-year passports to prove identity
- A sworn affidavit prior to your date of travel, declaring that both you and your fiancé are free and single to marry
- A Decree Absolute if one or both of you are divorced
- A death certificate of one or both of your former spouses if you are a widow or widower
- A stamped affidavit from the Notary Public if one or both of you are under 21 years of age, declaring the parents or guardian has given consent that you may marry
- Legal proof if one or both of you have changed your name
- Adoption papers if one or both of you have been adopted
- A letter stating legal names, occupations, ages, marital status, present addresses and fathers' names
- Proof of membership of a church if you wish to have a church wedding

The fee for a marriage license is US$50. If you have a specific date in mind for your wedding, you need to make the Registry aware prior to your arrival on the island. A local minister, Justice of the Peace, marriage officiant or Registrar may marry you.

Conclusion

We would greatly appreciate you emailing us after your honeymoon to let us know how your wedding went and how much *1001 Most Popular Wedding Questions from WedSpace.com* helped you in planning your event. We will use this information to continue improving this extensive wedding planner, and we may even use your story in our upcoming book about wedding experiences if you permit us to. We might even ask you to participate in some of our future radio and TV tours where you can tell your own story to the public!

Dear Elizabeth & Alex,

I want to tell you that *1001 Most Popular Wedding Questions from WedSpace.com* (helped a lot), (helped a little) in planning my wedding. I especially liked your section on_____. My wedding was on_____, and it was (a complete success), (a wild party), (a boring event), (a complete disaster), (the most stressful day of my life).

My comments about your book are:
- I wish your book had given me information about:
- The best thing about my wedding was:
- The worst thing about my wedding was:
- The funniest thing about my wedding was:
- What made my wedding special or unique was:
- My wedding would have been much better if:

This is to authorize WS Publishing Group to use our story in any of their upcoming books. WS Publishing Group (can), (cannot) use our name when telling our story. I also (am), (am not) interested in participating in a radio/TV interview tour.

Please provide the following information:
- Bride's Name:
- Groom's Name:
- Address:
- Home Number:
- Work Number:
- E-mail:

E-mail your stories to: info@WedSpace.com.
Or mail them to: WedSpace.com; 7290 Navajo Road, Suite 207; San Diego, CA 92119

Remember!
If you have a wedding planning question that you did not see in this book, log on to WedSpace.com. Our website is updated with new questions and answers on a daily basis. Still can't find your answer? No problem! You can also post your question on our Q&A/Forums section and get answers from wedding professionals and other couples just like you!

....
....
....
....
....
....
....
....
....
....
....
....
....
....
....
....
....
....
....
....
....
....
....
....

Notes

....

....

....

....

....

....

....

....

....

....

....

....

....

....

....

....

....

....

....

....

....

....

....

....

···

···

···

···

···

···

···

···

···

···

···

···

···

···

···

···

···

···

···

···

···

···

···

···

Notes

....
....
....
....
....
....
....
....
....
....
....
....
....
....
....
....
....
....
....
....
....
....
....
....
....
....
....

....
....
....
....
....
....
....
....
....
....
....
....
....
....
....
....
....
....
....
....
....
....
....

WeddingSolutions.com

Everything You Need to Plan Your Dream Wedding!

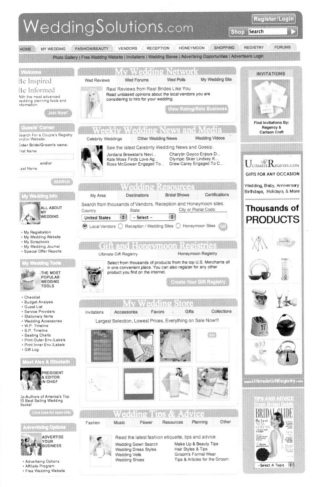

- The Latest Wedding Gowns
- Most Comprehensive Wedding Planning Tools
- Articles, Tips & Advice
- Thousands of Local Vendors
- Beautiful Reception Sites
- Honeymoon Destinations
- Largest Online Wedding Store
- Wedding Forums
- Personal Wedding Website
- Honeymoon & Gift Registry
- Polls, News, Videos, Media
- Much More

Log on to www.WeddingSolutions.com for more information

ULTIMATEREGISTRY.COM

Create a gift registry for any occasion!

Choose from over one million products from the top U.S. merchants

- Gifts from the top U.S. merchants
- Compare products and prices
- Simplified notification process saves you time
- Same Merchants, Same Products, 1 Registry!

Already have everything you need or want?

Help those in need through our Charity Registry

Request that your guests donate much-needed products to the charity of your choice in lieu of wedding gifts.

"Give a Gift" allows your guests to donate much-needed products to the charity of your choice.

Your guests will be able to select from hundreds of national and local charities and see their "wish list" of items they need most, such as blankets, office supplies and more.

Your guests can then purchase these products in your name and they will be sent directly to the charity of your choice.

Log on to www.UltimateRegistry.com for more information